Oregon
Real Estate Pre-License

Law

2nd Edition

Oregon Real Estate Pre-license Law

Executive Editor: Sara Glassmeyer

Project Manager: Arlin Kauffman,
LEAP Publishing Services

Developmental Editor: Molly Armstrong-Paschal

Art and Cover Composition: Chris Dailey

Cover Image: ProSchools

For product information and technology assistance, contact us at
OnCourse Learning and Sales Support, 1-855-733-7239.
For permission to use material from this text or product.

Library of Congress Control Number: 2015951045

ISBN-10: 1629801410
ISBN-13: 978-1-62980-141-4

OnCourse Learning
3100 Cumberland Blvd, Suite 1450
Atlanta, GA 30339
USA

Visit us at **www.oncoursepublishing.com**

Printed in the United States of America
2 3 4 5 6 7 20 19 18 17 16

Closing Process

Overview

In this lesson we review the closing process. Highlighted are the concepts of clear, marketable title, title insurance, escrow functions, and who can legally serve as an escrow agent.

Objectives

Upon completion of this lesson, the student should be able to:

1. Describe a chain of title.
2. Explain the purpose of title insurance.
3. Describe the different types of title insurance policies.
4. Define the terms "closing," "escrow" and "settlement" as they relate to a real estate transaction.
5. Describe escrow instructions.
6. Identify the participants in a closing.
7. Describe the role of the escrow agent in the closing process.

Title Insurance

A person who buys real estate usually gets a warranty deed from the seller. This renders the seller liable for damages for breach of warranty if the title being conveyed is not marketable or has defects not disclosed in the deed. However, the deed does not provide evidence that the title is marketable. To be **marketable** (or **merchantable**), the title must be free from reasonable objections.  This means there are no serious defects, liens or encumbrances clouding the title. A **cloud on the title** can be any item limiting or restricting ownership of the property. It could include:

- encumbrances, such as unpaid liens, liens paid but not having proof of payment, judgments, recorded or unrecorded agreements of sale, or easements for rights of way.
- title defects, such as claims of interest in property by missing heirs, or breaks or gaps in the chain of title where ownership cannot be traced from one owner to the next.

The **chain of title** is a complete record of all recorded instruments affecting the subject property traced back to the original source, which was often a conveyance from the government to a private person. It consists of all recorded title transfers, encumbrances, satisfactions of liens, and court proceedings pertaining to the land and the owners.

Clouds on title may be removed in a number of ways:

- An unpaid lien can be removed by payment of the lien and recording a satisfaction of lien to show payment.
- A claim of a missing heir or a gap in the chain of title might be resolved through a quitclaim deed negotiated for a price.
- In the event persons are not cooperative in removing title defects, legal action can be taken to remove the cloud. Court action taken to remove a cloud on title is called **quiet title action**.

----- TITLE INSURANCE -----

Title Evidence

A prudent buyer wants to have evidence of marketable title and assurance that someone other than he will take whatever action is necessary to make the title marketable, if the need arises. There are a number of forms of **title evidence** that are in use:

- An **abstract of title** is a digest in chronological order of the title history to a particular parcel of real estate. It is a full historical summary of all matters affecting the title, but it provides no guarantee or insurance of title. A person receiving an abstract will obtain an attorney's opinion, certifying the legal nature of the title and any defects or other rights disclosed in the abstract.
- A **certificate of title** is an opinion of the title without the title abstract. The certificate states that the title company's abstractor has searched the public record,

studied the title records and found the title properly vested in the present owner, subject to the encumbrances cited in the certificate.

- Title registration (also known as the **Torrens system)** may be used in a few states. In some of these states, the purported owner may submit an abstract of title to the court and file a quiet title suit. If the court determines that the applicant has title, the court decree and all other legal documents submitted as evidence are given to the county registrar of title.

- **Title insurance** is the most widely used type of title evidence. It is an instrument or document that protects insured parties (subject to specific exceptions) against loss by encumbrances, defective title, or adverse claims to title, resulting from defects in the title company's examination of the title record and against hidden risks. It does not cover defects arising after the effective date of the policy. Title insurance guarantees that the insured party will be defended free of charge against all covered title claims and paid up to the amount of the policy to satisfy any valid claims.

Title Insurance Companies

There is no law requiring that anyone be given title insurance or any other evidence of title. However, it is the common practice for a seller to provide title insurance for a buyer and for a borrower to provide it for a lender, as assurance that the title to the property is marketable.

Title insurance policies are issued by **title insurance companies**. These companies are regulated by a state insurance commissioner.

When a title insurance company receives a request for title insurance, a title examiner performs a **title search** in their **title plant** (a collection of records affecting title) and in the recorder's office in order to determine the condition of the title to the real property. He traces the conveyances and encumbrances relating to the real property in order to discover any flaws in the recorded title to that property, including encumbrances, liens, judgments, title defects and other matters affecting title to the land or the ability of the seller to convey a marketable title.

When the search is completed, the title insurance company issues a **preliminary title report** or **title commitment**, disclosing the current status of the title to interested parties contemplating a transfer of title or interest or a new loan affecting the real property.

> **NOTE:** In some instances, the lender or title insurance company may require a property survey to determine the exact location of the home and lot line, as well as easements and rights of way. A survey would be the best method of ensuring there are no encroachments on the property.

Title Policies

Title policies are designed to suit different needs. An **owner's title insurance policy** is used to protect a buyer (a grantee), who receives a deed to the property upon closing, against adverse claims to the ownership of the property, except those exclusions listed in the policy. The policy is issued in the amount of the full purchase price paid for the real property (not including the value of any personal property included in the sale). The policy ordinarily protects only the party named as the insured party in the written policy, his heirs and his devisees. It does not cover the lender or subsequent purchasers.

A **purchaser's title insurance policy** is designed to protect a buyer (vendee) purchasing real estate under a contract for deed (or land sales contract). This policy is issued at the time the contract is initiated in the amount of the contracted purchase price.

A **mortgagee's title insurance policy** is issued to protect a lender (a mortgagee or beneficiary) whose lien is secured by the borrower's property. It also insures any person to whom the mortgage or deed of trust is assigned. The policy assures him that the title vests in the borrower and that the mortgage lien has the priority required. This policy insures the lender against loss, up to the amount of the mortgage balance; therefore, coverage lasts until the debt is paid in full, but declines as the mortgage balance is reduced.

A **leasehold title insurance policy** is used to protect a tenant (or lessee) who is entering into a long-term lease. Coverage extends for the term of the lease. The amount of coverage is for the value of the property if the lease were for 50 or more years, or for the total amount of the rent or the value of the tenant's improvements, whichever is greater if the lease is for less than 50 years.

The cost of a title insurance policy is a one-time premium. Coverage will protect the insured party's interest forever (as long as he has liability) and need not be renewed. The premium is based on the amount of coverage provided. For an owner's or purchaser's policy, the premium is based on the cost of the property; for a lender's policy, it is based on the loan amount.

There are two basic forms of title insurance coverage available. These are the standard coverage policy and the extended coverage policy.

Standard Coverage
Usually, standard coverage is provided in the owner's policy. The form, developed by the American Land Title Association (ALTA) protects the insured against loss caused by:
- title to the estate or interest in the property being vested at the date of the policy other than as stated in the policy.
- any defect in or lien or encumbrance on the title.
- unmarketability of the title.
- lack of a right of access to and from the land.

The **standard coverage** policy insures the insured party against any item affecting title that has been made a matter of public record, such as a recorded mortgage, unless it is excluded or excepted from coverage in the policy.

It also insures against hidden risks. These are matters that are off the record and not disclosed in a recorded document, such as:

- false impersonations of grantors.
- forgeries of recorded documents in the chain of title.
- lack of competency or legal capacity of a prior grantor or his agent to convey title.
- claims of undisclosed or missing heirs challenging a conveyance after probate was closed.
- lack of intent to deliver an earlier recorded deed.
- judgments or decrees of courts without proper jurisdiction.
- defective recording, powers of attorney, foreclosures, or probate.

It also pays the cost of attorney's fees and expenses incurred in the defense of the title.

The policy excludes from coverage any loss arising from any law, ordinance, governmental regulation, eminent domain, or defects created or known by the insured prior to the date of the policy, and any loss due to the following matters if not on the public record:

- Taxes or assessments
- Any facts, rights, interests, or claims which could be ascertained by an inspection of the land or by making inquiry of persons in possession of the land, such as a claim of adverse possession or a claim of ownership by a person with an unrecorded deed or unrecorded contract
- Easements and claims of easements or encumbrances
- Discrepancies, conflicts in boundary lines, shortage in area, encroachments, or any other facts a correct survey would disclose
- Unpatented mining claims
- Water rights and claims of title to water
- Any lien, or right to a lien, for services, labor or material

Extended Coverage

Extended coverage is usually used in mortgagees' policies. The ALTA lender's policy provides all of the coverage of the standard policy, plus coverage of matters not shown by public records. These may include items requiring an inspection of the property to discover (e.g., rights of parties in possession such as adverse possessors and owners with unrecorded deeds, unrecorded easements, encroachments and observable defects). To determine if there might be problems, the title company has a **spot survey** performed, showing the location of easements, encroachments and improvements. This coverage may also extend to losses caused by unrecorded deeds and unrecorded liens.

Like the standard policy, the extended coverage policy excludes loss caused by public land use controls (such as zoning and building restrictions), any other government rights of police power or eminent domain, or defects created or known by the insured prior to the date of the policy.

Closing and Escrow

----- CLOSINGS -----

Generally, in the real estate sales agreement there is a date by which time both the buyer and seller are called upon to fulfill their obligations and a time is of the essence clause, requiring that both parties comply with all deadlines. If they cannot, they need to sign an addendum extending the deadline. When they finally are ready to fulfill their obligations, the seller provides the closing agent with a deed, and the buyer provides the funds necessary to close. This is called the closing or the **settlement process**. **Closing**, or settlement, is completed when the deed is recorded and the sales proceeds are delivered to the seller.

Settlement Meetings

The legal closing process varies somewhat throughout the country. In many parts of the country, closing takes place at a settlement meeting (a "table" closing). This meeting may be attended by the buyer and the seller, their representatives, representatives of any lenders involved, representatives of the brokers, and attorneys representing various parties. At the meeting, papers are signed and delivered, the closing statement is reviewed, and funds are disbursed.

When and where the meeting occurs is determined by agreement of the buyer and seller in the sales contract. It may take place at the lender's office, a broker's office, a title company, or a closing attorney's office. In states considered **attorney states**, lawyers carry out the closing functions at settlement meetings.

Escrow Functions

In other states, the closing process is conducted through escrow. **Escrow** is the process by which a deed or other written instrument is delivered to a third person, to be delivered by him to the grantee only upon the performance or fulfillment of a certain condition. The deposit in escrow places an item beyond the control of the depositor. Because of this, death or future incapacity of either party in the transaction does not prevent the completion of the transaction. A deed is considered to be delivered when placed in escrow. Death of the grantor afterward would not affect the deed's validity.

The purpose of escrow is to enable principals to the transaction (e.g., the buyer and seller) to deal with each other without risk. Responsibility for handling funds and documents is given to the neutral third party, the escrow agent in a sales transaction. The escrow agent receives and holds trust funds and documents and instructions from the buyer. He also receives documents and instructions from the seller. Through the use of escrow, the parties have:

- a place of safekeeping of funds and documents until the transaction is closed. When the seller delivers a deed to escrow, title remains with him until the escrow instructions have been met.
- a means of paying existing indebtedness.
- a means of clearing clouds on the title.

In order to represent the parties in a transaction, the escrow agent must have a binding contract and written instructions. In a contract, such as a sales contract, lease, option, or exchange agreement, the buyer and seller select the escrow company to close the transaction. The contract demonstrates a meeting of the minds and is a complete agreement between the parties. The escrow officer makes sure that the terms of the contract are carried out, prepares a computation of the necessary prorations and performs the necessary clerical work. In the event of a dispute between the buyer and seller, the escrow agent looks to this document for guidance.

The **escrow agent**, also called an **escrow officer,** prepares escrow instructions based on the purchase and sale agreement. These instructions create a separate agreement between the buyer and escrow and the seller and escrow; they may amend the sales agreement. The buyer's instructions indicate:

- the property being purchased.
- the sale price and terms.
- how items are to be paid.
- the condition of the title he is to receive.
- the prorate date.

The seller's instructions indicate:

- how much he will collect.
- the form of payment.

The escrow instructions also provide for the payment of:

- taxes;
- existing encumbrances;
- the broker's fee;
- the document preparation fees; and
- the escrow fee.
- the **prorate date**. This date must be the same for both the seller and buyer.

The escrow company has an attorney prepare documents and arrange for a title search and the issuance of title insurance. The escrow agent prepares **closing statements** for both the buyer and seller. A buyer's closing statement sets out the buyer's closing costs and credits in detail so that he will know what is expected of him at closing. The seller's closing statement provides the seller with a complete accounting of his own closing costs and credits and the amount of money he will receive from the proceeds of the sale.

The escrow agent acts as a dual agent, representing the buyer and the seller in the transaction. This imposes on him a fiduciary responsibility to both parties, requiring that he protect the interests of each party and take certain precautions in performing his duties:

- He must be confidential.
- He cannot give legal advice.
- He may fill in the blanks in deeds, mortgages and satisfactions of liens, but he cannot advise the parties as to which document to use or how to fill out the documents.
- He must be impartial.
- He must comply strictly with the escrow instructions, performing only as instructed by the principals (the broker is not a principal). If the instructions differ from the original sales agreement, they take precedence. If they cannot be followed, he must obtain amendments to them from the principals. Any deviation from the written instructions must have the mutual consent of both principals or the consent of the party affected.
- He must obtain all necessary signatures.
- He cannot deliver (disburse) any funds or documents unless the escrow conditions have been strictly met or unless the principals give written authorization to do so.

With a commercial transaction, there may be a tenancy statement, also called an **estoppel certificate**. When signed by both the buyer and seller, this instrument prevents one party from claiming different facts than those set out in the instrument.

----- CLOSING COST ESTIMATES -----

As part of its function, escrow will prepare closing statements for the seller and the buyer. A **buyer's closing statement** presents the buyer's closing costs and credits in detail so that he will know what is expected of him at closing. The **seller's closing statement** provides the seller with a complete accounting of his own closing costs and credits and the amount of money he will receive from the proceeds of the sale.

In any real estate transaction, there are **closing (or settlement) costs**. These are moneys that the buyer and seller pay to close the transaction. What is included, the amount, and who pays, depends on the transaction and its terms, the existence of any liens against the parties or the real estate, and the type of financing to be used in the sale. In a transaction with conventional financing, the party responsible for payment of various closing costs is determined by agreement of the parties.

In the accounting performed on a closing statement, the buyer and seller each have a series of debits (charges) and credits.

Buyer Entries

For the buyer, any items that must be paid for out of his account at closing are charges (debits). Every check written by escrow (such as to pay closing costs) to be paid out of the escrow account is a debit.

All funds put into the account to pay off those charges are credits. Therefore, every check written by someone other than escrow (the lender's check for a new loan, the buyer's check to close, etc.) is a credit. The buyer's credits are:

- items for which he paid before closing.
- items for which he will not pay until after closing.
- items which are owed him by the seller.
- cash he pays to close the transaction.

BUYER CREDITS (paid into his account)	BUYER DEBITS (paid out of his account)
<ul><li>Earnest money</li><li>Assumptions of existing encumbrances</li><li>New loans</li><li>Prepaid items received by seller</li><li>Check he pays at closing</li></ul>	<ul><li>Purchase price</li><li>Prorated share of property taxes paid in advance by seller</li><li>Property insurance</li><li>Recording fees</li><li>Legal fees and escrow fees</li><li>Reserve account</li><li>Mortgagee's title policy (for new loan)</li><li>Loan origination fee, appraisal fee, credit report, tax registration, mortgage insurance, staking or survey</li><li>Assumption fee</li><li>Interest adjustment charges</li><li>Judgments</li><li>Personal property not included in sales price</li></ul>

Seller Entries

Credits to the seller are all amounts he is to receive at closing, such as the purchase price and reimbursement for prepaid expenses. For the seller, any item that is paid into his escrow account is a credit. (Money into the account is a credit.)

The debits reflect how the funds owed him are to be disbursed. Any item that is paid out of his account, even if paid to him, at closing, is a charge or debit. (Checks written by escrow are debits.)

SELLER CREDITS (paid into his account)	SELLER DEBITS (paid out of his account)
• Selling price	• Owner's title policy
• Prorations of taxes paid in advance	• Commission (unless a note or property)
• Insurance premiums refunded	• Recording satisfaction of liens
• Rent not yet collected	• Legal fees and escrow fees
• Refund of interest paid in advance	• Discount points paid for buyer
• Refund of reserves	• Judgments
• Personal property added to sales price	• Purchase money mortgage or contract
	• Termite inspection/treatment
	• Survey
	• Excise tax
	• Rents collected in advance, security deposits, last month's rent
	• Obligations owed
	• Existing loan
	• Unpaid interest, taxes
	• Loan prepayment penalty
	• Amount seller will receive from closing

Settlement Items

The selling price is the price agreed to in the sales contract between the buyer and the seller. This is both a charge (debit) to the buyer and a credit to the seller.

If the buyer and seller agree that the buyer will purchase some items of personal property such as drapes, refrigerator, etc., for a price which is not included in the sales price, the price for the personal property increases the amount due from the buyer, and the amount to be paid the seller. Therefore, it is a debit to the buyer and a credit to the seller.

Anything the buyer uses to pay off the sales price is a credit to the buyer:

- earnest money.
- new loan obtained from a lender.
- purchase money mortgage given to the seller.
- contract for deed (real estate contract) taken from the seller.
- loan assumed by the buyer.
- check from the buyer.

Some of these items are also debits to the seller, while some do not even appear on the seller's closing statement.

For Example	Earnest money paid by the buyer, whether cash or other property, is a credit to the buyer. If the earnest money is cash, it would not appear on the seller's statement, as it neither increases nor decreases the amount of cash the seller receives at closing. If, however, the earnest money is property, the value of that property would be a debit on the seller's statement, as it would reduce the amount of cash paid to the seller.

The amount of any new loan obtained from a lender is a credit to the buyer (as it is paid into his closing account) and does not appear on the seller's statement.

The amount of any financing provided by the seller, whether in the form of a purchase money mortgage or a contract for deed, and the amount of any loan or other encumbrances (unpaid taxes, special assessments, deeds of trust, etc.) assumed by the buyer are credits to the buyer and debits to the seller.

Any encumbrances not assumed by the buyer that are paid off at closing by the seller would appear as debits to the seller.

The buyer may also have to pay for a home inspection and/or pest and dry rot inspection. Often, loan and inspection fees are paid for at the time of the inspection or the loan application. If not, the buyer is debited the cost at closing.

Another possible charge, which could be paid by either the buyer or the seller, is for a home warranty.

If the buyer assumes the seller's existing loan, he would be credited the amount of the loan balance being assumed and credited for unpaid interest from the date of the last payment, but debited the cost of an assumption fee charged by the lender for processing the paperwork.

Loan-Related Items

In general, items payable in connection with a loan (the fees lenders charge to process, approve and make the mortgage loan) are debits to the buyer, adding to the cost of acquiring the property. These items are neither credits nor debits to the seller.

Items related to a new loan include:

- a loan origination fee to cover the lender's administrative costs in processing the loan.
- an appraisal fee to pay for a statement of property value for the lender, made by an independent appraiser.
- a credit report fee to cover the cost of a credit report.
- an inspection fee to cover inspections made by personnel of the lending institution or an outside inspector.
- a mortgage insurance premium to pay for mortgage insurance to protect the lender from loss due to payment default by the borrower.
- a hazard insurance premium to pay for property insurance to protect the buyer and lender against loss due to fire, windstorm, and other natural hazards. The buyer needs to pay at least the first year's premium at closing. The lender will require the coverage to be for at least the full amount of the loan.
- a flood insurance premium to pay for flood insurance, if the property is within a special flood hazard area identified by FEMA.
- discount points as a one-time charge to adjust the lender's yield on the loan. This charge depends on how much the borrower wants to reduce the interest rate, as each point buys about a 1/8% reduction in the interest rate. Each point is equal to one percent of the mortgage amount.

For Example

If a lender charges four points on a $200,000 loan, this amounts to a charge of $8,000. $200,000 x 4% = $8,000.

- interest that accrues on the new loan from the date of settlement to the beginning of the period covered by the first monthly payment (normally the first day of the month following closing). If the closing is close to the end of the month, the lender may ask escrow to collect interest for the remainder of the month and the entire following month and then start the loan repayment period the month after that.

For Example

A closing takes place on April 16. The first monthly payment is due on June 1, including the interest charges for the month of May. At closing, the lender collects interest for the period from April 16 to May 1. In calculating the amount, the first step is to calculate the annual interest (by multiplying the loan balance by the interest rate). The second step is to multiply the answer by the number of days from closing to the end of the month of closing and divide by 365. If the loan amount were $120,000 @ 6% interest, the buyer would be charged $295.89 ($120,000 x 6% x 15 ÷ 365).

If a sale closed April 29, the buyer could be charged interest on the loan for 2 days in April and the entire month of May. Then the first loan payment would be July 1, to cover the month of June.

- reserves (or escrow or impound) deposit if the buyer is paying 1/12 of the estimated annual insurance premiums, property taxes, special assessments and homeowner's association assessments in his monthly mortgage payments. At closing, the borrower makes an initial deposit into the reserve account so that with the regular monthly deposits added, there is enough to pay the annual taxes, premiums, and assessments when due.
- a tax service fee for the cost of having a tax service company procure the city and county tax bills and special tax district improvement assessment bills each year for the lender, and verify the taxing description with the loan identification.

Title Charges

At closing, there are also title charges covering a variety of services performed by title companies and others directly related to the transfer of the title (title examination, title search, document preparation), as well as fees for title insurance, legal charges and settlement fees (also called closing fees or escrow fees).

In some states, attorneys may be allowed to prepare a chain of title, in lieu of using a title insurance company.

In escrow states, as opposed to attorney states, the escrow fee is the fee charged by the escrow agent to have the legal documents prepared and recorded, to collect funds, and to then disburse them to the parties entitled to receive them. This fee is based on the dollar amount of the transaction, so the greater the transaction amount, the greater the fee.

Included in this fee may be the cost for reporting the transaction to the IRS on a 1099-S form. A real estate reporting entity (such as escrow) must file an information report (Form 1099-S) showing the sale price on a real estate sale or exchange, unless the transaction involves a principal residence with a sales price of $250,000 or less for an individual or $500,000 or less for a married couple, and a signed 1099 certificate is obtained from each person.

In transactions involving the sale of property by a non-resident alien, the **Foreign Investment in Real Property Tax Act** requires that the buyer withhold 10% of the gross proceeds, unless he uses the property as a residence and the purchase price is less than $300,000. For transactions involving a foreign seller, the listing agent should have the seller sign an affidavit that he is a resident alien, if this is the case, and have the affidavit furnished to the buyer.

In closings involving settlement meetings, there is no escrow fee, but there may be a number of additional separate charges for title search, document preparation, notary fee and attorney's fee:
- A document preparation fee covers the cost of preparation of final legal papers, such as a mortgage, note or deed.
- A notary fee is charged for the cost of having a licensed person affix his name and seal to various documents authenticating the execution of these documents by the parties.
- Attorneys' fees may be charged for legal services provided to the lender in connection with the settlement.

An item that may be debited to both buyer and seller at closing is the cost of title insurance. In most areas, the buyer provides the lender with a lender's title policy. Custom in the area dictates whether the seller pays for the buyer's title insurance or not. There are also government recording and transfer charges. Normally the buyer is responsible for paying fees for recording instruments pertaining to the ownership of the property and the seller is responsible for fees for recording instruments to clear title.

In some states, a conveyance or excise tax is charged to the seller. The amount charged by the state is a percentage of the sales price.

Commission

If there was a broker in a transaction, the seller usually pays the listing broker a sales commission. It is usually a percentage of the selling price of the property, negotiated between the seller and the broker. When several brokers work together to sell a property, the commission may be split among them, but the split may not be shown on the closing statement.

Legal Advice

If an attorney is called upon to provide advice or to draft a contract, the party represented by the attorney is debited the cost of the attorney unless there is an agreement otherwise.

Existing Encumbrances

The seller may also have debits resulting from existing encumbrances. The amount of the existing loan is debited to the seller whether the loan is paid off from the sales proceeds or the buyer assumes the loan, since in either case, the seller receives less cash after closing.

The seller will also be debited for the interest on the existing loan from the date of the last payment to or through the date of closing. This is because loan payments pay interest for the past month, not the current month:

- If a loan is paid off at closing, the seller is charged interest through the date of closing.
- If a loan is to be assumed, the seller is charged interest to the date of closing and the amount charged the seller is in turn credited to the buyer, so it may be included in the buyer's next loan payment.

For Example

There is a $100,000 loan balance. The interest rate is 5%. The sale is to close on the twentieth of the month. If the loan were paid off, the seller would be debited for 20/365 of 5% of $100,000.

5% x $100,000 = $5,000
$5,000 x 20/365 (multiply by 20 and divide by 365) = $273.98

This would be paid to the lender. If the loan were assumed, the seller would owe the buyer for 19/365 of 5% of $100,000, or $260.28. This would be debited to the seller and credited the buyer.

Money in an existing reserve account is a credit to the seller, as it will be refunded to the seller either by the lender or by the buyer. When a loan is paid off, the lender returns the money. When a buyer assumes the loan, he also assumes the seller's reserve account, and reimburses the seller for the funds in the account. In that instance, the amount in the reserve account would be a debit to the buyer as well as a credit to the seller.

Insurance Premiums

The seller also receives money back for advance premiums paid for the policy insuring his property. Since insurance premiums are typically paid in advance, for at least one year, the seller is entitled to a refund of the portion of the premiums that applied to the period after closing. The amount refunded the seller is a credit.

> **For Example**
>
> If the policy cost $365 and the buyer assumed the policy the 200th day after the policy went into effect, the seller would be entitled to a refund of the premium paid for day 200 through 365 (166 days) or $166. This would be a credit to the seller and a debit to the buyer.

Property Taxes

Property taxes are usually prorated between the seller and the buyer. If the seller has prepaid taxes to cover a period beyond the date of closing, the buyer will refund to the seller the portion of the taxes covering the period from the date of closing to the end of the payment period. This amount would be a debit to the buyer and a credit to the seller.

If the seller has not paid taxes for the entire period prior to closing, the seller pays the buyer an amount to cover the time the seller had been in possession of the property from the lien date to the day of closing. This amount is a debit to the seller and a credit to the buyer. If the taxes are late or delinquent, the seller may also owe late fees and penalties. These would be debited to the seller and paid to the county.

Rent in Advance

In a closing of a rental property there is a proration of rents. Normally an owner will collect rent in advance and a security deposit, plus perhaps last month's rent, a cleaning fee, and/or a non-refundable fee. All deposits, fees and prepaid rents should be credited to the buyer and debited to the seller at closing, in their entirety. Current rents would be prorated.

Buyer's and Seller's Checks

When all of the buyer's credits have been subtracted from his debits, the result is the amount of cash the buyer needs to close. This is normally covered by a wire transfer to the buyer's escrow account or by cashier's check paid at closing. This check is a credit to the buyer. When it is added to the other credits, the total of the buyer's credits will equal the buyer's debits.

When the seller's debits have been subtracted from his credits, the result is the check the seller will receive from closing. This check is a debit to the seller. When it is added to the other debits, the total of the seller's debits will equal his credits.

Closing Statements

Buyer		Seller	
Debits	*Credits*	*Credits*	**Debits**
To be paid at closing	How debits paid before, at or after closing	To be received at closing	How credits disbursed at closing
Sales price	Earnest money	Sales price	Closing costs
Closing costs	Financing	Prorates	Seller financing, assumption, pay existing loan
Prorates	Check to close		Check from closing

Remember that a seller may not require a buyer to use a particular title company, or under the rules of RESPA, the seller would be liable for three times the title insurance cost, as damages to the buyer. The seller may negotiate with the buyer, and buyer and seller most often agree on which title insurance company to use. If the buyer and seller use the same company, the total cost is less.

Brain Teaser

Reinforce your understanding of the material by correctly completing the following sentences:

1. To be marketable (or _____), title must be free from reasonable objections.

2. When a title insurance company receives a request for title insurance, a title examiner will perform a title _____ in their title _____ and issue a preliminary title _____ .

3. An _____ is the process by which a deed or other written instrument is delivered to a third person, to be delivered by him to the grantee only upon the performance or fulfillment of a certain condition.

Brain Teaser Answers

1. To be marketable (or **merchantable**), title must be free from reasonable objections.

2. When a title insurance company receives a request for title insurance, a title examiner will perform a title **search** in their title **plant** and issue a preliminary title **report**.

3. An **escrow** is the process by which a deed or other written instrument is delivered to a third person, to be delivered by him to the grantee only upon the performance or fulfillment of a certain condition.

Review — Closing Process

In this lesson we discuss the closing process.

Evidence of Title

Title insurance is the most widely used type of title evidence. Unlike a title abstract, which merely provides a history of ownership of the property, a title policy is an instrument or document that insures parties, subject to specific exceptions, against loss by encumbrances, defective title, or adverse claims to title, resulting from defects in the title company's examination of the title record and against hidden risks, such as forgeries. Title insurance guarantees that the insured party will be defended free of charge against all covered title claims and paid up to the amount of the policy to satisfy any valid claims.

When a title company receives a request for title insurance, a title examiner will trace the conveyances and encumbrances in the chain of title (title search) in its collection of records (title plant) affecting title in order to determine the condition of the title to the property. The chain of title is a complete record of all recorded instruments affecting the property, including all recorded title transfers, encumbrances, satisfactions of liens, and court proceedings pertaining to the land and the owners. If the title examiner discovers any clouds on the title, such as unpaid judgments, unsatisfied contracts for deed, or unused easements, the title company will attempt to obtain a quitclaim deed or, if necessary, take legal action to quiet the title and remove the cloud.

Title Insurance

There are several types of title insurance policies, including:
- owner's title insurance.
- purchaser's title insurance.
- mortgagee's title insurance.
- leasehold title insurance.

An owner's title insurance policy protects a buyer who receives a deed to the property upon closing. Its cost is based primarily on the cost of the property. A purchaser's title insurance policy protects a buyer purchasing real estate under a contract for deed. A mortgagee's title policy protects a lender whose lien is secured by the borrower's property. Its cost is based on the loan amount. A leasehold title policy protects a tenant who is entering into a long-term lease.

Standard coverage, usually provided in an owner's policy, insures the insured party against any item affecting title that has been made a matter of public record, such as a recorded mortgage, unless it is excluded or exempted from coverage in the policy, as well as hidden risks. Hidden risks are matters that are off the record and not disclosed in a recorded document, such as lack of intent to deliver a deed, false impersonations, forgeries, missing heirs, and lack of competency of grantors.

Extended coverage is usually used in mortgagees' policies. It provides all of the coverage of the standard policy, plus coverage of matters not shown by public records, such as items requiring an inspection of the property to discover, and losses caused by unrecorded deeds and unrecorded liens.

Note: Neither standard nor extended coverage protects against government regulation of the use of the subject property.

Generally, a real estate transaction concludes at closing or settlement, when the seller receives the purchase price and the buyer receives the deed giving him title. In escrow states, this occurs through escrow; in attorney states, normally an attorney closes the transaction. The use of escrow enables closing to take place without the buyer and seller needing to be present at closing at the same time. The selection of the title and escrow company is made by the buyer and seller.

Escrow

Escrow is the process by which a deed or other written instrument is delivered to a third person who will deliver it to the grantee upon fulfillment of a certain condition. Appropriate documents are recorded, and funds are disbursed. The deposit in escrow places an item beyond the control of the depositor. A deed is considered delivered when placed in escrow. Therefore, once the deed has been placed in escrow, death or future incapacity of either party in the transaction would not prevent the completion of the transaction. However, the title remains with the seller until all escrow conditions have been met.

An escrow agent must have a contract and instructions in order to represent the parties in a transaction. Escrow instructions create a separate agreement between the buyer and escrow and the seller and escrow and may amend the sales agreement:

- The buyer's instructions tell him what property he is getting, for how much and under what terms, how the items are to be paid, the condition of the title he is to receive, and the prorate date.
- The seller's instructions tell him how much he will collect and in what form.

The instructions also provide for disbursements for taxes, payment of existing encumbrances, the broker's fee, the cost of preparing documents, and the escrow fee. They also show the prorate date.

The escrow agent is a dual agent representing the buyer and seller. He must be confidential; he cannot give legal advice; he may fill in blanks, but he cannot draft legal documents or advise the parties as to which document to use or how to fill out the documents; he must be impartial; he must comply strictly with the escrow instructions and cannot make any changes without the written consent of both parties; he must obtain all necessary signatures; and he cannot disburse any funds or documents unless the escrow conditions have been strictly met.

Conveyances and Deeds

Overview

In this lesson, the ways in which real property title may be transferred from one owner to another are reviewed. Voluntary and involuntary transfers are discussed, including transfers upon death, through a will and through intestate succession. Elements essential to a valid deed and types of deed forms are identified. Finally, the significance of recording a deed is highlighted.

Objectives

Upon completion of this lesson, the student should be able to:

1. Define the term "title" as it pertains to real estate.
2. Identify and describe how title may be transferred:
    *   to and from the government.
    *   by physical action.
    *   by adverse possession.
    *   upon death.
    *   by court action.
3. Describe the basic requirements for a valid conveyance.
4. Identify and describe various forms of deeds.
5. Explain the differences between constructive notice and actual notice.
6. Define recordation and explain why it is important in a real property transaction.

Ways to Transfer Title

The conveyance or transfer of title from one owner to another involves alienation of title by the current owner and acquisition of the title by the new owner. **Alienation** is the transfer or conveyance of the title to real property to another. Every property owner has a right of alienation, that is, the right to transfer his interest in the property to another.

Alienation may be voluntary or involuntary:

- Voluntary alienation refers to such actions as the sale, gift, or will of property to another.
- Involuntary alienation refers to transfer of ownership of the estate by operation of law (or court action).

----- TITLE TRANSFERRED TO AND FROM GOVERNMENT -----

Forms of transfer of title to and from the government include patents, forfeiture, dedication, and eminent domain.

Patent

A **patent** is a conveyance of title from the government, or sovereign power, to private owners. After claiming all the land through discovery, occupancy, conquest, or purchase, the government conveyed title to much of it to private owners through instruments called patents. If one were to trace back the record of ownership of a parcel of real estate, the first grant one would find in the chain of title is a patent issued by the government.

Forfeiture

Property may be forfeited to the government if it was used in the commission of a crime.

Dedication

Dedication is the gift or donation of property to the public without consideration. This may occur through dedication in public records, a deed or a will.

Through statutory dedication, a developer may be required to turn over land in a proposed subdivision to a public use, e.g., streets and public areas, in order to obtain approval for the development.

Through common law dedication, a local government may declare property to have been dedicated for public use, due to a property owner allowing the public to use the property for an extended period.

Technoproducts, Inc. has a private street running through its property. The street is not marked as private and is open to public traffic. Unless the owners occasionally block off access to indicate a claim of ownership, the street may be declared to have been dedicated for public use.

Eminent Domain

Eminent domain is the government's right to acquire title to property for public use by paying just and fair compensation to the owner. The two critical elements of eminent domain are public use and fair compensation.

The land must be taken for public use, e.g., for streets, highways, airports, public buildings, parks, etc.:

- A district school board may seek property for a public school through the power of eminent domain.
- A city can acquire property to widen a road from the owners of abutting property under the exercise of eminent domain.

The land can be taken by the government itself or by an authorized private entity, generally a public utility or public service corporation (for instance, a power company, railroad, communication company, or water company).

When Dusty Rhodes refused to allow a privately owned public utilities company to cross his property with a power line, the utilities company sought to acquire a right of way through use of eminent domain.

The process by which property is taken for public use under eminent domain is **condemnation**. When an owner of land refuses to sell the land at the price offered under the right of eminent domain, the government may require the owner to sell the land through condemnation proceedings.

Just compensation must be paid to the landowner. Therefore, while a landowner generally cannot expect compensation from the government for loss of use of land due to land use restrictions, such as zoning, he may expect compensation for the physical taking of his land through eminent domain. Just compensation can include:

- compensatory damages in the amount of the fair market value of the property taken, at the time of the taking.
- severance damages for the loss in value to the portion of the property not taken.
- consequential damages for loss in value due to surrounding property taken. If the loss in its value or use is too extensive, the owner may sue for **inverse condemnation**, to require the government to take and pay for the property.

----- PHYSICAL ACTION -----

Accession

Title to real property may be affected by physical action. The term for any additions to land or property, whether by natural or man-made causes, is **accession**.

Man-made additions include the **annexation** of fixtures. When an owner builds a house on his land, that house becomes part of the title to the land. If a neighbor mistakenly puts a structure on another person's land, that structure can become part of the title to the land on which it is placed.

The addition to one's land by the gradual deposit of soil through natural causes is **accretion**. For example, the owner of property on a shore or riverbank would acquire soil deposited (or accreted) on his land by the natural action of water and wind.

When a property boundary is the high water mark of a body of water, the property owner may acquire title to additional land by reliction. **Reliction** is the gradual recession of water from its usual high water mark so that the newly uncovered land becomes the property of the adjoining riparian property owner.

Loss

Just as a person can acquire title to soil by accretion, a person can lose title to soil through erosion. **Erosion** is the gradual loss of soil due to natural causes, such as currents, tides, winds or changes in temperature. It is the opposite of accretion.

When the natural loss is not gradual, but a sudden tearing away or removal of land by action of water (e.g., the removal of land when a stream suddenly changes its channel after a flood), the loss is called **avulsion**. Because the loss is sudden and perceptible, title to the land is not automatically lost, and the owner can claim the original boundary and reclaim the lost land, if that is possible.

Gained Land	Lost Land
• Accession: Any addition to land • Accretion: Natural gradual addition to land • Annexation: Man-made addition to land	• Avulsion: Rapid loss of land by water • Erosion: Natural gradual loss of land

----- ADVERSE POSSESSION -----

Title may be lost and acquired through adverse possession. **Adverse possession** is a means of acquiring title where the occupant of the land has been in actual, open, notorious, hostile, exclusive and continuous possession of the property for a required statutory period of time.

- Actual possession means the possessor actually uses or occupies the land as if he were the owner.
- Open and notorious possession means the land is used in such a manner that the owner knew about it or should reasonably have known about it.
- Exclusive possession means the adverse possessor has exclusive control of the subject property.
- Hostile means the adverse possessor claims ownership, rejecting the claims of others. Possession is not hostile if the owner has ever given the occupant permission (i.e., a license) to occupy the land, even if that permission is later withdrawn. Therefore, the true owner could prevent a claim of adverse possession by asserting ownership rights and giving a license granting revocable permission to use the land.
- Continuous possession means that all elements required for adverse possession existed for a continuous period of at least the number of years required under state law. In some states, this period is shortened if the adverse possessor paid the property taxes on the land during the period of his possession. However, the possession need not be by the same person throughout that period. Through **tacking**, an adverse claimant can achieve the required period of possession by adding the time of his possession to that of any previous adverse possessors.

A claim of adverse possession would be defeated if during the required number of years:
- the adverse use were discontinued even temporarily at any time.
- the true owner asserted ownership rights and resumed actual possession.
- the true owner took legal action to have the adverse possessor removed.

In many states, the adverse possessor must also be in possession under a claim of right or color of title:
- A **claim of right** means the adverse possessor claims ownership of the land.
- **Color of title** means the adverse possessor claims title under a written conveyance of the property or by operation of law from another person claiming title under a written conveyance. For example, a person who occupies the land under an invalid deed, while believing the deed to be valid, would have color of title.

Title generally cannot be acquired by adverse possession when the true owner is:
- under legal age.
- incompetent or insane.
- the government (although the government can take title to private property by adverse possession).

In order to get marketable title to property, an adverse possessor would have to obtain a quitclaim deed from the ousted owner or take quiet title action to obtain a judicial decree clearing the title to the property. A **quitclaim deed** passes any interest the signer may have in the property, but does not tie him to any warranty. **Quiet title action** is a lawsuit to determine and resolve all adverse claims to ownership of the property.

A person who merely uses another's property, openly, notoriously and hostilely, for a continuous state-specified number of years cannot claim title by adverse possession, but can claim an easement giving him a permanent, irrevocable right to use that property. Acquisition of an easement through adverse use is called **prescription**. Therefore, a person driving across another's land for a certain number of years without permission could get a permanent right of way through prescription, but not title by adverse possession.

----- Death -----

Upon a person's death, his property may pass on to others either through probate or without probate.

No Probate

If a person owns property as a joint tenant with a right of survivorship, his interest will automatically pass to any surviving co-owners named in the deed, upon his death.

If a couple owns property as tenants by the entirety, upon the death of one the estate passes to the other to be held as a tenant in severalty.

If a person has a life estate, upon the death of the person on whose life the estate is based, title will either:
- revert to the grantor or to the grantor's heirs or devisees, or
- pass to the remainderman, as specified in the deed.

In these instances probate would not be required.

Probate

Probate is the process by which a court:
- collects the deceased's assets.
- pays the legal claims of his creditors.
- distributes the remainder of his estate to those entitled to it.

Upon the death of a person who is a tenant in severalty or a tenant in common, his interest would be probated, whether he died testate (leaving a will) or intestate (not leaving a will).

A **will** is an instrument used to dispose of a person's property (the estate) upon death. Since the legal term for a will is a testament, a person who dies leaving a will is called a testator and is said to have died testate.

Generally, to be valid, the will must be a witnessed will. This is a will made by a mentally competent person who has reached majority, normally 18 years of age. The will needs to be signed by or for the testator in front of at least two witnesses, who also sign it. The will becomes effective when the testator dies. Prior to death the will is "ambulatory," meaning that it can be changed at any time. Changes to the will are called codicils.

Some states recognize what is called a holographic will. This is a will entirely handwritten by the testator, but not witnessed. Some states recognize an oral (nuncupative) will, normally only if it is made while the testator is on his deathbed with witnesses present and is to dispose of personal property of minimal value.

When a person dies **testate**, the will is probated to ensure it is valid and its terms are carried out. An executor named in the will distributes the estate. Persons receiving ownership of real property through a valid will are called **devisees**. Personal property will pass by bequest or legacy to **legatees**.

In community property states, when a married person dies testate, half the community property passes to the surviving spouse, and the other half of the community property and all separate property will pass by will. If there were no will, a surviving spouse would be entitled to all of the community property.

When the deceased dies **intestate**, the estate is transferred by descent to the decedent's heirs. The estate is probated to assure that it is distributed to the appropriate heirs. The court will appoint an administrator to distribute the estate to the deceased's heirs under the state laws of intestate succession. If no heirs can be found, any real property will revert to the government through escheat. This is very rare.

A general term used to refer to either an executor or an administrator is personal representative.

----- COURT ACTION -----

Court action can result in a conveyance of title:
- A co-owner may have his interest separated from that of the others through a partition suit.
- Divorce decrees may result in the transfer of title from both spouses to one of the spouses or require that the property be sold.
- Bankruptcy courts may require property to be sold to satisfy the claims of creditors.
- Courts may have property sold to pay off judgment creditors by means of an **execution sale.** To get paid, the creditor can request the court to sell whatever property is necessary. The court order that requires the sheriff to sell property is a **writ of execution**, so the sale is termed an execution sale.
- Real property used as collateral for a debt can be lost through foreclosure if the debt is not repaid according to its terms.

Foreclosure can result from failure to pay mortgages, construction liens, contracts for deed, property taxes, or special assessments.

In a **judicial foreclosure**, upon default, the creditor requests the court to foreclose on the property.
- In some states, the request may be for **strict foreclosure**. This foreclosure would terminate the property owner's rights and give the title to the creditor.
- In most cases, the request is for **foreclosure and sale**, which terminates the owner's rights and causes the property to be sold by the sheriff to the highest bidder.

A **nonjudicial foreclosure** is allowed when the mortgage or deed of trust (or trust deed) used to make real property security for a loan has a power of sale provision, giving the lender or a trustee the power to foreclose and sell the property without going to court.

Generally, a property owner has an **equitable right of redemption** in foreclosure actions. This is the right to keep the title by paying off the entire debt prior to the date of the foreclosure. In some states, the property owner will also have a **statutory right of redemption**, allowing him to buy back the property by paying off the entire debt within a specified period after the foreclosure.

----- FORFEITURE UNDER CONTRACT FOR DEED -----

Property may also be lost as a result of forfeiture under the terms of a contract for deed. A **contract for deed** (also called other names throughout the country, including real estate contract or land sales contract) is a contract under which a buyer (vendee) agrees to pay the seller (vendor) for the property over a period of time. If the buyer satisfies his contractual obligation, the seller will give him a deed. Often the contract will include a provision allowing for forfeiture of the vendee's interest if the vendee defaults, so the vendor can reclaim the property without having to resort to foreclosure.

Real property may also be alienated as a result of a gift or a sale by means of a deed. This is the most common means of a title transfer.

Deeds

A **deed** is the formal written instrument by which an owner conveys title to real property during his lifetime. The main purpose of a deed is to provide clear evidence of a change in title or transfer of an interest in real property. Because the deed shows the transfer, it is often called a **conveyance**.

The deed is evidence of title to the property, but not title itself. The term "**title**" refers to the intangible rights of ownership. There is no document called title that shows ownership of real property. Instead, the deed is evidence that one has rights of ownership.

> **For Example**
>
> A deed could be a piece of paper on which is written "I, Mimi Mine, convey to Hubie Nice, the real property described as Lot 12, Block 6, Allen Subdivision, Clark County, Washington. This is my voluntary act, Mimi Mine (signed)." When delivered, the deed is valid.

While requirements may differ by state, the following elements are generally required in order for a deed to be valid.

----- ELEMENTS OF DEEDS -----

	Essential Elements of a Deed
1.	Be in writing
2.	Have words of conveyance
3.	Describe the property
4.	Identify the parties to the deed
5.	Be signed by the grantor
6.	Have a legally competent grantor
7.	Be delivered

In Writing

The Statute of Frauds requires that a transfer of an interest in real property be evidenced in writing. Therefore, to be valid, a deed must be in writing.

Granting Clause

In order to convey title to real property, the deed must contain words of conveyance, a **granting clause**. The wording must indicate that the grantor is making a transfer of the title or interest to the grantee. Words of conveyance include such words as "conveys," "transfers," "grants," "releases," etc.

Following the granting clause there might be a **habendum clause**. This clause defines or limits the quality and quantity of the estate being conveyed. It is only needed when the grantor is conveying less than a fee estate. Without a habendum clause, the deed is presumed to convey fee simple title. If the deed were intended to convey a life estate, a habendum clause would be needed. It begins with the words, "to have and to hold." For example, "to John Doe, grantee, to have and to hold, a life estate in…"

Habendum Clause	
	• "To have and to hold" • Limits QUANTITY and QUALITY of estate • Not required in deed

The conveyance may include **deed restrictions**, restricting the grantee's use of the property. These may be covenants or conditions. They are generally referred to as CC&Rs, or Covenants, Conditions, and Restrictions:

- A **covenant** is a promise by the grantee to either do something or to not do something with regard to the property

> **For Example**
>
> Sandy Loam was deeded property with a covenant that provided she had to build a house of at least 2,000 square feet and not build within 10 feet of the lot line. If she builds a smaller house or a house within 10 feet of the lot line, she will need to make changes or tear the house down.

- A **condition** is a qualification of the estate being granted

> **For Example**
>
> Bea Ware willed her property to ABC Church with the condition that it may hold the title as long as the property is used for church purposes. When the church leased the property for commercial retail use, it violated the condition. Because the reverter clause in the condition provided that the church would lose the title, the title would revert to Bea's heirs.

Covenants and conditions may not be used for the purpose of illegal discrimination. Any illegal discriminatory covenant or restriction in a real estate document would be null and void, as a matter of public policy.

Property Description

To be valid, a deed must contain a description adequate to identify the property being conveyed. This is usually a legal description based on a survey.

The description may include exceptions and/or reservations:
- A deed **exception** leaves out, withholds, or excepts a part of the real property described in the deed.

Al Paca conveyed "Lot 4, Block 5, Sunset Subdivision, excepting the north 10 ft." to Noah Count. This allowed Al to keep the north 10 feet across the lot and convey to Noah the rest of the lot.

- A **reservation** reduces the rights conveyed by creating a new right in favor of the grantor. This would be used if the grantor wanted to keep an easement or the mineral rights on the land he is conveying.

Identify the Parties

A deed must properly identify (name) the grantor and grantee. In a real property sales transaction, the seller would be the grantor and the purchaser would be the grantee. If there are a number of grantors or grantees, all must be named. Legal phrases *et al* (meaning "and others") or *et ux* (meaning "and wife") should not be used as identification.

Competent Grantor

The grantor must be legally competent, that is, alive, mentally competent, and legally authorized to convey title, at the time the deed is delivered.

A deed would be voidable (i.e., enforceable but able to be voided), by a grantor who was a minor or who was determined after the fact to be incompetent at the time of delivery of the deed.

Signature

The grantor, or a lawful agent of the grantor acting under written authority, must sign the deed. If there is more than one owner of the property, all must sign as grantors. The signatures need not be witnessed. The deed can be signed by an attorney-in-fact acting on behalf of the grantor if there is a written power of attorney authorizing this, recorded in the county in which the property is located. If the grantor is a corporation, an officer authorized by the board of directors or by vote of the stockholders would sign for the corporation. If the grantor is a trustee representing an unincorporated group, he must have written authority granted by the charter and bylaws of the group to act on its behalf.

Delivery

The deed will not convey title until it is delivered to the grantee and accepted. Acceptance is presumed if the grantee does not reject the deed. For **delivery** to be effective the grantor must:
- intend delivery. Delivery depends upon the intention of the grantor.
- intend the title transfer to be immediate, not in the future.
- give up control of the deed by:
  o giving the deed directly to the grantee.
  o recording the deed.
  o giving the deed to an escrow agent with instructions to deliver the deed to the grantee or to record the deed after certain conditions are met.

A deed may be used only once. Once a deed is delivered, it cannot be used again to convey any interest in the property. It cannot be assigned, transferred or endorsed to another. If after delivery, the grantor and grantee were to decide to cancel the transaction, the grantee would have to prepare a new deed, naming himself as grantor, and sign the deed as the grantor.

Other Items Required for Validity or Recording

In a few states, the deed must be acknowledged in order to be valid. In most states, however, acknowledgment of the deed by the grantor is required only in order for the deed to be recorded. An **acknowledgment** is signing before a notary or other eligible official authorized to take acknowledgments of deeds that the conveyance is voluntary.

A deed will generally show the grantee's consideration for the interest (property) being transferred. In some states this is required for validity. In other states, it may be required in order for the deed to be recorded. The consideration may be required to be shown as the actual amount paid for the property for tax assessment or conveyance tax purposes. In the case of a gift, it may be shown as a nominal amount, such as $10, or simply as "a gift" or "for love and affection."

Grantee

A grantee need not be competent or sign a deed. The only requirement of the **grantee** is that he be either a living person or a legal person (e.g., an existing corporation) capable in law of accepting delivery of the deed. The grantee cannot be a fictitious person created to defraud others; however, a grantee could be an actual person using a fictitious, or assumed, name.

----- DEED FORMS -----

There generally are four deed forms available for use:
1. Warranty deed (or general warranty deed)
2. Special warranty deed
3. Bargain and sale deed
4. Quitclaim deed

These deed forms differ with regard to the warranties or covenants of title they contain. These warranties relate only to the condition of the title being conveyed. They do not provide assurances as to the condition of the structure or provide for reimbursement if a structural defect is discovered.

Warranty Deed (General Warranty Deed)

The type of deed generally required of a seller is a **warranty deed** (or general warranty deed). From the grantee's point of view the general warranty deed is the most desirable type of deed. This is because it provides the greatest protection for the grantee and creates the greatest liability for the grantor.

Normally, the warranty deed states or implies the following warranties or covenants:

- **Covenant of seizen**. This guarantees the grantor owns and possesses the property, has a fee simple absolute interest, has no conditions restricting the title, and has the right to convey the title. The grantor would be liable for the full price of the property if there were an undisclosed condition, or he had only a life estate.
- **Covenant against encumbrances**. This guarantees there are no tax liens, mortgages, assessments or other liens except as stated in the deed.
- **Covenant of warranty**. This provides the grantor will defend the title against all persons who lawfully claim the title.
- **Covenant of quiet enjoyment**. This warrants that the grantee will not be disturbed by a person with a lien or better claim to the property.
- **Covenant of further assurance**. This warrants that the grantor will perform any additional act or provide any document needed to provide the title promised.

Special Warranty Deed

A **special warranty deed** is a limited warranty deed. It limits the covenants by the grantor. In this deed the grantor conveys and specially warrants to the grantee the real property free of encumbrances created or suffered by the grantor except as specifically set forth in the deed. It has the same effect and warranties as the general warranty deed, except that the covenant against encumbrances is limited to those created or suffered by the grantor. If an owner were not certain that the property he was selling was completely unencumbered but he was willing to guarantee the title against defects arising from any action, by, through or under himself, he could offer the buyer a special warranty deed.

Bargain and Sale Deed

A grantor willing to convey title, but without any warranties of title, may use a **bargain and sale deed**. This deed simply states the grantor conveys the real property to the grantee. It does not provide any warranties or covenants of title to the grantee or the grantee's successors. Therefore, it will not protect the grantee against title defects.

Quitclaim Deed

The **quitclaim deed** creates the least protection of any deed for the grantee and entails the least liability to the grantor. It passes any interest the signer may have in the property but does not tie him to any warranty. The interest could be fee simple, an easement, a claim of adverse possession, color of title, or any other interest the grantor may have. This deed states that the grantor transfers any interest he might have, although he may have no interest at all, and someone else may have a stronger claim. Therefore, the quitclaim deed might convey no ownership rights at all. It merely releases any claims of the grantor to rights in the property.

For this reason, a quitclaim deed is most commonly used to remove a cloud from the title. A **cloud on the title** is an encumbrance, charge, or claim against the property, which could make it legally impossible for the owner to convey marketable title.

Types of Deeds		
Greatest Protection ▲	Warranty	
	Special Warranty (Limited)	
	Bargain and Sale	
Least Protection ▼	Quitclaim	

----- OTHER DEEDS -----

There are a number of other forms of deeds. In some states (such as California) **grant deeds** are used instead of warranty deeds. Deeds may be referred to by their purpose:

- A **reformation deed** (or correction deed) has wording stating that the deed is given to correct a specific error in a previous deed.
- A **gift deed** is used to make a gift of real property. The consideration given is good consideration (i.e., love and affection), rather than valuable consideration.
- A tax deed is used to convey title as a result of tax foreclosure.
- A sheriff's deed is used to convey title to property sold by the sheriff under a court foreclosure or execution of a judgment.
- An **estoppel deed** (or deed in lieu of foreclosure) is given by a delinquent borrower to the lender in order to avoid foreclosure.
- A **mining deed** conveys mineral rights or an interest in a mine.
- A **trustee's deed** is given by a trustee to the purchaser of property sold at a trustee's sale, resulting from the default on a deed of trust.

----- RECORDATION -----

In order to be able to keep track of who has what interest in a parcel of real property, state statutes permit the recording of documents relating to real estate. **Recording** enables persons to give public notice concerning documents affecting the title to real estate. Once recorded, the information in a deed or other document is available for public inspection.

Recording System

Recording of documents affecting title to real estate must be performed in the county in which the property is located. The recording system:

- enables a person to provide constructive notice to the world of the interests in a particular parcel of real estate.
- helps prevent forgery in recorded documents by requiring acknowledgement by a grantor in front of a notary public.
- establishes legal priority of interests. Generally, whoever records first and is without notice of a prior claim of right has priority. The date and time stamped establish legal priority for those interests that are recorded first.

----- NOTICE -----

While an unrecorded deed is valid and binding between the parties to the deed (the grantor and the grantee), it would be void against the rights of a bona fide purchaser who first records his deed. A **bona fide purchaser** is a purchaser who pays valuable consideration in good faith and has no notice of the existence of another person's claim to the title. A person is without notice if he has no actual knowledge of another's rights to the property and has no reasonable means of obtaining that knowledge.

A person has notice of a prior claim of right when he has either constructive notice or actual notice.

Constructive Notice

When an owner of land provides the public with a means of obtaining knowledge of his rights in the land, that owner is providing **constructive notice** of his interest in the land.

A person can provide constructive notice in two ways:
1. Take possession of the land. Possession of land by a person other than the grantor gives constructive notice. A grantee who has an unrecorded deed provides constructive notice upon taking possession of the property by:
   - occupying the property.
   - renting the property to a tenant who occupies the property.
   - any other means that would enable an interested person to determine that perhaps the owner of record is not the current owner.
2. Properly record the deed. A better way of protecting one's rights is to record the deed. If an instrument is recorded, a purchaser cannot successfully claim that he did not know about the contents of the recorded document. Recording helps to forestall actions arising from persons with unrecorded interests in the land by giving priority to the person who records first.

Actual Notice

A person who has actual knowledge of a fact is said to have **actual notice**. A person has constructive notice of ownership when a deed is recorded and has actual notice when he actually sees the recorded deed. While he has constructive notice when a person is in possession of property, he has actual notice when he knows the person is in possession of the property, or knows of the person's right to possession.

NOTICE	
Constructive	**Actual**
Record	See recorded deed
Take possession	Know person has unrecorded deed

Brain Teaser

Reinforce your understanding of the material by correctly completing the following sentences:

1. _____ is the transfer or conveyance of title to real property to another.

2. _____ _____ action is a lawsuit to determine and resolve all adverse claims to ownership of the property.

3. A court order that requires the sheriff to sell property is a writ of _____.

4. The Statute of _____ requires that a transfer of an interest in real property be evidenced in writing.

5. The _____ of seizen guarantees the grantor owns and possesses the property, has a fee simple absolute interest, has no conditions restricting the title, and has the right to convey the title.

Brain Teaser Answers

1. **Alienation** is the transfer or conveyance of title to real property to another.

2. **Quiet title** action is a lawsuit to determine and resolve all adverse claims to ownership of the property.

3. A court order that requires the sheriff to sell property is a writ of **execution**.

4. The Statute of **Frauds** requires that a transfer of an interest in real property be evidenced in writing.

5. The **covenant** of seizen guarantees the grantor owns and possesses the property, has a fee simple absolute interest, has no conditions restricting the title, and has the right to convey the title.

Review — Conveyances and Deeds

In this lesson we discuss conveyances of title and deeds that provide evidence of title.

Conveyance of Title

The conveyance or transfer of title from one owner to another involves alienation of title by the current owner and acquisition of title by the new owner. Alienation is the transfer or conveyance of title to real property to another. It may be voluntary, through sale, gift, or will of property to another. It is involuntary when transfer of ownership of the estate occurs by operation of law (naturally or by court action).

Title may be transferred to and from the government a number of ways:
- A patent may convey title from the government to private owners.
- Forfeiture gives possession of property to the government.
- Dedication is the gift of property to the public.
- Eminent domain is the right of the government or a company authorized by the government, such as a utility company, to acquire title to property for public use by paying compensation to the owner, through the process of condemnation.
- Escheat is the right of the government to take property when a person dies intestate and without heirs.

Title to real property may be affected by physical action. Accession involves any additions to the land or property by any man-made or natural cause. Annexation of fixtures is a man-made addition. Accretion is the addition to one's land by the gradual deposit of soil through natural causes. Avulsion, the sudden tearing away of land by action of water, does not automatically cause a loss of title.

Title may be lost or acquired through adverse possession when an occupant has been in actual, open, notorious, hostile, exclusive, and continuous possession of the property under a claim of right for the required statutory period of time. Hostile means the adverse possessor is claiming ownership of the land. The owner can defeat a claim of title by adverse possession or an easement by adverse use (prescription) by asserting his ownership rights, taking legal action to evict the claimant, or giving permission for use, within the statutory period.

Upon a person's death, his property may pass to others through probate or without probate. When a person dies testate, an executor named in the will distributes the real property in the estate to devisees and the personal property to legatees. When a person dies intestate, the court will appoint an administrator to distribute the estate, and title will transfer by descent to heirs entitled to it under the laws of intestate succession.

Court action can also result in a conveyance of title. A partition suit will separate a co-owner's interest from others; a divorce decree may result in transfer of title from one spouse to the other spouse; and bankruptcy courts may require property to be sold to satisfy claims of creditors.

Understanding the Term Title

The term "title" refers to the intangible rights of ownership. A deed is not the title, but is a written instrument by which an owner conveys or transfers title to real property during his lifetime. The main purpose of a deed is to provide clear evidence of a change in title or transfer of an interest in real property. It automatically conveys fee title unless it has a habendum clause that defines or limits the quantity or quality of the estate, by specifying the estate the grantee is to "have and to hold."

What Makes a Deed Valid?

To be valid, a deed must be in writing, have words of conveyance, adequately describe the property, identify the grantor and grantee, be signed by the grantor, have a competent grantor, and be delivered. Upon intended delivery (by recording, placement in escrow or manual delivery), title passes immediately. The grantee must exist, but need not sign the deed or be competent.

Types of Deeds

There are many types of deeds. A general warranty deed provides the greatest protection for a grantee and creates the greatest liability for the grantor. It has a covenant of seizen (that the grantor is the owner and possessor of the property with the right to convey the title), a covenant against encumbrances (that the property has no liens or other encumbrances except as stated in the deed), and a covenant of warranty (that the grantor will defend the title).

A special warranty deed limits the warranty against encumbrances to only those defects arising from actions by, through, or under the grantor. A bargain and sale deed conveys title without any warranties or covenants. A quitclaim deed releases any claims of the grantor to rights in the property. While it will convey the grantor's existing interest in the property, it may convey no ownership rights at all. It is generally used to convey partial interests and to clear clouds on the title by releasing a claim of one of the parties claiming an interest.

A deed may have reservations and exceptions. A reservation allows the grantor to keep rights (such as mineral rights) in the property, while an exception excludes part of the property (such as the west 15 feet) from the conveyance.

Recording Deeds

An unrecorded deed is valid between the parties, but may be void against bona fide persons who are without notice and record a deed first. State statutes allow documents relating to real estate to be recorded in the county or counties in which the property is located so there is a way to keep track of interests in the property. The recording system enables a person to provide constructive notice of his interest in a particular parcel of real estate and establish the legal priority of his interest. It also helps prevent forgery, as a document transferring rights, such as a deed, must be acknowledged by the person giving the rights, before the document can be recorded. Acknowledgment includes declaring and signing before a notary that the transfer is his voluntary act.

A person has notice of a prior claim of right when he has either constructive notice or actual notice. He has constructive notice when he has a means of obtaining knowledge of rights in land. This notice is provided when an owner takes possession or records a deed. A person has actual notice when he has actual knowledge of a fact, such as when he sees a recorded deed or knows a person has an unrecorded deed.

Encumbrances

Overview

In this lesson we discuss nonmonetary encumbrances as well as monetary encumbrances, called liens. Restrictions, encroachments, easements, and licenses are reviewed. Types of voluntary, involuntary, statutory, equitable, general and specific liens are defined. Differences between general and special tax assessments are clarified.

Objectives

Upon completion of this lesson, the student should be able to:

1. Define the term "encumbrance" and give examples.
2. Define the terms "lien," "restrictions," "encroachments," "easements," and "licenses" and give examples of each.
3. Describe the creation and the termination of easements by necessity, prescription and condemnation.
4. Define the following forms of liens: voluntary, involuntary, statutory, equitable, general and specific.
5. Explain the effects of a lien as an encumbrance on title to real property.
6. Describe the priority of liens on title.
7. Explain attachments and judgments.
8. Describe the purpose of the homestead exemption.
9. Describe the effect of a mechanic's lien.
10. State the differences between general taxes and special assessments.

Deed Restrictions and Easements

An **encumbrance** is any interest or right to land held by third persons which affects the title and possibly the value of the property. It could include a claim against clear title resulting in a cloud on the title. Some encumbrances adversely affect the title by limiting the owner's rights and, therefore, diminishing the value of the property. Other encumbrances have no effect on value. Still others, such as subdivision restrictions and utility easements actually result in an increase in the property value.

There are two types of encumbrances:
1. Some encumbrances affect the physical condition of the property or affect the use of the property. These include deed restrictions (private limitations on the use of land), easements, and encroachments.
2. Other encumbrances are financial; they involve money. Such encumbrances are called liens. A lien is a charge against property, making that property security for payment of a debt.

----- NONMONETARY ENCUMBRANCES -----

Nonmonetary encumbrances include deed restrictions and several types of easements.

Deed Restrictions
Deed restrictions may be conditions or covenants:
- A condition is a restriction that provides for ownership of the property to revert to the former owner if the condition is violated. It creates a defeasible fee estate.
- A covenant is a promise to do or to not do something:
  - Subdivisions have covenants that establish set back lines, limit types of structures that may be built, etc.
  - Persons adversely affected by a violation of a covenant, those (benefiting) from the restriction, may sue for damages or seek an injunction to force correction of the violation.

Easements
Real property is encumbered when persons other than the landowner hold rights to use the land.

An **easement** is an irrevocable right to use all or a portion of another's land for a specific purpose. It is a nonpossessory right, as it gives the holder the right to limited use, but not to possession, of another's real property.

The owner of property A was given a permanent right to cross over property B. While his legal rights include the right of use and enjoyment of the land for passage, they fall short of ownership of, or an estate in, the land belonging to owner B.

Because an easement is a right to use and not to possess, it is usually nonexclusive. The landowner has the right to use the portion of the land on which the easement lies in any manner that does not interfere with the rights of the easement holder.

The electric company and telephone company have easements to run their lines across the back of Smith's lot. Smith still has the right to use that portion of his land as long as he does not disturb those lines or interfere with the right of the companies to maintain and repair those lines.

Servient Tenement

An easement is an encumbrance, but it is not a lien, as it does not involve money. Because the easement belongs to someone other than the owner of the land on which it lies, the easement is an encumbrance on the title to that land. As a result, that property would be subject to the easement. Land that is subject to, and therefore encumbered by, the easement is called a **servient estate** or **servient tenement**.

Because the easement is irrevocable, the owner of servient tenement cannot terminate the easement, even if the easement causes him great inconvenience. Furthermore, sale of the servient tenement has no effect on the easement. The purchaser of a servient tenement would receive title encumbered by the easement, even if it is not mentioned in the deed.

Depending on who has the easement right, an easement may be an easement in gross or an easement appurtenant.

Easement in Gross or Easement Appurtenant

An easement that is the right of an individual or company, held for the benefit of that person or company, is called an **easement in gross**. An easement in gross is personal property of the easement holder. It attaches to him personally and not to his land. The easement could be noncommercial or commercial.

Fred sold land bordering a park and reserved an irrevocable right to have access to the park through the land he sold. He has a noncommercial easement in gross. His easement is nonassignable and will terminate with his death, unless it is specified otherwise.

The same would hold true if a person sold a property that bordered a beach and reserved the right to cross the property to access the beach.

A commercial easement in gross is usually used by a utility company to install its lines under or over a privately owned property. Since almost all property has such lines, the easements in gross are the most common forms of easement. A commercial easement in  gross would also be created if a person had a right to maintain a billboard on another's property. A commercial easement in gross can be sold, assigned and mortgaged.

With an easement in gross there is only one parcel of real estate involved: the servient estate.

When a person has a right to enter the property and remove soil or other resources, such as sand, gravel or timber, his right may be called a *profit a prendre*, or simply, a profit.

With an **easement appurtenant** there are at least two parcels of land under separate ownership. This easement is a burden on one property (the servient estate) and a benefit or appurtenance to another property (the **dominant estate** or **dominant tenement**).

> **For Example**
>
> Ward has an easement appurtenant for ingress (a way to get in) and egress (a way to get out) over Taylor's acre, to enable him to reach the public road. Taylor's land is the servient tenement. Ward's land is the dominant tenement. This right runs with the land, so it will pass with the title from Ward to the next owner and successive owners whenever the title is transferred.

Because an easement appurtenant is a property right, and not a personal right of the holder, it is considered a real property interest rather than a personal property interest. Because it is appurtenant to the dominant estate, it runs with the land and will pass with the dominant estate when the title to that property is conveyed.

A dominant tenement need not adjoin the servient tenement at any borders.

> **For Example**
>
> A right of way over four parcels has been granted to a fifth parcel. That fifth parcel, the dominant estate, borders one of the servient estates, but not the other four.
>
> George's property has an easement for passage of light, air and heat over a hilly parcel that is not adjoining his property.

Affirmative and Negative Easements

An easement appurtenant may be an affirmative easement or a negative easement. An **affirmative easement** is a right to physically use the servient tenement. It could be:
- a party wall connecting adjoining townhouses.
- a right of way providing ingress and egress over an adjoining parcel.
- an easement to run a sewer line across neighboring property.

A **negative easement** is a right held by the dominant estate, which restricts the use of the servient estate. This would include:

- a view easement prohibiting the owner of the servient estate from constructing or growing anything which would block the view from the dominant estate.

- a solar easement prohibiting blockage of the sun's rays from reaching a portion of the dominant estate.
- an aviation easement prohibiting the owner of a servient estate near an airport from doing anything to interfere with flight patterns.

Creating an Easement

An easement may be created in the following ways:

- **Express grant**. The holder of the servient estate grants the easement in writing, either in a deed or a written agreement between the parties. This could be considered an easement created by mutual agreement.
- **Express reservation**. The grantor of the property reserves an easement in the property being conveyed.
- **Eminent domain** (condemnation). The government, private utilities and public transportation companies may take easements in private property if the property owner will not give them voluntarily, as long as fair compensation is provided.
- **Dedication**. A subdivider must dedicate streets and other areas in a subdivision to the government and easements to utility companies in order to receive subdivision approval.
- **Implication**. This results when an easement is not specified but is obviously necessary for a person to exercise rights received by grant or reservation, e.g., in most states a person can be sold mineral rights, and if no easement is specified to allow him to get to the minerals, an easement is implied.
- **Necessity**. An easement by necessity is a type of implied easement, created when justice or necessity make it necessary that an easement be provided for access (ingress and egress) to and from the property.

For Example

If Jones divided his land and sold the portion with no access to the street to Smith, Smith or purchasers from Smith could claim an easement by necessity.

- **Prescription**. This is unauthorized, nonexclusive, open, notorious and visible, hostile, continuous and uninterrupted use of another's property for a period set by state statute. It may result in the user obtaining an irrevocable right to continue the use, called a **prescriptive easement** or **easement by prescription**.

Terminating an Easement

An easement may be terminated in the following ways:

- **Written release** signed by the easement holder (i.e., the holder of the dominant estate or the holder of an easement in gross). It may be in the form of a quitclaim deed or an agreement between the easement holder and the owner of the servient estate.
- **Clear and intentional abandonment** by the easement holder, e.g., by building over the land leading to a right of way easement, so that access to that right of way was no longer possible.
- **Merger** of the servient tenement and dominant tenement under one owner, since that owner will no longer need a right to use someone else's land.
- **Expiration** of a specified time period for which the easement was created.
- The **purpose for which the easement was created ceases to exist**, e.g., when access to a new street makes an easement by necessity unnecessary or when telephone lines are relocated off the property.
- **Prescription** (adverse use) by the servient estate holder for a specific number of years.

For Example

If the servient estate holder builds over a right of way and the easement holder does nothing about it for a specified number of years, the easement could be terminated.

- **Eminent domain**, with the government taking the right away upon payment of fair compensation.
- **Destruction of the servient tenement**. For example, an easement given for a party wall or utility lines through a building would terminate if the building were destroyed.
- **Nonuse of a prescriptive easement** for a specified number of years.

NOTE: Nonuse will result in loss of the easement only if it was originally obtained by prescription. Nonuse would not terminate a deeded easement

An easement is not terminated:

- at the will of, or revoked by, the possessor of the servient estate.
- by the sale of either the dominant estate or the servient estate, even if it is not mentioned in the deed transferring the title to the dominant estate.
- merely because it created an inconvenience to the servient tenement impinging on the quiet enjoyment of the property.

License

A less formal right to use another's property is a **license**. A license is a personal, revocable, nonassignable right to use the property of another. Because it is personal, it could be terminated by death of either party and by sale of the property. It gives a person permission to use land for some limited purpose, but gives no other rights in that land. It is like a noncommercial easement in gross, except that it is revocable and need not be in writing.

A right, given orally, to enter upon the property of another to have a shortcut to a park bordering the property would be a license. If the same right were granted in writing as an irrevocable right, it would be an easement in gross.

Encroachment

An **encroachment** is the unauthorized intrusion of a building or other improvement onto  one's land. For example, if Walter built a wall, fence or eave that extended onto Scott's land, the wall, fence, or eave is an encroachment. Since the use of the land encroached upon is adversely affected by the existence of those improvements, the encroachment is an encumbrance, clouding the title. Most often, an encroachment is unintentional, but it is illegally entering onto another's property without authority or permission of the owner, so it is a form of trespass. The property owner could sue for ejectment to have the encroachment removed. Usually, an encroachment is discovered as a result of a survey.

ENCUMBRANCES – USE	
CC&Rs	▪ Covenants – Promises ▪ Conditions – Reverters ▪ Restrictions
Easement	▪ Irrevocable ▪ In Gross or Appurtenant ▪ Negative or Affirmative
License	▪ Revocable ▪ Personal Permission
Encroachment	▪ Intrusion onto Adjacent Property

Monetary Encumbrances

----- LIENS -----

When one person owes money to another, the creditor can place a lien against the debtor's property so that if the debt is not paid, the creditor can have the property sold to get his money. The **lien** is a security interest of the creditor in the property of another. It is a charge against property, making that property security for payment of a debt. In most cases, the priority of a lien on real property is established by the date it is recorded.

Liens include property taxes, special assessments, mortgages, deeds of trust, attachments, judgments, income tax liens, and mechanic's (or construction) liens. Some of these liens are voluntary; others are involuntary.

Liens may be specific or general. A **general lien** is an involuntary lien that applies against a person and all of the property of that person, except property exempted by statute. Judgment liens, debts of decedents, income tax liens and estate tax liens are general liens.

A **specific** (or **special**) **lien** is an encumbrance against one or more specified parcels of real estate. A mechanic's lien, a property tax lien, a special assessment, or a mortgage applying to three parcels would be a specific lien.

A **voluntary lien** is a **contractual lien**. It is created by a voluntary contract, such as a mortgage or a deed of trust, entered into by the debtor and creditor. A mortgage would create an encumbrance in the form of a voluntary lien against the property by pledging the property to secure the debt.

Involuntary liens are imposed by operation of law, without the owner's consent. These would include a real property tax lien, a mechanic's lien for work done on property, a special assessment for public improvements benefiting property, an income tax lien, an estate tax lien, or a money judgment of a court resulting from a lawsuit.

Involuntary liens may be statutory or equitable. **Statutory liens** are those authorized by state statute, such as mechanic's liens and property tax liens. **Equitable liens** are those imposed by courts of equity, often as a result of breach of contract.

General Liens

Upon the death of a person, general liens for debts of the decedent are created when
 creditors file claims against the decedent's estate. Federal and state governments may also impose estate or inheritance taxes on the estate. These taxes may result in a lien against the estate in order to ensure payment before estate proceeds are distributed to heirs, devisees or legatees. Since these are general liens, the

debts are paid first from any personal property of the deceased not specifically bequeathed, then paid from the rest of the personal property. If any debts remain outstanding, the real property may be sold.

The **income tax lien** is a general lien created when a government files a tax warrant in the county in which property of a delinquent income taxpayer is located. Once recorded, this lien applies to all of the taxpayer's property in any counties in which the lien is filed. The lien has priority as of the date the lien was recorded.

A **judgment lien** is a general involuntary lien resulting from a judgment *in personam* (against a person). The judgment is a court order resulting from a lawsuit, to enforce a contractual or legal right to receive a payment of money due, determining that a person is indebted to another and fixing the amount of the indebtedness. Because the lien is against the person, it is a lien against all of that person's property (real and personal), rather than any particular items.

A judgment becomes a lien upon any of the judgment debtor's real and personal property in the county in which it is recorded. It remains a lien against that property for the number of years specified by state law, from the time the judgment is rendered.

During the lien period, the judgment debtor cannot convey clear title to his real property, unless the lien is satisfied, as the judgment would remain on the property even if the property were sold. If the debtor can satisfy the judgment before it is enforced, he would obtain from the creditor a satisfaction of judgment and record it to show that the judgment has been paid and is no longer a lien on the debtor's real property.

Any time during the lien period and before the judgment is satisfied, the judgment creditor may seek to have the judgment enforced by a process referred to as execution. The creditor would ask the court for a **writ of execution**, ordering the sheriff to sell the debtor's property to satisfy the judgment.

Normally, all of the judgment debtor's personal and real property would be subject to the execution, except for items exempt by law (such as, clothes, household goods, or cars below certain values).

Homestead Exemption

Many states have a provision for a **homestead exemption**, which provides protection from foreclosure due to unsecured liens (meaning liens in which the property was not originally offered as security for the debt). The laws provide that, in the event of a foreclosure, the debtor must be able to receive a certain amount of equity from the sale. The amount varies by state. The exemption does not defeat foreclosure of secured liens such as mortgages or deeds of trust, or homeowners' or condominium association liens.

Specific Liens

While general liens affect all property of the owner, specific liens affect only specified properties.

Attachment

An **attachment** is a specific lien placed against property of a defendant in a lawsuit for money damages. The attachment arises in those situations, at the start of or during the progress of a legal action, when it may be necessary to protect the creditor against the removal of the defendant's property from reach of the court before a judgment is rendered. In the attachment process, a writ is issued by the court ordering the seizure of certain property of the defendant in the action as security for the satisfaction of any judgment the plaintiff may recover. The **writ of attachment** is used primarily against the property of absconding or fraudulent debtors.

Because the attachment is placed before a judgment is rendered in order to make sure the defendant's property will be available if the plaintiff obtains the judgment, it is not dependent upon a judgment being rendered.

Lis Pendens

Because there may be a considerable period of time between the filing of a lawsuit and the actual rendering of a judgment, in an action affecting title to real property, the plaintiff may record a notice of the pending suit, called a **lis pendens**. The lis pendens may be recorded at or after the time of filing the lawsuit. The recording gives constructive notice to any future purchaser of the property that he will be bound by all proceedings after the filing of the notice as if he were a party to the action. The result is that any future judgment resulting from the lawsuit would date back to the date of the recording of the lis pendens and would have priority over claims of persons who had constructive notice of the possible judgment.

Mechanic's Lien

Another specific lien is a **mechanic's lien** (or materialman's lien or **construction lien**). This lien results from statutory law, as opposed to common law, so it is considered a **statutory lien**. The law gives those who have furnished work or materials for the improvement of real property the right to place a lien on that property if they are not paid. This allows contractors, subcontractors, laborers, material suppliers and equipment renters to file such liens.

For Example	John Smith installs a swimming pool on Mr. Brown's land. He is not paid. He can file a mechanic's lien on that parcel of property.

These liens do not arise automatically as a result of work done. They must be filed within a specified time period after the work has ceased or materials have been delivered. Once recorded, the construction lien is valid. However, unlike any other private liens, the effective date might not be the date of recording. Depending on state law, the effective date may be the day the contractor filing the lien started work, the day he finished work, or the day the entire job was finished. In some states it is the day anyone on the job started work (so that all contractors working on one job would share the same priority date). In those states, if a construction lien was recorded May 1, but work started January 2, the lien would date back to January 2 and would have priority over any private lien recorded after that date. Lenders may require an inspection of the property before giving building loans to be sure that work has not started before their lien is recorded.

Once a construction lien is recorded, the contractor has a statutory number of months in which to file a suit for foreclosure, if he is not paid. If he does file for foreclosure, the court could order the property sold by the sheriff to satisfy the lien. If the lien is not foreclosed within the time allowed by state law, the property can no longer be used as security for the debt and cannot be foreclosed upon. However, the claimant can file for an unsecured judgment against the property owner himself.

If property is encumbered with a construction lien and the contractor is paid, the owner should obtain and record a satisfaction of the lien in order to clear the lien from the records.

Special Assessments
A **special assessment** is a governmental lien placed against real property to pay all or part of the cost of a local improvement that will benefit the property. Cities, towns, and counties have the right to make local improvements based on the request of the property owners, or without their consent when the improvements are in the public interest. Such improvements include paving and creating curbs, sewers, and sidewalks; installing water mains, drains, sewers, street lighting, and other items. If the property owner does not pay for the work in a lump sum payment, the cost becomes a lien as of the time the assessment is determined and remains a lien until it is paid in full.

Property Taxes
Property tax liens are a major source of income for local (city and county) governments. They are specific involuntary liens and have priority over all other liens, including liens filed before the lien date. This means in the event of foreclosure they are paid first. Property taxes become a lien on property on the first day of the tax year and remain a lien until paid. If the real property is sold during the tax year and there is no agreement as to who will pay the taxes, the law provides that the buyer and seller will each be liable for a prorated amount.

Property taxes are direct and proportionate taxes. They are proportionate because the dollar amount of taxes varies according to the value of the property. Because property taxes are imposed according to value, they are considered to be **ad valorem** taxes.

Property taxes generally involve assessment of the property by the county assessor. The assessor will determine what real and personal property is taxable, assess it and get it listed on the tax rolls. In many states, the assessed value is supposed to be 100% of the true and fair value. Other states may use a **tax ratio**. This means that the assessed value is less than 100% of the market value of the property. In a state with a tax ratio of 80%, the assessed value is 80% of the market value. In such a state, a property worth $100,000 would have an assessed value of 80% of $100,000, or $80,000. Since it is not possible for the assessor to actually physically inspect each taxable parcel of real property each year, between physical inspections, the assessor may adjust the value of the property based on trend data and submit data relating to the sale or improvement of the property since the last assessment.

The property tax rate is obtained by dividing the budget for a tax district by the total assessed value of all taxable property in the district. This rate may be expressed as an amount per thousand dollars of value or as **mills**.

> **For Example**
>
> The total assessed value of property in a fire district is $80,000,000. The budget for the fire district is $500,000. To determine the tax rate, divide the budget, $500,000 by the assessed value of property, $80,000,000. The tax rate is .00625. This rate can be expressed as 6.25 per thousand dollars of value, or as 6.25 mills. One mill is one-tenth of a cent, or one–one thousandth (.001). So, a mill is the same as saying "per thousand."

The property tax is calculated by adding the tax rates for all the taxing bodies that affect a particular parcel of property, and then multiplying that total by the value of the property.

> **For Example**
>
> The total of the various rates for a property equals .01175 ($1.175 per thousand dollars of value or 1.175 mills). The property is worth $300,000 and assessed for tax purposes at $250,000. The tax would be .01175 x $250,000. The property tax is $2,937.50.

Taxes generally may be paid in installments. If they are unpaid for a number of years, the county will foreclose.

Brain Teaser

Reinforce your understanding of the material by correctly completing the following sentences:

1. An _____ is any interest or right to land held by third persons which affects the title and possibly the value of the property.

2. An _____ is an irrevocable right to use all or a portion of another's land for a specific purpose.

3. A _____ is a charge against property, making that property security for payment of a debt.

4. To be valid, a _____ (or construction) lien must be filed within a specified time period after the work has ceased or materials have been delivered.

Brain Teaser Answers

1. An **encumbrance** is any interest or right to land held by third persons which affects the title and possibly the value of the property.

2. An **easement** is an irrevocable right to use all or a portion of another's land for a specific purpose.

3. A **lien** is a charge against property, making that property security for payment of a debt.

4. To be valid, a **mechanic's** (or construction) lien must be filed within a specified time period after the work has ceased or materials have been delivered.

Review — Encumbrances

In this lesson we discuss encumbrances.

Encumbrance Basics

An encumbrance is any interest or right to land held by third persons which affects the title and possibly the value of the property. Encumbrances could adversely affect title, may have no effect on value, or may result in an increase in the property value.

Encumbrances affecting the physical condition of the property include deed restrictions, easements, and encroachments.

Deed Restrictions

Deed restrictions include conditions and covenants. A condition is a restriction that provides for ownership of the property to revert to the former owner if the condition is violated. A covenant is a promise to do or not do something.

Easements

An easement is an irrevocable right that gives the holder the right to limited use of all or a portion of another's land for a specific purpose. The land burdened or encumbered by any easement is called the servient estate.

An easement giving a person the right to use another's land, such as a right of way held by a public utility company, is called an easement in gross.

An easement belonging to a parcel of real property is called an easement appurtenant, as it is appurtenant to the land benefiting from it (the dominant estate), and transfers or runs with the property when it is sold. The servient and dominant estates need not be adjoining.

Easements may be created by:
- express grant (in writing).
- express reservation.
- eminent domain (or condemnation).
- dedication.
- implication.
- necessity (if the property is landlocked and the owner needs access over adjacent property).
- prescription (similar to adverse possession, and often referred to as adverse use).

An easement may be terminated by:
- written release (through a quitclaim deed) from the easement holder.
- clear and intentional abandonment by the easement holder.
- merger of the dominant and servient estates under one owner.
- expiration of a specified time period.
- the purpose for which the easement was created ceasing to exist.
- destruction of the servient tenement.
- prescription (adverse use by the servient estate holder).
- eminent domain.
- nonuse (but only if the easement had been acquired by prescription).

Licenses
A less formal right to use another's property is a license. It may be created in writing, orally, or by implication, to give a personal, revocable and nonassignable right to use another's land for some limited purpose, with no other rights in that land.

Encroachment
An encroachment is the unauthorized intrusion of a building or other improvement onto one's land. The encroachment is an encumbrance, clouding the title to the property encroached upon. Most often, an encroachment is unintentional, but it is illegal and a form of trespass (entry on land without the owner's permission). It is usually discovered as the result of a survey.

Types of Liens
An encumbrance that involves money is called a lien. It is a charge against property, making the property security for payment of a debt. It is voluntary when it is created by a contract entered into by the debtor and creditor, pledging the property to secure the debt, like a mortgage or deed of trust. It is involuntary when it is imposed by operation of law, such as property tax lien, a construction (or mechanic's) lien, a special assessment for public improvements benefiting property, an income tax lien, an estate tax lien, or a judgment lien resulting from a lawsuit. It is statutory when authorized by state statute. A mechanic's lien is an example of a statutory (authorized by state statue) lien. It is equitable when imposed by a court of equity.

A lien is either general or specific. A general lien (e.g., a judgment lien, debt of a decedent, income tax lien or estate tax lien) applies against a person and all of his property, except property exempted by statute. A specific (or special) lien is an encumbrance against one or more specified parcels of real estate. A mechanic's lien, a property tax lien, a special assessment, or a mortgage applying to three parcels would be a specific lien.

A judgment lien is a general involuntary lien resulting from a judgment against a person. A judgment is a court order determining that one person owes another a certain amount of money. Upon filing the suit, the plaintiff may record a lis pendens (notice of suit pending), providing constructive notice of the potential judgment lien's priority over transactions occurring after the date of recording. He may also seek a writ of attachment from a court, ordering the sheriff to seize the defendant's property to make sure it will be available to satisfy the potential judgment. If the court issues a judgment against the defendant, he will not be able to convey clear title to his real property unless the lien is satisfied. Any time during the lien period, the judgment creditor may seek to have the judgment enforced by obtaining a writ of execution, ordering the sheriff to sell the judgment debtor's property.

A mechanic's (or construction) lien results from statutory law that gives a person who has furnished work or materials for the improvement of real property the right to place a lien on that property if he is not paid. It must be filed within a specified time period after the work has ceased or materials have been delivered.

A special assessment is a charge upon real property to pay all or part of the cost of a local improvement that will benefit the property. Such improvements include paving and creating curbs, sewers, and sidewalks; installing water mains, drains, sewers, street lighting, and other items.

Property tax liens are specific involuntary liens and have priority over all other liens, including liens filed before the lien date. This means in the event of foreclosure, they are paid first. The tax is based on the assessed value, with the rate generally expressed in dollars per thousand, or mills.

Estates

Overview

In this lesson we explain how an estate differs from other interests that people or entities may have in real estate, for example, liens and easements. Two different types of estate classes are outlined: freehold and nonfreehold (leasehold). Clear examples of different kinds of fee estates and life estates are provided. Finally, the four main types of leasehold estates are defined.

Objectives

Upon completion of this lesson, the student should be able to:

1. Describe the two types of estates in land.
2. Define fee simple, determinable fee and fee simple subject to condition subsequent.
3. Describe a conventional life estate and differentiate between remainder interests and reversion interests.
4. Describe and compare the following four types of leasehold estates: estate for years, estate from period to period, estate at will and estate at sufferance.

Estates Explained

A real estate agent attempting to negotiate a real estate transaction for a client must be aware of the estate in the property held by the owner in order to ensure that the owner has the right to sell or lease the property under the terms negotiated by the parties. The estate held by the owner signifies the degree, quantity, nature and extent of the owner's title, right or interest in real property.

An **estate** is a possessory right or ownership interest in real property. A person has an estate when he has a possessory right or ownership interest in real estate. Therefore, a person has an estate when he owns or leases property. In either instance, the holder of the estate would have the right to use and possess (control) the property and the right to dispose of his interest in the property. More than one person may hold an estate in a particular property at the same time. If Mr. and Mrs. Smith were co-owners of a property, they would hold the estate together at the same time. A person who holds an estate is called a tenant, and the way in which he holds the estate is called a tenancy.

Other persons or entities may hold interests in real estate that give them rights, but these rights do not include the right to possess the property. These interests would then be short of an estate.

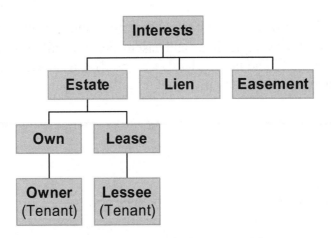

<table>
<tr><td rowspan="5" style="writing-mode: vertical-rl">For Example</td><td>A lienholder would have an interest in a property, but would not have an estate. A lender may hold a mortgage or trust deed as security for a loan. This gives the lender a lien against the property, but not a right of possession. Therefore, the lender (called a mortgagee if he holds a mortgage, or a beneficiary if he holds a trust deed) does not have an estate.</td></tr>
</table>

A person holding an easement or a license to use somebody else's land would not have an estate, since the right to use the land is not the same as the right to possess the land.

A right to possess is not the same as possession. If a person has possession, but does not have the right of possession, he would not have an estate. Therefore, a trespasser who has adverse possession of property with no legal right to possess it, does not have an estate. Also, a person does not have to have actual possession in order to have an estate, as long as he has the right of possession.

The holding of an estate does not always give a right of immediate possession. It could give a person a present right of possession or a future right of possession.

<table>
<tr><td>For Example</td><td>When an owner leases property to a tenant, the tenant has the right of possession until the lease is terminated and the owner has the right of possession after the lease has terminated, so both hold estates.

One person could hold the right to own and possess the property for a lifetime, while another holds the right to own and possess the property upon the death of the first person.</td></tr>
</table>

An estate may be created in a number of ways, including the following:
- Grant to another
- Reservation
- Operation of law

An estate in real property (other than a lease for one year or less) can only be created by operation of law or by a written instrument, such as a deed, a will or a lease. Contracts containing an agreement to create an estate in real property, such as a real estate purchase contract, need to be in writing.

Estates are divided into two broad classes based on their length of duration. These classes are freehold and nonfreehold:
1. **Freehold estates** are estates that last indefinitely for one or more lifetimes or in perpetuity. These estates involve ownership of the property. They are considered real property interests. They include fee simple, life, reversion and remainder estates.
2. **Nonfreehold estates** are estates which last for a lesser and temporary period of time. These estates involve the lease or rental of real estate. They include an estate for years, periodic estate, estate at will and estate at sufferance.

Freehold Estates

Fee Simple

The most common type of freehold estate is the **fee simple estate**. This may also simply be called a **fee estate**. Unless a deed or will specifically indicates a different type of estate, it is presumed that the owner has a fee estate. A fee estate is the maximum estate and the greatest interest that a person may hold in land. This is because it is of indefinite and unlimited duration, the most freely transferable and inheritable estate.

A fee estate is an estate of inheritance. It has no restrictions as to inheritance of the estate. It may be transferred by will; such a transfer is referred to as a **devise**, and those receiving the estate by devise are called devisees. The estate may pass to the estate holder's heirs upon his death, even if he leaves no will, through the laws of descent. As a result, the estate may pass on in perpetuity (forever).

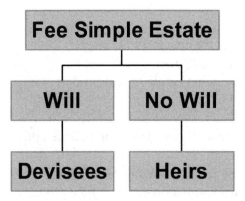

The estate may or may not be free of encumbrances. Virtually all real property is encumbered by rights or claims of others to an interest in the property. The most common encumbrances include property tax liens, mortgage or trust deed liens, and utility easements. The presence of these encumbrances does not alter the nature of the fee estate. A person holding a fee estate:

- holds title to the property.
- has the right to dispose of it through sale or gift during his lifetime or through will or inheritance upon his death.
- may impose conditions or restrictions on future use which would apply to all persons who later acquire the estate.

He may convey a fee estate to another with or without conditions, or even convey a lesser form of freehold estate, called a life estate. If he gives a life estate, he gives the new owner title for a lifetime and designates the party to whom the estate would pass at the end of that lifetime. That party could be himself, or his heirs, or some other person.

A fee simple estate may be absolute or it may be qualified. A **fee simple absolute estate** is the most complete form of ownership our law recognizes today. The term "absolute" indicates that the estate cannot be taken from the estate holder due to the occurrence of any event other than the death of the estate holder without any living heirs. In other words, there are no conditions imposed on the estate. Unless there are words to indicate that there are conditions placed on the estate, a fee estate would be absolute. Therefore, the terms fee estate or fee simple estate could be used to refer to a fee simple absolute estate.

A **qualified fee estate** (also called a **conditional fee**, a **defeasible fee**, or **fee simple defeasible estate**) is an estate of potentially unlimited duration and does not terminate upon the death of the owner. However, the estate has certain qualifications (conditions). The term "defeasible" is used to indicate that, if the event specified in the conditions were to occur, the estate would or could be defeated.

For Example	The conveyance of title with the condition that the land not be used for any purpose other than a nature preserve would create a fee simple defeasible estate. If the land were used to create an owner's residence, the estate may be terminated.

The wording of a **condition** in a defeasible fee estate could provide that the termination would be automatic or it could provide that the estate would be terminated at the discretion of the person creating the condition or his heirs. When the wording indicates that the estate would terminate automatically, the estate is either fee simple determinable or fee simple subject to executory limitation. The conveyance of an estate in fee simple determinable creates the possibility of automatic reversion of title. If the condition were violated, the estate would automatically terminate and revert (return) to the grantor (the giver) of the estate or the grantor's heirs.

For Example	Assume Barb Dwyer owned fee simple title to a vacant lot adjacent to a school. She decided to make a gift of the lot to the school. She wanted to have some control over the use of the lot, so her attorney prepared a deed to convey ownership of the lot to the school as long as it was used for educational purposes. After completion of the gift, the school will own a fee simple determinable estate.
	Assume Perry Noyd devised a piece of property through his will to City Hospital for so long as the property was used for medical purposes. Several years later, the City Hospital conveyed this property to a real estate development company. As a result, the development company has lost its interest in the property, and the property will revert to the heirs of Perry Noyd.

A fee simple subject to executory limitation also is subject to automatic termination. However, upon the happening of the specified event, the estate would pass to some person other than the grantor or the grantor's heirs.

When a defeasible fee estate could be terminated, but termination is not automatic, the estate is fee simple subject to condition subsequent. In this case, if the condition is violated, the grantor or his heirs have the right to re-enter and take possession of the estate, but loss of the estate is not automatic.

All defeasible fee estates are inheritable and include the same bundle of rights as a fee simple absolute estate as long as the conditions of ownership are not violated and conditions imposed by the original grantor will run with the land and be effective against any future owners of the property.

Life Estate

Freehold estates might also be noninheritable. Noninheritable freehold estates are called **life estates**. A life estate is a freehold estate, since it is an ownership estate. However, it is not a fee estate, since it is not inheritable. A life estate may be measured by the life of the holder of the life estate (the life tenant).

For Example	Wilson willed his widow, Willow, the use of the family home for the rest of her natural life, with the provision that the title would go to their children upon her death. Willow is the life tenant, holding the life estate. Willow's estate will exist only as long as she is alive. After Willow remarried and had two more children, she went to her attorney to have a will drafted leaving the home to her spouse and their children. When she learned she had no right to pass the estate to her heirs or devisees upon her death, Willow wept.

When a person holds a life estate for his life, his heirs would have no estate or interest in the property.

For Example	Dell conveyed a house to Meadow for life, then to Lea. Meadow's heirs would have no estate or interest in the property. Once Meadow dies, the property passes to Lea, and not to Meadow's heirs.

Not all life estates are for the life of the life tenant. A life estate may be measured by the life of someone other than the holder of the life estate. In such a situation, the life estate could extend beyond the life of the life tenant.

For Example	Basil deeds Blackacre Ranch to Rosemary for the life of Sage. Rosemary is the life tenant and holds the life estate for as long as Sage remains alive. Sage has no interest or estate at all in the property. However, when Sage dies, Rosemary's life estate is terminated, and she loses the right of possession. If Rosemary were to die before Sage does, the estate would vest in Rosemary's heirs until Sage died.

A life estate may be measured by the life of more than one person.

Because a life tenant has a freehold estate, he has an exclusive right of possession in the property. Unless there exists a deed restriction to the contrary, he may rent or lease the property, use the property to earn profits, or encumber the property, such as by using it as security for a loan. He can even sell his life interest in the property. If he does, the buyer's interest will be a life estate for the same life as the seller's life estate was.

Why might a person buy a life estate, give a loan secured by a life estate, or lease property from a life tenant? A person who wants the use of the property for an indefinite period could buy or lease the property for less than it would cost if the owner had a fee estate. In addition, he could obtain life insurance on the life measuring the life estate so that he could get his money back when the estate was over. A lender whose loan was secured by the estate could have the borrower purchase life insurance that would pay off the loan upon termination of the life estate.

There are a number of limitations on the bundle of rights held by a life tenant, which exist in order to protect the rights of the person who will acquire the title when the life estate is terminated. The person holding a life estate for his life could not devise (will) the estate. The only time a life tenant could devise his interest would be when he holds the estate for the lifetime of another person and he dies before that person does. Even this is a limited action, as the devisees would hold the estate only until it was terminated. A life estate holder cannot make any changes or alterations in the property that could create waste or damage to the property. In fact, he is responsible for maintaining the property and paying all taxes and assessments on the property.

Finally, he can convey only those rights he has. If he sells, mortgages, or leases the property, the transaction is effective only to the end of the term of the life estate, and the sale, mortgage or lease would terminate automatically upon termination of the life estate.

A person may determine the estate an owner has, so he does not unknowingly buy a life estate, by reviewing the owner's deed or by having the owner provide:

- a title report that will show the estate he has.
- a title insurance policy that will guarantee the accuracy of the title report.

A life estate may be created by deed or will. The deed or will would establish what would happen upon termination of the life estate. There are two possibilities.

One possibility is that title will revert (go back) to the grantor who created the life estate in the deed, or to his heirs, or to the heirs of the devisor who created the life estate in a will. Title will revert if the deed or will states that the title will revert, or if nothing is mentioned. When nothing is stated, the implication is that the title will revert.

> **For Example**
>
> A deed from Angio Gramm states, "to Polly Gramm for her life." This implies that the title will revert to the Angio, the grantor, upon Polly's death. During the entire period of the life estate, Angio has an interest in the property known as reversion or as an estate in reversion.

Reversion is the right to future possession by the grantor creating the life estate. Reversion means the land will return to the grantor of the estate.

> **For Example**
>
> In a deed in which the grantor, Sam Count, states "to Noah Count for his life, and then back to Sam Count," Sam would have a reversion interest.

The second possibility is that the deed or will provides that, upon termination of the life estate, title will pass to a specified third party. That third party, called a **remainderman**, holds a remainder interest or estate in remainder during the entire term of the life estate. With an **estate in remainder**, upon termination of a life estate, title passes to a specified third party.

Miller willed the benefits of his real property to Baker for Baker's lifetime, after which the property will pass to Smith. Smith has an estate in remainder.

An owner of a fee simple estate can change his ownership to a life estate by conveying and reserving to himself a life estate in the property, and granting to a remainderman a remainder interest. Upon the death of the life tenant, the remainderman will get fee title to the property even if the life tenant had sold the life estate.

Willow, a life tenant, sells her estate to Laurel. When Willow dies, Laurel's interest will be terminated and title will be in the remainderman.

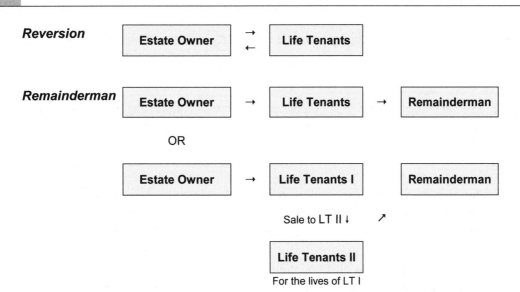

There is always more than one estate existing in property owned by a life tenant: the life estate and either an estate in reversion or an estate in remainder. The estate in remainder or estate in reversion would exist only while the life estate exists. Once the life estate is terminated, the estate in reversion or estate in remainder will usually change to a fee simple estate; however, it is possible to give a remainderman a life estate.

Earl Lee gives a life estate to Burl Lee, with the provision that when Burl dies, the estate will go to Pearl Lee, and upon Pearl's death, it will go to Shirl Lee. Pearl is a remainderman who will get a life estate and Shirl is a remainderman who will get a fee estate.

A life tenant and a remainderman could agree that one will sell his interest to the other, or agree to mutually sell their interests to a third party. The result of either type of transaction would be a merger of the estates, and the new owner would have a fee estate.

Life estates have a number of uses:

- They can serve as a "poor man's will." A person who owns property in fee simple title can deed property from himself as fee estate holder to himself as life estate holder, naming his son as remainderman. Thus, the property would still be his for the remainder of his life, but would pass to the son automatically upon his (the life tenant's) death.
- They can be used to tie property up for future use.

For Example	A person interested in a property could buy an estate in remainder, thus acquiring the right to the property upon the death of the owner. The owner would change ownership from fee estate to life estate and name the purchaser as the remainderman. The remainderman then acquires ownership of the fee estate upon the death of the life tenant. The price paid for the remainder interest would be based in part on the life expectancy of the life tenant.

- They can be used to gift property to a charity or other nonprofit organizations.

For Example	The fee owner changes his ownership to a life tenancy, naming his college as the remainderman to receive it upon his death.

- They can be useful in second marriage situations where an owner may want to provide a surviving spouse with a place to live for the remainder of his or her life, but may not want the property to pass to the heirs of that surviving spouse. The fee owner could will the surviving spouse a life estate in the property instead of a fee estate, and name a child of the fee owner as the remainderman. If the fee owner were to just will the property to the surviving spouse, upon the death of the surviving spouse, the property would be devised to whomever that spouse wished or would pass to that spouse's heirs.

The common element involved in all freehold estates, whether fee estates or life estates, is that they are of indefinite duration and involve ownership of a real property interest.

Nonfreehold Estates

----- NONFREEHOLD ESTATES -----

Freehold	Nonfreehold (Leasehold)
Indefinite Duration	Limited Duration
Real Property Interest	Personal Property Interest

Nonfreehold estates (also called **less than freehold estates**, **leasehold estates**, or **chattels real**) are limited in duration and are considered to be personal property interests.

These estates may be created by a lease. A lease exists whenever one person holds possession of the real property of another under an express written or oral agreement, or under an implied agreement. The person who owns the real property and permits the occupation of the premises could be called the **lessor** or **landlord**. The person who occupies the property is called the **lessee** or **tenant**.

> **Helpful Tip**
>
> Givers are identified with "or" at the end of the word, while receivers are identified with "ee" at the end. A **grantor** gives a freehold estate; a **grantee** receives it. A lessor gives a lease; a lessee receives it. A mortgagor (borrower) gives a mortgage; a mortgagee (lender) receives it.

The term **lease** may be used to refer to:
- a conveyance of a leasehold estate in land to the lessee;
- an agreement to occupy property for a specified period; or
- any document or instrument that transfers possession and use of real property for specific consideration, but does not transfer ownership.

The lessee's rights under the lease are contractual rights. Such rights are personal property, so the tenant has only a personal property interest or chattel interest in the real property. Since the lease conveys the right of possession to the tenant, there is a conveyance of an estate in the real property. Therefore, the lessee's interest in the leased property by virtue of the lease can be described as chattel real. An old-fashioned term used to indicate the conveyance of a leasehold estate is demise. **Demise** refers to an estate that will end.

In any lease transaction there will exist at least two estates. The lessor will keep a freehold estate (or leased fee) in the property while giving the lessee a leasehold estate. This gives the lessor a reversionary interest in the property during the term of the leasehold, as he has the right to retake possession of the property when the lease expires. In addition, he has the right to receive rent while the leasehold exists.

The lessee receives a leasehold estate, giving him the right of use, possession and quiet enjoyment of the property. His leasehold estate is:

- inheritable (so he can will it or leave it to his heirs).
- transferable by sale or assignment (so he can sell or assign it).
- of certain duration, as it is either limited in time or by the desire of the parties.

	4 Types of Leasehold Estates
1.	Estate for Years (for a fixed period)
2.	Periodic Estate (from period to period)
3.	Estate at Will
4.	Estate at Sufferance

Estate for Years

An **estate for years**, despite its name, has nothing to do with years. This estate is a tenancy of definite duration. It may run for any length of time (e.g., a day, a week, a month, a year, or any number of days, weeks, months or years). The distinguishing feature of an estate for years is that it is for a definite and fixed period of time. It has a fixed and definite termination date that can be clearly established at the beginning of the tenancy.

> **For Example**
>
> If Chad agreed to lease a beach house to Molly for the summer months of June, July and August, Molly would have an estate for years.
>
> If a tenant rented a building from April 1 to March 31 of the following year, he would have an estate for years.

Unless the lease provides otherwise:
- an estate for years will not terminate on the death of either the lessor or the lessee. If either dies, his rights and obligations pass to his heirs.
- if the lessor sells the property, the new owner must continue to honor the lease.

If a lease contains a termination date, no advance notice of termination is needed to terminate it. The lease would automatically terminate on the stated expiration date.

Generally, an estate for years is referred to as a lease, while any other tenancy may be referred to as a rental agreement.

Periodic Estate

A **periodic estate** or (**periodic tenancy**) is a tenancy which automatically renews itself on the last day of the term for another term of the same duration until it is terminated by either party with proper notice. It does not have a fixed termination date, as it automatically renews at the end of each term.

Periodic tenancies typically run from month to month, week to week, day to day, or year to year. A periodic tenancy is automatically created when premises are rented for an indefinite time, with monthly or other periodic rent reserved. The tenancy would be considered a month-to-month tenancy if rent is payable monthly. When rent is payable at any other interval, the tenancy is from period to period in which the rent is payable.

<table>
<tr><td>For Example</td><td>A lease states that the lessee will pay the lessor $20,000 a year to rent his property. This is not an estate for years, as the agreement does not state that the lease will end after one year. This is an estate from year to year. It would continue for a year and automatically renew for another year and for each year thereafter. To terminate the tenancy, either the landlord or the tenant would have to give advance notice to the other.</td></tr>
</table>

While a month-to-month tenancy may be oral, a year-to-year tenancy must be created by express written contract. Often a periodic tenancy can be terminated by either party giving written notice a statutory number of days prior to the expiration of the period for which rents are to be paid, unless the rental agreement is one to which a residential landlord and tenant law were to apply.

<table>
<tr><td>For Example</td><td>In some states, if a commercial tenant has paid rent the 1st of every month and wishes to terminate the month-to-month tenancy, the tenant may be able to terminate as of October 31 if he gave written notice to the landlord by the 1st of October. If he gave notice on October 2, the earliest he would be able to terminate the tenancy would be November 30.</td></tr>
</table>

Estate at Will

Under an **estate at will** or (**tenancy at will**) the tenant is in possession at the will of the owner. An estate at will is created when a person enters into possession of real estate with the consent of the owner and without the intention of creating a freehold interest. It is a leasehold estate that continues for an indefinite period of time, so long as both parties consent. There is no fixed period, and there are not even any renewal periods.

<table>
<tr><td>For Example</td><td>An estate at will exists when a tenant agrees to occupy a property until it is sold or rented to another person, or until the owner constructs a new building, or until the owner needs the land for his own use, or until the tenant can find a new home, while a holdover tenant and landlord negotiate a new lease after an estate for years has terminated, or when an owner allows a relative to occupy a property.</td></tr>
</table>

If there is no specific rent agreed upon, the tenancy may be terminated at any time by either party. The tenant however, must be given a reasonable time to relocate, following notice from the landlord. Unlike other tenancies, a tenancy at will is not assignable or inheritable. Therefore, it would terminate upon the death of either the landlord or the tenant.

Estate at Sufferance

An **estate at sufferance** (or **tenancy at sufferance**) is created when a person retains possession of premises without the consent of the owner or any other person having the right to give possession. In other words, if a tenant stays after expiration of a lease without the consent of the landlord, the tenant is considered a holdover tenant and holds a tenancy at sufferance.

Noah Count had a one-year lease on a residence that expired on July 31. When he stayed on after that date without the consent of the landlord and did not pay rent, he held a tenancy at sufferance. If he had paid the rent but the landlord refused it, he would still hold an estate at sufferance.

A tenancy at sufferance is created when a tenant remains wrongfully. If a tenant were to pay rent and the rent was accepted, the tenant would not be a tenant at sufferance.

Al Packer had a one-year lease on an apartment, which expired on January 1. He stayed on after this date with the consent of the landlord and began to pay rent on a monthly basis. He then held a month-to-month tenancy.

A tenant at sufferance is legally liable to pay reasonable rent for the actual time he occupied the premises and must, on demand, surrender the possession to the owner. His right to possession terminates immediately upon such demand, without prior notice.

From the point of view of a lessee, a tenancy at sufferance is the weakest possible tenancy, as no notice is required to terminate the tenancy, and the tenant has no right to remain. The tenant can be evicted immediately.

Estates

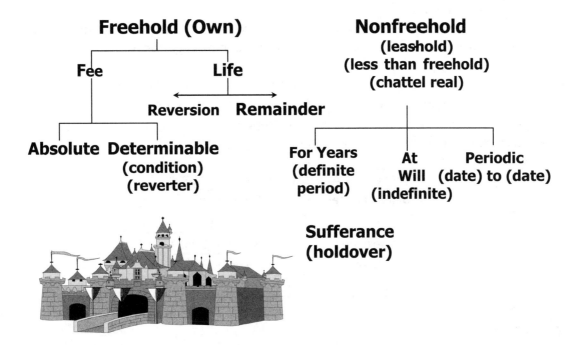

Estates in real property include freehold estates, which are real property interests, as well as less than freehold estates, which are personal property interests. An owner of real estate, e.g., the owner of a condominium, would have a freehold estate and a real property interest. A lessee of an apartment would have a less than freehold estate and a personal property interest. Thus, while they have a different legal relationship with the property, what they do have in common is that they each have an estate in real property.

----- SALE-LEASEBACK -----

One can have a freehold estate, dispose of various interests in the property, and still have the freehold estate. In most states, a property owner could sell the air, mineral or oil rights in property to a third party. A property owner could lease the land on a long-term lease, convey an easement for a right of way over the land, or assign a right of way to a railroad; none of these actions would alter the fact that he has a freehold estate.

However, a freehold estate could be converted to a less-than-freehold estate by a **sale-leaseback arrangement**. In this arrangement, an owner sells the property, terminating his freehold estate. At the same time he agrees to lease the property back from the purchaser under a long-term lease. This would result in him having a less than freehold estate. The seller/lessee gives up the title to the real estate to the buyer/lessor, and at the same time is able to retain possession of the property.

The sale-leaseback is used as a financing technique. It enables the seller to:
- get cash for the value of the property to use for other purposes.
- possess the property.
- deduct the entire rental payment from his taxable income, if the property is used for business purposes.
- improve the balance sheet by converting a fixed asset (real property) to a liquid asset (cash) and eliminate a major liability (the mortgage debt).

The advantage of the arrangement to the buyer/lessor is that he is able to:
- receive rent payments over a long term from a reliable tenant.
- realize appreciation in the value of the property.
- declare depreciation on the building for tax purposes.

SALE–LEASEBACK ADVANTAGES	
Seller (Lessee)	Buyer (Lessor)
Cash	Rent
Possession	Reliable Tenant
Tax Deduction	Appreciation
Improve Balance Sheet	Tax Depreciation

Brain Teaser

Reinforce your understanding of the material by correctly completing the following sentences:

1. An _____ is a possessory right or ownership interest in real property.
2. Unless a deed or will specifically indicates a different type of estate, it is presumed that the owner has a _____ estate.
3. Noninheritable freehold estates are called _____ estates.
4. Leasehold estates are considered to be _____ property interests.

Brain Teaser Answers

1. An **estate** is a possessory right or ownership interest in real property.

2. Unless a deed or will specifically indicates a different type of estate, it is presumed that the owner has a **fee simple (or fee)** estate.

3. Noninheritable freehold estates are called **life** estates.

4. Leasehold estates are considered to be **personal** property interests.

Review — Estates

In this lesson we review various estates that may be held in real estate.

Estate Basics

An estate is a possessory right or ownership interest in real estate. This includes owning or leasing property. It does not include the interest created by an easement or by a lien, such as property taxes or a mortgage. The estate held by the owner signifies the degree, quantity, nature, and extent of his title, right, or interest in the real property. Estates are divided into two broad classes based on their duration: freehold and nonfreehold.

Freehold estates, that last indefinitely for a lifetime or forever, involve ownership of property and are considered real property interests in real property. Nonfreehold estates last for a specified or temporary period of time, involve the lease or rental of real estate, and are considered personal property interests in real property.

Freehold Estates

The fee simple estate is the most common type of freehold estate. Unless a deed or will specifically indicates a different type of estate, it is presumed that the owner has a fee simple estate. Fee simple is an estate of inheritance and is the maximum estate one may hold, as it is of indefinite and unlimited duration and is freely transferable to others. It may be absolute or qualified:

- If it is absolute, there are no conditions imposed on it.
- If it is qualified or determinable, certain conditions or qualifications attached to it create the possibility of automatic reversion (or return) of title to the grantor of the estate or the grantor's heirs, upon the occurrence of an event specified in the condition.

Upon termination, all leases, encumbrances, and sales that had occurred or been placed on the property after creation of the qualified fee estate become invalid.

A life estate is a noninheritable freehold estate, created in writing by deed or will. It is ownership for a definite time period that is measured by the life span of a particular person or persons.

The deed or will creating the life estate establishes what will happen upon termination of the life estate. Two possibilities exist. One is reversion, which is the right to future possession by the creator of the life estate, called the grantor. In the case of reversion, the title will revert (go back) to the grantor or the heirs of the grantor who created the life estate. The second possibility is that a third party holds a remainder interest, or estate in remainder, during the entire term of the life estate. Upon termination of the life estate, the title passes to the third party, who is called a remainderman, specified by the grantor.

Nonfreehold Estates

Nonfreehold estates are also referred to as less-than-freehold estates, leasehold estates, or chattel real. They are commonly created by a lease. The person who rents out the property is the lessor, while the person who occupies the property is called the lessee or tenant. The lessor has a reversionary interest while the lessee holds a leasehold interest.

There are four types of leasehold estates: estate for years, periodic estate, tenancy at will, and estate at sufferance.
1. An estate for years, generally called a lease, is a tenancy of definite duration that is clearly established at the beginning of the tenancy.
2. A periodic estate is a tenancy that automatically renews itself on the last day of the term for a further term of the same duration until it is terminated by either party with proper notice.
3. An estate or tenancy at will is created when a person enters into possession of real estate with the owner's consent and continues for an indefinite period of time at the will of the owner, as long as both parties consent.
4. An estate at sufferance, the weakest possible tenancy, is created when a person retains possession of the premises without the owner's consent, such as when a tenant holds over after the expiration date of a lease without the consent of the landlord.

Sale-Leaseback

A freehold estate can be converted to a less-than-freehold estate through a sale-leaseback. This is a financing arrangement, whereby the owner sells the real estate to another person, and rents the property back from the new owner. This enables the seller to get cash for the value of the property to use for other purposes, while still being able to possess the property. It is the only way a freehold estate is changed to a less-than-freehold estate.

Land Use Restrictions

Overview

In this lesson we review private and public land use restrictions. Valid private restrictions are itemized, and definitions and examples of covenants and conditions are provided. Public restrictions, including compliance with community comprehensive plans and zoning regulations are detailed. A list of environmental laws is provided. Finally, building codes, subdivision regulations, and land sales regulations are explained.

Objectives

Upon completion of this lesson, the student should be able to:

1. Identify methods by which land use is controlled.
2. Discuss the control of land through private restrictions.
3. Describe the aspects of police power that enable public use and control of land.
4. State the purpose of a comprehensive plan.
5. Explain how zoning can affect land use.
6. Identify federal environmental legislation.
7. Describe how federal and state laws control the division and sale of undeveloped land.

Private Restrictions

Before subdividing (dividing raw land into smaller parcels) or developing (building structures on parcels and then selling the parcels) a subdivider or developer must determine what public and private restrictions have been placed on the use of the land. Prior to building any type of structure or even a fence around a property on the property line, a property owner should check both private and public restrictions:

- Public restrictions include local building, housing and health codes, zoning restrictions and subdivision regulations.
- Private restrictions include covenants and conditions found in deeds and other written agreements.

Usually there will be private restrictions and zoning restrictions on the same property. When there is a difference in the degree of restrictions between the two, whichever is the most restrictive (i.e., most stringent) has priority:

- If a zoning regulation permits a specific use of a property, but a private restriction in the deed limits that use of the property, the deed restriction would prevail.
- If the deed permitted a specific use, but the zoning regulation limits that use, the zoning regulation would prevail.

----- PRIVATE RESTRICTIONS -----

A property owner has a right to restrict the future use of the property he gives or sells to another. When he does so, he creates a private restriction. Private restrictions are considered to be encumbrances. They are restrictions not created by any government entity, but created in deeds or other written agreements by property owners.

Creation
Private restrictions may be created by:

- a grantor and placed in a deed upon sale of the property. Through this **deed restriction,** the seller is able to limit or control the buyer's use of the property. The restriction may then remain on the property forever, binding all future owners even after the property is resold.
- a testator and placed in a will.
- an agreement between two or more landowners.
- a developer or subdivider as general plan restrictions at the time of filing a subdivision plat. These may be listed in a recorded declaration of restrictions, often called CC&Rs (for conditions, covenants and restrictions), or in some cases, shown on the plat itself. When this is the case, the individual deeds will not contain the restrictions but will refer to the recorded declaration instead.
- a lessor in a lease to restrict the lessee's use of the property.

Purpose

Private restrictions may be for any purpose that is not illegal or against public policy:

- Restrictions that restrict the owner's right of alienation (i.e., the right to transfer title to the property) are against public policy and would be void and unenforceable.
- In 1948 (Shelley v. Kraemer), the U.S. Supreme Court declared restrictions that limit or restrict the use or occupancy of real property by a person or group of persons based on race to be unenforceable. Since then, federal and state laws have added restrictions based on national origin, religion and physical or mental handicap to the types that are void. Therefore, a restriction in a deed limiting sales to Caucasians or to Protestant families only, or prohibiting sales to members of a particular minority group would be void and unenforceable.

The existence of an unenforceable restriction does not have any effect on the conveyance of the title. The restriction will be unenforceable, but the remainder of the deed will be valid.

Valid restrictions may be:

- personal restrictions created by the grantor to satisfy a personal concern, e.g., a restriction that no alcoholic beverages can be consumed or sold on the premises, or that certain plants or trees must remain on the land. These can be enforced by the grantor or his heirs.
- for the benefit of land retained by the grantor, e.g., a building or tree height limitation that preserves the view from the grantor's property. These restrictions can be enforced by the grantor or any future owner of the grantor's property.
- for the benefit of the property sold, restricting the use of the property retained by the grantor to enhance the value of the property sold. These restrictions can be enforced by any future owner of the property sold.
- general plan restrictions (CC&Rs), created by the subdivision developer, to enhance the marketability of the property in the subdivision by prohibiting incompatible uses of the property within the subdivision. These restrictions can be enforced by any owner affected by the restrictions.

Covenants and Conditions

Private restrictions may be covenants or conditions. Most restrictions in the CC&Rs are covenants. A **covenant** is a promise to not violate the restriction. It may be a promise to perform a certain act or to do something in the future, or to not do something.

It may:
- control the style, height, size and location of homes to be built on the lots.

- specify a minimum cost of construction for improvements (but such a restriction is difficult to enforce).
- control appearance, e.g., limit the choice of colors for exterior paint, limit the size and type of fences, prohibit parking of vehicles other than cars on the street or in driveways, restrict placement of satellite dishes, etc.
- limit the number and type of pets in the neighborhood, e.g., prohibit animals other than cats and dogs.

Often the developer will establish a homeowners' association to review building plans and alteration proposals and to assure violations do not occur.

Because general plan restrictions run with the land, they apply to all future owners of the property, not just the initial owners. However, they usually have a time limit, often equal to the useful life of the original buildings. At the end of the time period, the restrictions would expire unless extended by approval of a specified percentage of the current property owners. During the period the restrictions are effective, they may be subject to amendment or removal with approval of 100% of the lot owners, or with approval of a lesser percentage as stipulated in the declaration of restrictions.

Since these restrictions are for the benefit of the subdivision lot owners, each lot owner has the right to enforce them. In the event a restriction is violated, the customary procedure to enforce the restriction is to apply to the court for an **injunction**. The injunction may be used to prevent a violation or to remedy a violation, e.g., repaint the house, tear down improvements built over the setback line, etc. If an injunction is not the appropriate option to pursue, the violator could be sued for damages to compensate those entitled to enforcement for any loss they may have suffered as a result of the violation.

However, enforcement of these restrictions may be denied by a court of law if:
- enforcement is not reasonable, e.g., the neighborhood has changed in character, from residential to commercial.
- there is an indication that the restrictions have been abandoned, e.g., there have been a number of violations which have been allowed to exist without challenge.
- there has been undue delay (referred to as "laches") in enforcing the restriction.
- the person seeking to enforce the restriction has violated any of the same restrictions.

A private restriction is a **condition** when it provides that a violation will cause the title to the property to revert to the grantor or his successors in interest (e.g., his heirs or his devisees). The condition, therefore, is a reverter clause. Upon learning of a violation, the grantor or his successors may declare a forfeiture of title and sue to recover possession of the property.

> **For Example**
>
> John willed property to the city for use as a park. If the city were to change that use, the property would revert to John's heirs without payment of compensation to the violator.

In addition, any encumbrances created by the violator may be ordered removed by the court before the property is returned to the person creating the condition. Since violation of a covenant will result in an injunction or payment of damages and violation of a condition results in loss of title, conditions are harsher than covenants.

A **condition** is a qualification of the estate granted. It creates a defeasible fee estate that will run with the land into the indefinite future. Since it gives the grantee title only so long as he complies with the condition, it can be imposed only in a document conveying an estate. On the other hand, a **covenant**, being only a promise, could be found in any type of agreement and may either bind the original grantee only or bind all future owners.

Public Restrictions

----- PUBLIC RESTRICTIONS -----

In planning for orderly development and use of their land resources, local governments will employ various public land use controls in the form of zoning restrictions, building codes, housing codes, subdivision regulations, and other restrictions. These controls all derive from the state's **police power** to protect the health, safety, morals and general welfare of the public. The right of the states to legislate for the public welfare is granted in the U.S. Constitution. The right of cities and counties to pass land use legislation is granted by the states in the form of enabling acts.

In most states, exercise of police power will not provide affected property owners with compensation from the government for loss of value or increased expense to the owners.

For example, when a local governing body re-zones an area, it may provide for more limited or lower density use, e.g., re-zoning land to allow four units per acre instead of the eight previously allowed. Such re-zoning is called **downzoning**. In most states, the owner of land affected by downzoning is not compensated for the loss in value or loss of profits caused by the downzoning to four units.

> **NOTE:** Re-zoning to provide for higher density use would be called upzoning.

Another means by which government may control land use is through direct public ownership. This may be the result of the negotiated purchase or exercise of another of the governmental rights: eminent domain. In either case, when the government desires that land needs to be acquired for a public purpose, it will compensate the owner for the physical taking of his land.

Comprehensive Plans

States may require local city and county governments to adopt **comprehensive plans** to provide for orderly development or redevelopment of the community so as to provide its residents with jobs, housing, and social, recreational and cultural opportunities. Comprehensive plans enable planners to make effective decisions regarding zoning changes and enable property owners to plan for future development of their properties.

Zoning

The main method of implementing a state or local comprehensive plan is through **zoning**. A zoning ordinance is a restriction on the use of private land. Zoning is not considered to be an encumbrance and does not make title unmarketable, but a violation of a zoning ordinance can create an unmarketable title.

While zoning ordinances do not independently create land value, zoning does have a huge effect on the value of real property. This is because zoning:

- regulates the use of land and the types and location of structures that can be built on the land through building height and size limitations.
- regulates the use to which a structure may be put.
- designates the land area a building may occupy, typically through setback requirements, lot size requirements, yard areas, and open spaces.
- designates the amount of off-street parking required.
- controls density of use, by dividing the land into zones (areas set off for a specific use) and regulating the type of activity that may be conducted on property in those zones.

Through **protective zoning**, communities are able to protect existing land users from encroachment by undesirable uses; through **directive zoning** they ensure that land uses in the future will be based on the highest and best use of the land and will be compatible with each other.

Often zones have major classifications (e.g., residential, commercial, industrial or multiple use) within which there are subclasses (e.g., residential areas may have subclasses for detached single-family dwellings, semidetached structures containing not more than four dwelling units, etc.). The zones are usually identified by code abbreviations, such as "R" for residential, "C" for commercial, and the subclass may be identified by a number. Because there is no uniformity from one city to another, the meaning of the zone identifications in any area needs to be checked.

As part of urban planning:
- **buffer zones** may be planned to provide separation of two incompatible zones (e.g., on land between a residential area and an area zoned for industrial use, a developer may be required to plant grass and trees).
- aesthetic zoning may require conformity with a certain type of architectural style.
- incentive zoning may specify that a portion of the land be devoted to a specific purpose in order to obtain approval for certain concessions (e.g., the developer may have to provide open space to get approval for the street floor of an office building to have retail businesses).
- bulk zoning may control the density of uses by limiting building size (e.g., by number of stories and/or height in feet) and/or lot size.
- cumulative zoning may allow less restrictive uses in an area, such as four-unit townhouses in areas zoned for apartment houses.
- inclusionary zoning may require certain uses to be included in a development, such as a certain percentage of the units for low- and middle-income families.
- exclusionary zoning may prohibit certain uses in an area, such as liquor stores or gun shops near schools.

Zoning requirements may:
- fix minimum front, side and rear yard **setbacks** (i.e., distances between the lot lines and improvements).
- limit the percentage of a lot that may be covered by a building.

- establish a minimum or maximum square footage of dwellings.
- limit the relationship of the floor area of a structure to the lot size (e.g., a floor area ratio of 2 to 1 means that 2 square feet of floor space may be developed on one square foot of land).
- specify a maximum number of living units per acre, a minimum lot area per living unit, and minimum living area within a unit.

To be valid and enforceable, a zoning ordinance:
- must serve a public purpose that relates to the public health, safety, morals or general welfare.
- must be exercised in a reasonable manner in accordance with the due process requirement of the 14th Amendment to the Constitution. It cannot be destructive, unreasonable, arbitrary, confiscatory, or discriminatory.
- cannot be retroactive.

When an ordinance takes effect, buildings and land uses that had been legal prior to that date will not conform to new zoning requirements, but they will not become illegal. Instead, they are considered legal **nonconforming uses**.

Nonconforming uses would include:
- an old grocery store located in an area re-zoned residential.
- a 12-story building constructed prior to enactment of a city ordinance prohibiting construction of buildings over 10 stories.

These nonconforming uses are allowed to remain under a grandfather clause in the zoning ordinance. They may continue to be used as they had been and need not be demolished, removed or changed. However, since the intent of re-zoning is often to eventually rid the area of nonconforming uses, restrictions may be imposed to:
- prohibit expanding or remodeling of the structure to extend its life.
- prohibit rebuilding the structure if it is destroyed or torn down.
- prohibit repairing extensive structural damage (but not prohibit basic repairs due to general wear and tear).
- terminate continuation of the nonconforming use if the owner voluntarily abandons the structure or discontinues the use.
- amortize termination of the use over a reasonable period of time.
- abate the use if it is a nuisance. A **nuisance** is a use that unreasonably interferes with the reasonable use of others' property (such as offensive noise or odor). If it affects a large area, it is termed a public nuisance and can be abated (removed) by government action; otherwise, it can be removed by abatement by a private party.

It is possible that zoning could be changed. Depending on the state and location, zoning changes may be made by amending the zoning ordinance or by obtaining a variance. Re-zoning is called **spot zoning** when it involves only a small parcel of land and the use classification differs significantly from that of the surrounding parcels (e.g., re-zoning of a lot in the middle of a residential zone to allow the operation of a laundry or barbershop would be considered spot zoning). Spot zoning may be allowed if it would serve a useful purpose for the area and not create a nuisance. Often courts will strike down such zoning because it does differ from the surrounding area and does create a nuisance.

In instances where strict compliance with a zoning restriction may serve to cause practical difficulties or unnecessary hardships, an owner may request a variance (also called an adjustment). A **variance** is special permission to allow a land use that would normally be in violation of current zoning, but it would not change the basic character of the area and would be consistent with the general objectives of zoning in the area.

For Example	An owner may request a variance if he needed to extend the side of his home beyond the normal 10' setback boundary required by the zoning in the area and build up to 7' from the lot line, or if he owned a parcel so irregular that he could not build a structure on it and still comply with setback requirements, or if a portion of his lot was so steep that a structure would have to be built nearer to the lot line than normally permitted, or if he had a 9,990 sq. ft. lot and 10,000 sq. ft. were the minimum size of a buildable lot.

Local governments also provide for exceptions to zoning restrictions through **conditional use permits** (or special use permits). Such permits allow a land use that does not conform to zoning requirements as long as it is within the strict limitations of the permit regarding size, traffic control, etc. Permits are generally granted for uses that do not fall into any particular zoning classification (i.e., child care centers, medical clinics, private schools, dog kennels, professional offices, etc.), yet which benefit the community.

ZONING	
Type	**Use**
Buffer Zone	Between Residential and Commercial
Downzone	Lower Density Use
Legal Nonconforming Use	Existing
Variance or Adjustment	New
Spot Zoning	Small Parcel, Significant Difference
Conditional or Special Use Permit	Benefit Community

Generally, requests for zoning changes or adjustments are referred to a planning commission or community planning board. The function of this board is to stimulate wider interest in community planning problems, coordinate civic developments, and stabilize property values and city growth.

Environmental Protection

Federal, state, and local environmental protection laws impose additional restrictions on land use:

- The **National Environmental Policy Act** requires federal agencies to prepare an **environmental impact statement** disclosing the effects of a development, whenever a proposed project would have a major impact on the environment.

- The **Comprehensive Environmental Response, Compensation and Liability Act (CERCLA** or the **"Superfund Act"**) makes past and present owners, and even lenders, jointly and severally liable for cleanup of hazardous substances, regardless of whether they were connected to the production, transportation, or disposal of the hazardous substances on the property, unless they can qualify as innocent purchasers or bona fide prospective purchasers who have not caused or contributed to hazardous waste contamination. Areas that have been abandoned or idled and underused industrial and commercial facilities, where expansion or redevelopment is complicated by real or perceived environmental contamination, are referred to as "brownfields."
- The **Clean Air Act** imposes standards for air quality.
- The Federal Water Pollution Control Act, also known as the **Clean Water Act**, imposes standards for water quality and wastewater treatment. States are required to implement plans for meeting those standards.
- The **Federal Coastal Zone Management Act** (known as CZM, or CZMA) provides assistance to coastal states to develop and implement programs for managing their coastal zones.
- The **Resource Conservation and Recovery Act** (RCRA) was enacted to deal with hazardous waste management. Its primary goals are to protect human health, protect the environment from hazardous waste disposal, conserve energy and natural resources, reduce waste, and ensure waste is handled in an environmentally sound way.

Some states have enacted legislation that regulates development within a certain number of feet of the high water mark on the coastal shoreline, large lakes, and large streams. Often a state will enact an environmental policy (or protection) act, requiring **environmental impact reports (EIRs)** for actions of state and local agencies, and for land use activities (e.g., re-zoning, building permits, subdivision plats, etc.), requiring approval of state and local agencies, which may have a significant environmental impact. These describe the proposed actions and their impact on the environment, identify unavoidable adverse environmental effects, assess feasible alternatives, etc.

The state, cities and counties also have laws regarding air, water, noise and solid waste pollution.

Building and Housing Codes

State and local **building codes** (or building ordinances) establish minimum material and construction standards for new construction and building alterations. They require that a person submit building plans and obtain a building permit before building, altering or repairing a building so that building code officials may determine whether the work would meet building code and zoning requirements. An owner/builder who builds without a permit could be forced to tear down the building. During the course of new construction, building inspectors must inspect the work to verify compliance with the code requirements. Upon inspection of the completed work, the building code department will issue a **certificate of occupancy** to allow occupancy if the building satisfies all code requirements.

Codes can be very elaborate. Plumbing, electrical and fire codes all have very specific requirements and measurements (approved materials, size of pipe, number and location of installed components, and so forth). Local governments also establish housing codes, that impose standards for use and maintenance of existing housing units, and health codes, that impose restrictions and requirements relating to the adequacy of water and sewage disposal systems. While building codes generally are not retroactive and apply only to new construction or new work, housing and health codes apply to structures without regard to whether there is any construction activity.

Subdivisions and Land Sales

----- SUBDIVISION REGULATIONS -----

When representing either sellers or buyers of subdivided lots, tracts or parcels of land, real estate agents must be familiar with all relevant **subdivision regulations** relating to the subdivision, platting and sale of land.

Cities and counties have authority to regulate the legal separation of land into smaller lots or parcels. They may adopt standards and procedures governing approval of plats. A plat includes a final map and other writing containing all the descriptions, locations, specifications, dedications, provisions and information concerning a subdivision.

These standards may include requirements for:
- placement of utilities.
- width and location of streets and other requirements to lessen street congestion.
- minimum lot sizes.
- securing safety from fire, flood, slides, pollution or other dangers.
- providing adequate light and air.
- preventing overcrowding of land.
- facilitating adequate provision of transportation, water supply, sewerage, drainage, education, recreation or other needs.
- dedicating to the public all common improvements, such as streets, roads, parks, sewage disposal and water supply systems, and easements for public utility purposes.

----- LAND SALES -----

Federal and state laws regulate the sale of land.

Interstate Land Sales Full Disclosure Act
The **Interstate Land Sales Full Disclosure Act**, administered by the office of Interstate Land Sales Registration in the U.S. **Department of Housing and Urban Development (HUD)**, regulates the sale or lease of undeveloped land through use of interstate commerce, the mail, or over the internet with certain exceptions. However, effective as of July 21, 2011, the Consumer Financial Protection Bureau (CFPB) has been given the job of enforcing ISLA.

Some of the major exceptions include:
- subdivisions with fewer than 25 lots. (These are exempt from both antifraud provisions and registration requirements; subdivisions of 25 to 99 lots that are part of a common promotional plan are exempt from registration, but subject to antifraud provisions.)
- subdivisions in which every lot has at least 20 acres.
- lots sold only to builders or developers.
- lots on which a building has already been erected or where a sales contract will obligate the seller to build one within two years.
- lots leased for a term of no more than five years.

If the law requires registration, the seller must file a statement of record with HUD, giving material information about the land and the condition of the title. If HUD determines that the information is complete, it will register the development so the land may be offered for sale. The seller must provide each buyer or lessee with a property report, which is a brief extract of the more detailed information in the statement of record. The buyer or lessee has a right:
- if given the report, to rescind the contract until midnight of the seventh day after signing the contract.
- if not given the report, to rescind the contract for two years after signing the contract.
- to sue for civil damages for losses caused by the seller's failure to provide the public report or by false statements in the report.

State Laws
Since federal law applies only to larger subdivisions and interstate transactions, the states have statutes to provide similar protection to purchasers of land in transactions not subject to the federal law.

These laws require developers to register the development (unless it is exempt) with a regulatory agency within the state prior to marketing it and to fully disclose all relevant facts concerning the property that are necessary to make an informed buying decision. If they fail to do so, the agency could take action to prevent any further advertising or sale of the land and impose civil penalties.

Just as the federal law does, state laws will require a developer or agent selling lots or interests in land to give a public offering statement to each buyer no later than the time of signing a purchase agreement and provide that the purchaser generally will have a right to review the statement and rescind the sales agreement within a specified period after signing it.

Brain Teaser

Reinforce your understanding of the material by correctly completing the following sentences:

1. Restrictions that limit or restrict the use or occupancy of real property by a person or group of persons based on race are _____.

2. The state's _____ _____ allows it to enact legislation to protect the health, safety, morals and general welfare of the public.

3. The Comprehensive Environmental Response, Compensation and Liability Act makes past and present owners, and even lenders, jointly and severally liable for cleanup of _____ substances.

Brain Teaser Answers

1. Restrictions that limit or restrict the use or occupancy of real property by a person or group of persons based on race are **unenforceable**.

2. The state's **police power** allows it to enact legislation to protect the health, safety, morals and general welfare of the public.

3. The Comprehensive Environmental Response, Compensation and Liability Act makes past and present owners, and even lenders, jointly and severally liable for cleanup of **hazardous** substances.

Review — Land Use Restrictions

In this lesson we discuss private and public land use restrictions.

Land Use Restrictions

Land use restrictions may be private, such as deed restrictions, or public, such as zoning. When more than one restriction applies, the most restrictive prevails. Violation of either can make the title unmarketable.

Private Restrictions

Private restrictions, also called deed restrictions or CC&Rs, are created by property owners in deeds and other written agreements, and are considered to be encumbrances. They run (transfer) with the land, so they enable a seller or devisor to limit or control future owners' use of the land.

Usually these restrictions would be covenants:
- A covenant is a promise to not violate the restriction.
- It can be enforced by a court injunction forbidding the violator from continuing the violation.
- A private restriction in the form of a condition provides that violation of the restriction will cause the title to the property to revert to the grantor or his heirs.
- Covenants and conditions are enforceable for any purpose that is not illegal or against public policy (such as to call for illegal discrimination).

Valid private restrictions may be created to satisfy a personal concern of the grantor; or for the benefit of the land retained by the grantor; or to enhance the value of the restricted property; or general plan restrictions created by the subdivision developer, intended to enhance the marketability of the property in the subdivision.

Public Restrictions

Public restrictions include zoning restrictions; building, housing, and health codes; and subdivision regulations. These restrictions are derived from the police power of the state and are exercised by local governments to protect the health, safety, morals and general welfare of the public. States may require local city and county governments to adopt comprehensive plans to provide for the orderly development or redevelopment of their communities.

Zoning is a restriction on the use of private land that sets off areas (zones) for specific uses and can have a huge effect on the value of real property. Zoning regulates the use of land and the types of structures that can be built on the land (through building height and size limitations and setback line requirements). A strip of land called a buffer zone might separate zones providing different types of use, such as residential and commercial areas.

To be valid and enforceable, a zoning ordinance must serve a public purpose that relates to the public health, safety, morals or general welfare, and cannot be retroactive.

- When an ordinance takes effect, pre-existing buildings and land uses that had been legal will not conform to new zoning requirements, but they will not become illegal. They are considered legal nonconforming uses.
- In instances where strict compliance with a zoning restriction may serve to cause practical difficulties or unnecessary hardships, an owner may request a variance (also called an adjustment) to allow him to improve his property.
- Local governments establish building, housing and health codes.
- Building codes require building permits in order to provide evidence of compliance with municipal regulations.
- Building plans must be submitted and a building permit must be obtained before building, altering or repairing a building, and work must be inspected.
- Housing codes impose standards for use and maintenance of existing housing units.
- Health codes impose requirements to insure the adequacy of water and sewage disposal systems.

Land Use and Sale Regulations

Cities and counties have authority to regulate the legal separation of land into smaller lots or parcels. They may adopt standards and procedures governing approval of plats. A plat includes a final map and other writing containing all the descriptions, locations, specifications, dedications, provisions and information concerning a subdivision.

The Interstate Land Sales Full Disclosure Act, administered by the Consumer Financial Protection Bureau, regulates the sale or lease of undeveloped land through use of interstate commerce, mail, or over the internet. It applies to subdivisions with 25 or more lots:
- The seller must file a statement of record with HUD, giving material information about the land and the condition of the title. If the information is complete, HUD will register the development.
- The seller must provide each buyer or lessee with a property report. If given the report, the buyer or lessee has a right to rescind the contract until midnight of the seventh day after signing the contract.

The states have statutes to provide similar requirements in transactions not subject to the federal law. These laws require developers to register the development (unless it is exempt) with a state agency prior to marketing it, to fully disclose all material facts concerning the property, and to allow a limited period during which the purchaser may rescind the transaction.

Oregon Liens

Overview

This lesson explores the influence of state statutes on liens against real property. The effects of the homestead exemption, construction lien law and the Bancroft Bonding Act are discussed. Details of the property tax process conclude the lesson.

Objectives

Upon completion of this lesson, the student should be able to:

1. Describe the purpose of the homestead exemption.
2. Describe the basic provisions of Oregon construction lien law.
3. Explain the purpose of the Bancroft Bonding Act.
4. Describe the Oregon property tax assessment and appeals process.
5. Describe the property tax payment schedule.
6. Identify property tax exemptions and deferrals.
7. Explain the property tax foreclosure process.

Types of Liens

----- HOMESTEAD EXEMPTION -----

An Oregon homeowner is provided with some protection against the forced sale of his personal residence due to a judgment lien in the form of the Oregon **homestead exemption**.

The homestead exemption applies only to judgment liens. It does not affect or provide protection against or prevent foreclosure arising out of construction liens, real property taxes, mortgages or trust deeds or any other specific liens.

The exemption applies automatically to the judgment debtor's personal residence. There is no need to file a claim for the exemption. The exemption can apply only to the actual residence of the debtor or his spouse, parent or child. The debtor cannot claim the exemption for any other property he owns. In addition, the exemption is limited to one block of city property or 160 acres of farm or rural property.

The exemption remains on the property until the debtor permanently leaves the property. It would not be affected by a temporary removal or absence if the debtor had the intention to reoccupy the property as a homestead. For example, an exemption would not be lost if the debtor were absent from his home as a result of being in jail.

The exemption may be lost after one year from the date of removal or absence from the property, e.g., as a result of foreclosure, abandonment or lease of the property to another. It may also be lost after one year from the date of the sale of the property. The proceeds of a sale would remain subject to the exemption so long as they were used to purchase another residence within the year following the sale. The exemption would be lost, however, if the debtor were to sell his home and reinvest the proceeds in anything else, such as an out-of-state business.

In order to sell the homestead on which a judgment lien exists, the owner must notify the judgment creditor that there will be a transfer of title and that the owner's equity is less than the exempted amount or that the amount received from the sale above the exempted amount will be used to pay off the creditor. The creditor has 14 days to request a hearing if he objects to any information presented in the notice.

The homestead exemption exempts from a judgment lien a certain dollar amount of equity in the debtor's home. If the home is a house, manufactured dwelling, or floating home, the amount is $40,000 for an individual debtor and $50,000 if two or more co-owners are debtors.

The exemption applies in the following way. It prevents a judgment creditor from foreclosing on the judgment lien unless there will be enough proceeds remaining from the foreclosure sale to apply to the judgment lien after payment of court costs, property taxes, all liens having priority over the judgment, and the full amount of the homestead exemption.

> **For Example**
>
> Joe owes Mr. Smith $90,000 as a result of injuries he caused in an auto accident, above the limit covered by his insurance. Smith obtains a judgment lien against Joe for the $90,000. Joe has a home worth $250,000. Prior to the effective date of the judgment lien, there has been recorded a trust deed, which currently has a balance of $230,000. Since there would not be enough from the sale to provide Joe with the $40,000 exemption amount, the judgment lien cannot be foreclosed by the Smiths. If a year later, the value of the property has risen to $290,000 and the loan balance has been reduced to $225,000, Smith could foreclosure $290,000 - $225,000 leaves $65,000. From that, Joe gets $40,000. Smith gets the remaining $25,000 as partial payment on his lien.

----- CONSTRUCTION LIEN -----

When a contractor, subcontractor, laborer, material supplier, architect, landscape architect, engineer or rental equipment dealer has performed work or provided material to improve a parcel of real estate on the order of the owner but has not been paid for the work, that person has a statutory right to record a notice of a **construction lien** (also called a mechanic's lien) and file a lawsuit to foreclose on the lien within a set period of time allowed by state law.

A construction lien claim must be filed in the county or counties in which the property is located in order to become a lien. The lien will be a specific, or special, lien against only the property or properties on which the work was performed. It will also be an involuntary lien since it was not placed on the property with the consent of the owner.

In order to prevent contractors or others from arbitrarily filing such liens against property, a claimant must follow a specific procedure set by statute.

First, if someone other than the owner requests the work, equipment or materials, (e.g., a general contractor), the claimant must give the owner a notice of the claimant's right to lien and the means by which the owner can protect himself. An exception to this requirement is a person who performs labor or rents equipment for a commercial improvement (i.e., an improvement that is not a one- to four-family dwelling to be occupied by the owner as a resident). The exception does not apply to providers or suppliers of materials.

The notice must be given while the work is being done and applies to all work done or materials delivered beginning eight business days before delivery of the notice. If the owner or lender demands a list of materials or a description of the labor supplied, the claimant must respond within 15 business days or lose the right to collect attorney fees and costs.

If not paid, a person has up to 75 days from the date of ceasing to provide labor, rental equipment or materials to file a lien. Other claimants (e.g. architects, engineers, landscape architects, etc.) have up to 75 days after completion of the construction project to file the lien. Completion of construction occurs when:

- the improvement is substantially complete;
- the owner, lender or original contractor conspicuously posts a completion notice at the site and records it after all original contractors have substantially performed their contracts; or
- the improvement is abandoned (i.e., no work has been done for 75 days or the owner or lender has posted and recorded a notice of abandonment).

Within 20 days after filing a lien claim, the claimant must mail a notice of the filing to the owner and lender. If not paid, the claimant will then have 120 days from the date of filing the claim to foreclose, or lose the right to do so, unless the owner was allowed additional time for extended payments.

The claimant must give the owner and lender notice of the intent to foreclose at least 10 days before beginning the foreclosure proceedings.

If there are a number of persons who performed on the same construction job and who properly file lien claims, all would have the same priority regardless of when they started work or recorded their claims. They would all share in the proceeds of the foreclosure sale based on their pro rata share of the total amount owed (e.g., if one contractor was owed ¼ of the total unpaid amount, he would get ¼ of the proceeds, up to the amount owed him).

In relation to other types of liens, a construction lien relating to construction of improvements generally has priority over all other prior encumbrances on the land on which the improvements are constructed, including mortgages and trust deeds. To enforce the lien, the claimant may sell the improvements separately from the land and have them moved within 30 days after the sale.

A construction lien relating to preparation of the land has priority over encumbrances which were recorded after or were unrecorded at the time the actual preparation or construction on the site began.

In either of these instances, a lien for materials and supplies would lose its priority over recorded mortgages or trust deeds if the lender is not given a notice of the right to a lien within eight business days of the delivery of materials or supplies and is not given a list of the materials or supplies within 15 business days of requesting it.

A construction lien claimed for alteration or repair of an existing improvement, which started after a mortgage or trust deed was recorded, will not have priority over that mortgage or trust deed unless the mortgage or trust deed secured the loan financing the alteration or repair.

In most instances construction liens will not result in foreclosure. Usually, the debt to the contractor will be paid in full, and the mechanic's lien would be removed from the public records by recordation of a release of lien. In instances where there is a dispute between the owner and contractor, the owner may have the property released from the lien by posting a bond or deposit equal to $1,000 or 150% of the lien claim, whichever is greater.

Property Taxes

---- BANCROFT BONDING ACT -----

In many instances, a local governing body will undertake public improvements which benefit only certain properties. Such improvements may include street paving, installation of curbs, sidewalks, sewers and street lighting. The local governing body will then impose a charge on the properties benefiting from the improvement to cover the cost of the work. This charge is called a **special assessment**.

In order to ease the property owner's financial burden of paying the assessment for such improvements which can amount to thousands of dollars, the **Bancroft Bonding Act**, provides that payments for special assessments may be paid in a lump sum or may be paid in installments. In order to take advantage of the Act, a property owner must apply for the installment option within 10 days after receiving a notice of the assessment. If he does choose to pay in installments, he would make periodic payments plus interest on the unpaid balance of the assessment over a period of from 10 to 30 years, as established by the governing body. If the owner takes advantage of the Act, the assessment will appear as a lien against the property until it is entirely paid off.

While the property owners are allowed to pay the assessment in installments, under the Bancroft Bonding Act the governing body may also issue bonds to raise the money to pay the costs of construction and then use the funds paid by the property owners to pay off the bondholders over a period of time.

----- PROPERTY TAXES -----

One type of lien which affects all real property is the real (general) property tax lien. **Real property taxes** that are not paid are specific (or special) involuntary liens. The property tax lien usually has priority over other interests in real property regardless of when it becomes a lien of record. Therefore, property tax liens would normally take priority over all other liens even if they had been previously recorded, such as:
- judgment liens.
- mortgage liens
- mechanic's liens.
- trust deed liens.

While income taxes are the major source of income for the federal government and the State of Oregon, property taxes are the major source of income for local governments and local taxing districts. Local taxing districts include school districts, fire districts, sanitary districts, park districts, library districts, as well as cities, towns and counties. As a result, the property tax bill for property will include allocations for a number of taxing districts.

The amount of property taxes imposed on property is based on two factors: the assessed value of the property and the tax rate. The annual property tax is equal to the value of the property, as determined by the county assessor, times the tax rate.

Assessment

Because the property is taxed according to its value, the property tax is considered an ad valorem tax. The term **ad valorem** means according to value. Oregon law requires that the assessed value of real property be the lesser of the real market value of the property as of the assessment date (January 1) or the maximum assessed value (i.e., the 1995 assessed value, as adjusted by law).

The real market value is the minimum amount in cash which could reasonably be expected by an informed seller acting without compulsion from an informed buyer acting without compulsion, in an arm's length transaction during the current tax year. The assessment of property for tax purposes is performed by county-designated appraisers.

Property values are usually adjusted based on a study of sales of similar properties in similar neighborhoods. For example, if the study shows property in the neighborhood sold at 10% above the sales prices the previous year, the assessor may adjust the assessed value of property in that neighborhood by increasing it 10%. The assessed value of improvements and land are shown separately on the property tax bill. The bill is mailed out to the property owner, or a person designated by the owner (e.g., the mortgage lender or a vendee under a land sales contract), by October 25.

Appeals

An owner of real property who believes the assessed value placed on his property by the county assessor is too high may appeal the assessment. In an appeal, the burden of proof in determining the valuation of his property rests on the taxpayer himself and not on the assessor. This means the taxpayer must present convincing evidence that the assessed value is wrong and that the value he is requesting is correct.

If the taxpayer disagrees with the value shown on the bill, he may discuss the matter with the assessor and check the data on which the assessment was based to determine whether there may have been any errors (e.g., wrong square footage, etc.). If still not satisfied with the amount of the property tax assessment, the taxpayer may file an appeal to the county board of property tax appeals by December 31.

In the appeal process, a taxpayer may send in evidence with the initial appeal paperwork or may appear at the hearing of the board in order to present the evidence personally. If not satisfied with the decision of the board, the taxpayer may, within 30 days, appeal to the Magistrate division of the Oregon Tax Court. He may, within 60 days, appeal a Magistrate decision to the regular division of the Oregon Tax Court.

Exemptions

Not all property is subject to taxation. Many types of property are tax exempt. The exempt property must be reasonably necessary and used in a way to achieve the organization's purpose. Any portion of the property that does not meet the requirements of the exemption program is taxable. Among these are properties owned by:

- government entities.
- religious organizations.
- nonprofit organizations.
- others when the property is used for tax-exempt purposes.

In addition, there are special tax exemptions which provide for reduced valuation of property for certain property owners or property uses. Those exemptions include the following:

- Veteran's property tax exemptions
- Residential property located in commercial or industrial zones
- Farmland
- Forest land

Veterans

Under the **veteran's property tax exemption**, eligible veterans and widows of veterans are entitled to exempt a certain portion of their homestead property's real market value from property taxation. The exemption amount is adjusted annually. To qualify for a veteran's property tax exemption, a veteran must reside on the property, and the veteran or the veteran's spouse must own it (although they need not own the property free and clear of encumbrances).

In addition, the veteran must have been honorably discharged from active duty in the armed forces after having served either 90 consecutive days during wartime, prior to February 1, 1955, or 210 consecutive days after that date, unless discharged earlier due to a service-connected injury or illness. The veteran must also be certified as being at least 40% disabled. If the disability is not service related, the veteran must have income below set limits and the exemption is for a lower amount than if the disability is service connected. The veteran must apply for the exemption by April 1 each year in order to claim the exemption for the coming tax year.

Residences in Commercial Areas

Another exemption exists to protect owner-occupants of residences located in areas re-zoned for commercial or industrial use. It provides that such property, if occupied by the owner, is assessed at the value for residential use rather than at its highest and best use. However, if the use is converted to another use or the property is no longer occupied by the owner, the owner would be charged the difference between the tax paid and the tax that would have been paid had the exemption not existed, for up to 10 years.

Farmland

A similar exemption applies to farmland in order to encourage the continuation of farming. Farmland used primarily to make a profit from farming may be assessed based on its agricultural value rather than its value at highest and best use. If the property is located in an exclusive farm-use zone, this land is automatically assessed as farmland until:

- it is no longer used as farm land.
- the owner requests a zone change.
- the owner creates a nonfarm dwelling.

If located outside of an exclusive farm use zone, the land is specially assessed only if:

- the owner applies for the assessment;
- the land has been used for farming for the past two years; and
- meet the income requirements for three of the past five years.

The special assessment is lost once the land:

- fails to meet the income test;
- is no longer used as farmland;
- is platted for a subdivision;
- is sold or transferred to an ownership making it exempt from property tax; or
- is requested to be removed from special assessment.

Once the farmland is no longer qualified for the special assessment, the owner will be charged the difference between the tax paid and that which would have been paid for up to five years, if the property was not in an exclusive farm use zone or was in an exclusive farm use zone located in an urban growth boundary, or for up to 10 years if it was in an exclusive farm use zone and not in an urban growth boundary. This additional tax need not be paid until the land is actually used for a purpose other than farming, even though the method of assessment would change as soon as the land is no longer used for farming.

Forest Land

Owners of forest land may also apply to have their land assessed at its value for forest use rather than its market value. These owners, however, are subject to a severance tax when timber is harvested from the land.

Mobile Homes

Mobile homes, structures more than eight feet wide and designed for highway transportation, are also subject to property tax. A mobile home used as a residence or for business, commercial or office purposes is assessed as personal property when the land under it is owned by someone other than the owner of the mobile home. A mobile home would be considered real property for purposes of property taxes when it is on land owned by the owner of the mobile home. In either case, the mobile home would be assessed based on its market value as of July 1. In order to move a mobile home on Oregon highways, the owner must get a trip permit from the Department of Motor Vehicles (DMV). To get the permit, he must present proof from the county that all current and delinquent taxes have been paid.

Tax Rate

The **property tax rate** for each taxing district is determined by dividing the district's tax levy (the amount of money to be raised from property taxes) by the total assessed value of property in that district.

> **For Example**
>
> The assessed value of all property in Smithville is $12,000,000. The city budget is $600,000. The tax rate would be $600,000 divided by $12,000,000 or .05. This figure can be expressed in two ways. In Oregon, the rate is expressed as dollars per thousand of assessed value. To arrive at dollars per $1,000, multiply the decimal figure .05 by 1000. .05 X 1000 = $50. Therefore, the tax rate is $50 per thousand. In other states, mills are used. One dollar per thousand is 1 mill. So $50 per thousand is 50 mills.

The tax bill prepared by the county assessor for each property in the county will show the tax rate for each taxing district as well as the total tax rate, determined by adding the individual rates together.

Tax Amount

To calculate the property tax amount, one would multiply the total tax rate by the assessed value.

> **For Example**
>
> If property is assessed at $740,000 and the tax rate is $13/1,000 of assessed value, use the formula: Tax = tax rate x assessed value. Therefore, the tax = 13/1,000 x 740,000. Change the fraction to a decimal by dividing 13/1000. This equals .013. Then multiply by 740,000. The tax is $9,620.

In some states, the assessed value might be set at a percentage of market value. Therefore, in those areas the tax would be figured by first calculating the assessed value:

- Multiply the assessed value ratio by the market value.
- The assessed value is then multiplied by the tax rate to get the tax.

> **For Example**
>
> A $498,000 home as assessed at 97% of its value and the combined tax rate is $17/1,000 of assessed value. To determine the annual tax, first calculate the assessed value. Assessed value = 97% x $498,000 value; it is $483,060. The tax is 17/1,000 x 483,060; 17/1,000 = .017; and .017 x $483,060 = $8,212.02.

Property Tax Calendar

The property tax year starts on July 1 and runs through the following June 30. This means that taxes on real and personal property in Oregon become a lien on July 1 of the year of assessment. When the property is sold, the buyer and seller will prorate their share of the tax bill, with the seller responsible for the amount of taxes from July 1 up through the day before the sale closes. The buyer is responsible for the amount starting the day of closing through the next June 30, unless they agree to some other arrangement.

If a sale closed on August 1, the seller's share of the annual tax would be 31/365 (for the 31days in July). The buyer's share would be 324/365 of the tax bill for the rest of the year.

Even though the lien date is July 1, taxes are not due until November 15. Taxes may be paid in full or in installments. If paid in installments, one third is due November 15, one third is due February 15 and the last one third is due May 15. If more than one third is paid on or before November 15, the taxpayer may be entitled to a discount. The discount is 3% if the full tax is paid on or before November 15 or 2% if two thirds is paid on or before November 15.

Frank Scott owed $2,400 in property taxes. He paid his tax bill in full on November 12. He would pay 3% less than $2,400 (or 97% of $2,400). $2,400 x 97% = $2,328.

There is no discount for paying one third since that is the amount due, and there is no discount for paying more than one third after November 15.

If payment of the property tax is not made when due, there is an interest charge. For real property, the charge is 1.33% of the amount due per month or fraction of a month until it is paid.

NOTE: The interest is imposed as of the 16th of November, February or May, so a month runs from the 16th through the 15th of the next month.

A property's tax is $2,400 for the year. Therefore, one third ($800) is due November 15, another $800 is due February 15, and another $800 is due May 15. If the tax is paid between November 16 and December 15, the taxpayer is charged one month's interest, or 1.33%, of the $800 tax that is late ($10.64). If the tax is paid between December 16 and January 15, the interest is 2.66%. If nothing is paid until September 19 of the following year, the interest will amount to 11 months x 1.33% of $800 for the November installment, plus 8 x 1.33% of $800 for the February installment, plus 5 x 1.33% of $800 for the May installment. This totals 24 x 1.33% x 800, or $255.36 in interest charged.

Personal property taxes become delinquent on the day taxes become overdue (November 16, February 16, or May 16). If not paid by the date shown on the delinquency notice, the tax collector may issue a warrant, creating a judgment against the taxpayer, may seize and sell the assessed property, or may charge the tax against real property owned by the taxpayer.

Real property taxes do not become delinquent until the day after the last installment is due. This is May 16.

Tax Foreclosure

Tax foreclosure of real property can occur three years after the earliest delinquency date; e.g., if taxes are delinquent May 16, 2012, the property is subject to foreclosure as of May 16, 2015. Prior to this, the taxpayer will have ample notice. Delinquent taxes owing and the year the taxes are subject to foreclosure are shown on the delinquency notice sent out when taxes are first delinquent as well as on each annual tax statement sent until they are paid. Three years after the delinquency, another delinquency notice is sent. By July the property is placed on a foreclosure list, which is published in the newspaper one month later.

The owner may have the property removed from the foreclosure list prior to publication by paying the full tax and interest for the year causing the foreclosure. He may have it removed after publication if, within 30 days, he pays the full tax and interest for the year causing foreclosure plus a penalty of 5% of the total tax and interest owed, or by filing with the Circuit Court reasons why the property should not be on the list.

The same day the foreclosure list is published the District Attorney will apply for a judgment and order through the Circuit Court. If the property is not removed from the list within 30 days, the court will issue the judgment and order foreclosing the property. After that there is a two-year statutory redemption period. After the property has been foreclosed by the county, the owner holds the title and has the right to redeem the property within the statutory **redemption period**.

The property may be redeemed by a person with an interest in the property as of the date of the order, or a lienholder, upon payment of taxes, interest, the 5% penalty, interest on the total judgment of 9% per year, plus a redemption fee.

Furthermore, unlike other foreclosures, during the redemption period following property tax foreclosure, the delinquent taxpayer has the right of possession. This means he can continue to reside in or retain possession of the property as long as he does not damage or destroy the property. He need not vacate or pay rent. However, taxes continue to accrue, so if he wished to redeem the property, he would have liability for the tax payments accruing during that period.

One year before the end of the redemption period, the tax collector will notify those with an interest on the property that the redemption period will end. Between 10 and 30 days after the end of the period, he will publish two notices of expiration of redemption period. At the end of the redemption period, he will deed the property to the county, and the taxpayer will lose the title and all rights to the property. The county may then sell the property back to the taxpayer at a private sale, for at least the amount needed to redeem the property, may keep the property or may sell it at public sale. At a public sale, the property is sold to the highest bidder if the bid satisfies the minimum price set by the county.

Tax Deferral

Disaster Area Deferral

There are some people who qualify for deferral of property taxes. For example, farmland in a disaster area, and adversely affected by the disaster, will qualify for a disaster area property tax deferral. If the owner applies for the deferral by September 1 of each year, the taxes would be deferred until the area is no longer considered a disaster area. After the deferral is ended, by November 15 of each year one-fifth of the deferred tax, plus interest of 9% per year, must be paid until the deferred taxes have been repaid.

Property Tax Deferral for Disabled and Senior Citizens

A disabled or senior citizen can "borrow" from the State of Oregon to pay property taxes to the county.

For qualified taxpayers, the Oregon Department of Revenue (DOR) will pay the county property taxes on November 15th of each year.

A lien will be placed on the property and DOR will become a security interest holder. Upon disqualification or cancellation from the program, the following must be repaid before the lien or security interest on the property will be released:

- The property taxes that have been paid by DOR.
- The accrued interest (six percent annually).
- The cost of recording and releasing the lien.
- A $55.00 filing fee on manufactured structures.

How is the value of the lien on my property determined?

The lien amount is an estimate of future taxes to be paid and interest to be charged based on current tax and life expectancy tables.

Who qualifies?

By April 15th the taxpayer must apply and meet all of the following requirements:

1. Be either:
   - 62 years old, or
   - A disabled citizen, who's receiving or is eligible to receive federal Social Security Disability benefits.
2. He must own or be buying the property; have a recorded deed or sales contract in his name or have a revocable trust; and he may not have a life estate interest in the property.

3. Have owned **and** lived on the property for at least five years. If he lived away from the property due to medical reasons, he must attach a medical statement on letter head from his health care provider.
4. Have homeowners insurance that covers fire and other casualties.
5. Household income must be less than the limit (2015 limit is $43,000.) Household income includes all taxable and non-taxable income of the applicant(s) and their spouse(s) that reside in the home for the prior calendar year.
6. His net worth is $500,000 or less. This doesn't include the value of the home under the Property Tax Deferral Program or personal property.
7. Either:
    - He doesn't have a reverse mortgage, or
    - He has a reverse mortgage and was on the Property Tax Deferral program prior to 2011.

Joint owners
- For the **Senior Citizen program**, if you own the property with someone else, **all** owners must apply jointly and meet all the qualifications.
- For the **Disabled Citizen program**, only one owner must be disabled, but all joint owners must apply and meet all of the other qualifications

For both programs, these requirements don't apply to joint owners who are married or registered domestic partners (RDP). The spouse or RDP isn't required to apply, but must qualify for the program if they do apply.

Farmland Tax Deferral
Land used for farming can qualify for a significantly reduced property tax. There is no minimum acreage size. The tax savings can be great, even on smaller parcels. Licensees need to remember that properties removed or disqualified from farm assessment can be subject to a one-time charge representing a payback of the benefit of the tax savings while under farm assessment. However, as long as the land continues to be farmed, even under new ownership the, special assessment continues.

Qualification of farmland for special assessment is determined as of January 1 each year and to qualify, the land must currently be used and have been used in the previous year exclusively for farm use, which means the current use of the land is for the primary purpose of making a profit by activities such as:

- Raising, harvesting, and selling crops
- Feeding, breeding and selling livestock, poultry or bees.
- Producing dairy and dairy products
- Stabling and training horses for income

These are but a few of the activities that would qualify a property for the special tax assessment.

Forestland Tax Deferral

This Oregon program is very similar to the Farmland Tax Deferral program. Many rural properties are eligible for a special assessment or deferral if the property is "used for the predominant purpose of growing and harvesting trees of a marketable species." The purpose of the program is to provide a financial incentive to property owners, in the form of reduced property values, for keeping their land in timber production. The assessed value is based on the productivity of the land for growing marketable trees. As with the Farmland Deferral, this program has a potential for tax payback if the requirements discontinue to be met.

More detailed information on any Oregon tax deferment program can be found at the county assessor's office in which the property is located.

Brain Teaser

Reinforce your understanding of the material by correctly completing the following sentences:

1. The homestead exemption applies only to _____ liens.

2. The _____ _____ Act provides that payments for special assessments may be paid in a lump sum or may be paid in installments.

3. Real property taxes become delinquent _____ ____.

Brain Teaser Answers

1. The homestead exemption applies only to **judgment** liens.

2. The **Bancroft Bonding** Act provides that payments for special assessments may be paid in a lump sum or may be paid in installments.

3. Real property taxes become delinquent **May 16**.

Review — Oregon Liens

This lesson explores the influence of state statutes on liens against real property.

Homestead Exemption

The homestead exemption applies only to judgment liens. The exemption applies automatically to the judgment debtor's personal residence, but is limited to one block of city property or 160 acres of farm or rural property.

The exemption remains on the property until the debtor permanently leaves the property. The homestead exemption exempts from a judgment lien a certain dollar amount of equity in the debtor's home.

Construction Liens

A construction lien claim must be filed in the county or counties in which the property is located in order to become a lien. If not paid, a person has up to 75 days from the date of ceasing to provide labor, rental equipment or materials to file a lien. Other claimants (e.g. architects, engineers, landscape architects, etc) have up to 75 days after completion of the construction project to file the lien. Within 20 days after filing a lien claim, the claimant must mail a notice of the filing to the owner and lender. If not paid, the claimant will then have 120 days from the date of filing to foreclose, or lose the right to do so, unless the owner was allowed additional time for extended payments.

If there are a number of persons who performed work on the same construction job and who properly file lien claims, all would have the same priority regardless of when they started work or recorded their claims, and all would share the proceeds of the foreclosure sale.

Property Taxes

In order to ease the property owner's financial burden of paying an assessment for such improvements as sidewalks, curbs and sewers, which can amount to thousands of dollars, the Bancroft Bonding Act provides that payments for special assessments may be paid in a lump sum or may be paid in installments. In order to take advantage of the Act, a property owner must apply for the installment option within 10 days after receiving a notice of the assessment. The Bancroft Bonding Act also enables the governing body to issue bonds to raise the money to pay the costs of construction and then use the funds paid by the property owners to pay off the bondholders over a period of time.

A property tax lien usually has priority over other interests in real property regardless of when it becomes a lien of record. Because the property is taxed accordingly to its value, the property tax is considered an ad valorem tax. An owner of real property who believes the assessed value placed on his property by the county assessor is too high may appeal the assessment, but the burden of proof in determining the valuation of his property rests on him and not on the assessor.

Eligible veterans and widows of veterans are entitled to exempt a certain portion of their homestead property's real market value from property taxation. To qualify, a veteran must reside on the property, and the veteran or the veteran's spouse must own it (although they need not own the property free and clear of encumbrances).

The property tax year starts on July 1 and runs through the following June 30. This means that taxes on real and personal property in Oregon become a lien on July 1 of the year of assessment. Even though the lien date is July 1, taxes are not due until November 15. If paid in installments, one third is due November 15, one third is due February 15 and the last one third is due May 15. The taxpayer is entitled to a 3% discount if the full tax is paid on or before November 15 or 2% if two thirds is paid on or before November 15.

Real property taxes become delinquent May 16. Tax foreclosure of real property can occur three years after the earliest delinquency date. If the property is not removed from the foreclosure list within 30 days, the court will issue a judgment and order foreclosing the property. After that there is a two-year statutory redemption period. During the redemption period following property tax foreclosure, the delinquent taxpayer has the right of possession.

A senior citizen may defer payment of property taxes on his homestead if he is 62 years old, has a recorded deed to the property or is buying the property under a recorded land sales contract (but a person with a life estate interest is not eligible), lives on the property, and has total household income below specified limits. The deferral will continue until the owner earns too much income, sells the property, moves to a new residence, or dies. A surviving spouse may apply to continue to defer the deferred taxes, if he is under 59½ years old, or continue to defer past and future taxes, if he is at least 59½ years old.

Oregon Property Law

Overview

This lesson explores the effects of Oregon laws on real property ownership and interests. Included are discussions relating to Oregon tenancies, inheritance and succession, and the use of deeds.

Objectives

Upon completion of this lesson, the student should be able to:

1. Explain the legal concepts behind Oregon water rights.
2. Describe the rights of tenants in severalty, tenancy in common and by the entirety in Oregon.
3. List the elements required for claiming title by adverse possession in Oregon.
4. Identify who inherits under Oregon's intestate succession laws.
5. Explain the role of a licensee in advising clients with regard to which deeds to use and how to complete them.
6. Identify and describe the various forms of statutory deeds.
7. Explain the basic requirements for recording a deed.

Water Rights

----- WATER RIGHTS -----

By virtue of state statute, water in Oregon is considered to be owned by the general public and not the person who owns the land through which the water passes. There is one exception to this: Spring water that surfaces naturally on the land, does not flow in a well-defined channel, and does not flow off the property onto which it surfaced belongs to the owner of the land as long as he does nothing to alter the opening artificially and does nothing to stop the water from flowing off the property.

Riparian Rights and Prior Appropriation

Although the public owns the water, a private person may obtain the right to use the water. In the United States, each state has its own system for granting and recognizing the right to use water. Some states subscribe to the common law doctrine of riparian rights. However, the ownership and use of water in states where water is scarce is often determined by the **doctrine of prior appropriation**. Oregon, like most western states, is an appropriation doctrine state and not a riparian rights state. In a **riparian rights state**, a person owning land over which water flows or which borders a waterway has the right to use that water automatically because of the location of his land.

In Oregon and other states operating under the doctrine of prior appropriation, a riparian owner does not automatically have the right to use water. Instead, the state grants, or appropriates, rights to use water to riparian and nonriparian owners. Therefore, if the state gives permission to a nonriparian owner of a farm to use water from a nearby lake, the owner will have received the right under the appropriation concept.

Legal Concepts

There are three legal concepts which serve as a basis for water rights in Oregon:
- Beneficial use
- First come, first served
- Appurtenance

Beneficial Use

The beneficial use of water is the basis, measure and limit for the use of water. The right to appropriate water for private use can be established through issuance of a water rights permit from the **Water Resources Director**. In the application to the Water Resources Department for the permit, the property owner must state the nature and location of the proposed use of the water. When issued, the permit will specify the maximum amount of water that may be used to meet the needs for the use and location for which the water right is granted. Therefore, if the water right is for irrigation of a 40-acre parcel, the water could be used only to irrigate those 40 acres.

After the owner actually uses otherwise unused water, the Department will replace the permit with a certificate of water right which remains valid as long as the beneficial use is continued. Failure to continue the beneficial use of the water may result in the loss of the right to use the water right. A person who holds a certificate of water right could have the right canceled through a statement of intentional abandonment filed with the Water Resources Department or could lose the right after a specified period of nonuse. An Oregon water right, once established, may be lost by nonuse over a continuous period of five years. It is subject to cancellation and may be invalidated after five consecutive years of nonuse, although cancellation is not automatic.

First Come, First Served

Water right priorities are established on a "first come, first served" basis. When a dry year does not produce enough water in a drainage basin to fill the needs of all the water right holders, those with the oldest valid rights are served first in order of the date of their permit applications. If they use all of the water available, junior water right holders may have to do without water during the deficit condition.

> **NOTE:** One type of use does not take precedence over another use when there is insufficient water for both, except when water right holders were issued permits with identical dates of claims.

If there is a conflict between two water right holders with the same priority because their permits have identical dates of claims, then a domestic user is favored over an industrial or commercial user.

Appurtenance

Once the certificate of water right is issued, the water right is appurtenant to the place of use for which the right was established. That means the property receives the water right, and title right passes with title. Therefore, the water right is not invalidated by a change in ownership of the property for which the water right was established. It passes with the title to the new owner. Also, the holder of the certificate may not use the water right on new property he acquires. The right applies only to the land for which it was established.

When a seller will be transferring a surface irrigation water right with the title, he must, upon acceptance of an offer for the property, disclose in writing whether or not a certificate of water right is available and verify that he will deliver the certificate at closing if it is available. This would be done in the earnest money agreement or an addendum. A real estate licensee can assist in checking on whether a water right exists and is not subject to cancellation due to nonuse by contacting either the local water master or the Water Resources Department in Salem.

Surface Water and Ground Water

Depending on the source of the water and the nature of the use of the water, there are instances in which a water right certificate is required and other instances in which it is not required. The Water Rights Act of 1909 controls the use of surface water.

Surface water controlled by this law is water on the surface of the earth (e.g., lakes, rivers, streams, creeks, etc.), as well as spring water which flows in a normal channel over a property or off the property on which it surfaces. Remember, the law related to public ownership of water does not apply to spring water flowing in an undefined channel and which does not flow off the property from which it surfaces. The law requires a water right permit in order to use surface water for most purposes, except for the following: use of water for certain types of fish protection, fire control, forest management, and land management practices; use of rainwater from an impervious surface; and stock watering directly from the water source, without any diversion or modification to the water source.

The Ground Water Act of 1955 controls the use of ground water. **Ground water** is water beneath the surface of the earth which is obtained through artificial openings or artificially altered natural openings. Therefore, spring water would be considered ground water if the natural opening were altered artificially. This law requires a water right permit on wells dug after 1955 but not on those dug prior to that date. However, it does not require a water right permit for all uses of ground water.

A **water right permit** is not necessary and therefore will not be issued for six uses of ground water:
1. Livestock watering. No use permit would be required on a proposed well used for livestock, regardless of the number of gallons to be pumped.
2. Watering a lawn or noncommercial garden ½ acre (21,780 square feet) or less. This exception applies no matter how much water is used. For example, a proposed well would pump 2,000 gallons of water per day for a 100-square-foot garden. Because the garden measures 100 feet by 100 feet and its total area is 10,000 square feet, no permit would be necessary.
3. Single or group domestic uses not exceeding 15,000 gallons per day. For example, no permit would be required on a proposed community well used to pump 6,000 gallons per day for six families.
4. Any single industrial or commercial use in an amount not exceeding 5,000 gallons per day. Therefore, a use permit *would* be required on a proposed well used to pump 6,000 gallons per day for a commercial use.
5. Down-hole heat exchange uses.
6. Watering school grounds of 10 acres or less in critical ground water areas.

> **NOTE:** A water right permit is not required for use of ground water for domestic, industrial or commercial use if the amount used will be less than the specified 15,000- or 5,000-gallon limits per day, while the permit is not required for livestock or lawn watering regardless of the amount used.

Tenancies

----- TENANCIES -----

In Oregon, a person may hold title by himself as a tenant in severalty or with others as tenants in common, tenants in partnership, tenants by the entirety, or joint tenants with the right of survivorship.

> **NOTE:** Not all states recognize tenancy by the entirety or joint tenancy or community property.

Severalty

A person who owns property to the exclusion of all other persons has a **tenancy in severalty** (or estate in severalty), whether that person is a natural person (a human being) or a legal person (e.g., corporation). Since Oregon does not recognize **community property**, in Oregon a spouse may own property in severalty. If two individuals accumulate real property in severalty while they are single, after they are married, the property remains as their separate property and will pass to their heirs or devisees upon their death.

> **For Example**
>
> Before they were married, Keith and Susan each owned a house. After their marriage they did not change the deeds but kept the houses as rentals and together bought a new house as tenants by the entirety. Two years later Susan died. The property Susan owned prior to marrying Keith then would be inherited by Susan's heirs, including Keith. Keith and Susan could have changed the title any time while they were married by deeding the property from one to both, either as tenants by the entirety or as tenants in common.

Tenancy in Common

A **tenancy in common** is created automatically whenever title to or an interest in real estate is conveyed or willed to two or more persons, other than to a husband and wife, or to executors or trustees, and there is no wording to declare that the tenants have a right of survivorship.

> **For Example**
>
> A deed conveying land to John Doe and Richard Doe creates a tenancy in common since it does not specify a right of survivorship. John and Richard are not husband and wife, and they are not trustees or executors.

A tenant in common is free to sell, transfer, convey or encumber his interest without the consent of any other co-owners. If two corporations and three unrelated individuals took title as tenants in common to a parcel of Oregon land, the corporations and the individuals would be able to sell their shares of interest without regard to the other tenants. When a tenant in common dies, his interest passes to his devisees, if he leaves a will, or to his heirs, if he does not. His heirs or devisees would then become tenants in common with the original surviving co-tenants.

Tenancy by the Entirety

A **tenancy by the entirety** can only be created between a husband and wife. It is a type of co-ownership where the parties must be husband and wife; no other persons may own property together as tenants by the entirety.

> **For Example**
>
> An Oregon deed is recorded naming Alfred Johnson and Barbara Johnson as tenants by the entirety, but Alfred and Barbara are, in fact, unmarried. Therefore, the title so conveyed would be held by them as tenants in common. The deed will still give them title but not as tenants by the entirety.

A husband and wife will usually hold real property in Oregon as tenants by the entirety. In fact, unless otherwise specified, a conveyance of property to a husband and wife will automatically be construed as a tenancy by the entirety. Therefore, if two purchasers who are husband and wife do not state in a deed how they wish title to be taken, title would be conveyed to them as tenants by the entirety.

> **For Example**
>
> David and Billie Pierson, a married couple, buy a home in Oregon. Although both of their names are specified in the deed, no mention is made in the deed concerning any preference for holding title. They will automatically hold the property as tenants by the entirety.

A married couple need not be tenants by entirety. They could choose to have one own the property in severalty, or they could have both own it as tenants in common by having the deed specify that they wished to be tenants in common. If a married couple has a parcel of land in Oregon and the deed indicates that each has title as tenants in common, then each party is entitled to sell an undivided interest in the land without the consent of the other party. If they were tenants in common when one died, the deceased spouse's share would be inherited according to that person's will or, in the absence of a will, under the descent and distribution laws of Oregon. The survivor would have no right of survivorship in the estate of the other and would not automatically become the owner of the whole ownership interest.

Unlike our neighboring states, Oregon does not recognize **community property**. In community property states, in most cases, property acquired by a husband and wife after marriage automatically is community property and owned by both spouses, even if only one spouse is named as the owner.

When a husband and wife have a tenancy by the entirety, each spouse has an equal interest in the property and holds title with a **right of survivorship** that cannot be destroyed by either party alone. Neither spouse may transfer his or her interest by will, since an interest in the entirety is not inheritable. Upon the death of one spouse, the surviving spouse will automatically become the owner of the whole property through the right of survivorship.

A tenancy by the entirety and right of survivorship may be dissolved in a number of ways:

- Joint conveyance by both parties (A husband and wife who own property as tenants by the entirety can together sell their interest and deed it to another. Both parties must sign any sales agreement, deed, lease, mortgage or other document for it to be legally binding upon both of them. One tenant cannot bind both of them.)
- Conveyance by one spouse of his or her interest to the other spouse by sale or gift
- Death of either spouse (When one spouse dies, that spouse's interest passes to the survivor, who then holds the entire ownership interest in severalty.)
- Divorce (When the owners of a tenancy-by-the-entirety estate are divorced, they become tenants in common; they cannot remain tenants by the entirety.)

For Example

If a couple were to obtain a divorce and thereby terminate their tenancy by the entirety of a section of Oregon land and nothing else were said as to their holding, the former husband and wife would each have an undivided half interest in the section as tenants in common. Since a section of land contains 640 acres, each would have a 1/2 interest in 640 acres. They would not each own 320 acres, unless they had the land partitioned so that each became an owner in severalty in half the property.

Title Transfer and Recordation

----- CONVEYANCES -----

Adverse Possession and Easement by Prescription

Oregon statute provides a person may acquire fee simple title to real property by **adverse possession** if he can prove by clear and convincing evidence that he and his predecessors in interest:

- maintained actual, open, notorious, exclusive, hostile and continuous possession of the property for 10 years; and
- upon first taking possession of the property, the person in possession had the honest belief that he was the actual owner of the property and that belief
  - continued throughout the 10-year period;
  - had an objective basis; and
  - was reasonable under the particular circumstances.

In a similar manner in Oregon a person can obtain an easement (an irrevocable right to use another's land) by **prescription**, if he had adversely used another's land openly, notoriously, hostilely (without permission), for a continuous and uninterrupted 10-year period.

Intestate Succession

Under Oregon's laws of **intestate succession**, when the decedent leaves a surviving spouse, the spouse gets the entire net estate if there are no children of the decedent, or if all the children are children of the decedent and spouse. Therefore if a husband dies and is survived by his wife and their child, the wife inherits the entire estate. If surviving spouse there are children of the decedent who are not children of the, then the surviving spouse gets one half of the net estate and the children share one half of the estate. If there is no surviving spouse, the entire estate passes to the decedent's children. If there are no children, it passes to the surviving parents. If there are no children or parents surviving, it passes to the decedent's brothers and sisters and their children. If there are none of these persons surviving, it passes to the decedent's grandparents and their children.

Deeds

In 1973, the Oregon legislature enacted laws establishing **statutory deed forms** for the voluntary conveyance of real property. These laws provide that, if a deed is written in the form specified in the statute, the effect of the deed will be defined in the statute rather than in the wording of the deed. The purpose of the laws were to create shorter deed forms, which could be uniformly interpreted. The laws do not require that a statutory form be used. These forms are not mandatory. The laws merely allow their use.

The four statutory deed forms are the following:
1. Statutory warranty deed
2. Statutory special warranty deed
3. Statutory bargain and sale deed
4. Statutory quitclaim deed

A real estate licensee may not advise a client on the selection of a statutory deed form to use. If the client is in doubt, the choice of which form to use should be made only after obtaining competent legal advice. Furthermore, if any deviations from or modifications to a statutory deed form are necessary, the client should be advised to seek the assistance of an attorney to make the changes.

Once the client has selected the form to use, a real estate licensee may help the client fill in blanks on the statutory deed form, as the filling in of blank spaces is not considered the practice of law.

Statutory Warranty Deed

The wording of a **statutory warranty deed** provides that the grantor conveys and warrants to the grantee the real property free of encumbrances except as specifically set forth in the deed. State statute provides that a deed in this form will convey as of the date of the deed the entire interest in the property and the grantor, the heirs, successors, and assigns of the grantor cannot assert at a later time that the grantor did not have that estate or interest to convey. In addition, the deed will pass any and all after-acquired title. **After-acquired title** is an interest the grantor obtains after delivery of the deed to the property to the grantee.

For Example	Jones held title under a forged deed. Not knowing this, he executed a warranty deed to Smith. When the forgery was discovered, Jones obtained a properly executed deed, thereby acquiring good title. Because Jones had given Smith a warranty deed, Smith would automatically acquire good title, as the warranty deed conveyed Jones's after-acquired title.

The statutory warranty deed also includes certain covenants of title, which run in favor of the grantee and the grantee's successors in title, as if they were actually written in the deed.

A **covenant of seizen** (or "seisin") warrants that at the time of delivery of the deed the grantor is seized of the estate in the property, which the grantor purports to convey. In other words, the grantor is the owner and possessor of the property being conveyed and has the right to convey the same. He would be liable for the full price of the property if he purported to convey a fee estate (belonging to the owner and transmittable to his heirs) and only had a life estate (held only during a person's life and not passable by inheritance).

A **covenant against encumbrances** warrants that at the time of the delivery of the deed, the property is free from encumbrances except as specifically set forth in the deed. This covenant guarantees there are no tax liens, mortgages, assessments or other liens except as stated in the deed. If the grantor desires to exclude any encumbrances or other interests from the scope of the covenants of the grantor, these exclusions must be expressly set forth on the deed. If an encumbrance were not disclosed, the grantee could sue the grantor for the cost of removing the encumbrance.

A **covenant of warranty**, also called a covenant of warranty forever, provides that the grantor warrants and will defend the title to the property against those who may lawfully claim the title. This makes the grantor responsible for actually defending the title and reimbursing the grantee, or the grantee's successors, for any loss resulting from lawful claims. The grantor's promise to defend the title does not expire with the death of the grantee. These warrantees extend back in time and are not limited to matters that occurred during the current grantor's ownership of the property.

For Example	Jones bought property and was given a deed on which the signature of one of the grantors was forged. When Jones later sold the property, he gave the buyer, Wilson, a warranty deed. Later, there is a claim to the property made by heirs of the grantor whose signature had been forged. Due to the warrantees provided, Jones would be liable for providing a legal defense of the title and/or for any loss suffered by Wilson.

Statutory Special Warranty Deed

In a **statutory special warranty deed**, the grantor conveys and specifically warrants (guarantees) to the grantee the real property free of encumbrances, arising during the grantor's ownership, except as specifically set forth in the deed. This deed has the same effect and includes the same warranties as the general warranty deed, except that:

- the covenant against encumbrances is limited to the encumbrances attributable to the grantor.
- the covenant of warranty limits the warranty and defense of title to persons who lawfully claim title by, through or under the grantor.

Therefore, both the warranty deed and the special warranty deed warrant undisclosed encumbrances placed on the property by the seller, but only the warranty deed will guarantee against undisclosed encumbrances placed on the property while the grantor was not the owner.

 A special warranty deed may be used by a trustee, executor, or administrator who would have no authority to warrant against acts of prior owners. It would be commonly used to convey title to property which had been sold under a land sales contract. A **land sales contract** is a contract in which the buyer agrees to pay the seller for the property over a period of time, and the seller promises to give the buyer a deed to the property once the buyer has paid off the amount of the contract. The seller keeps the title until that time but generally allows the buyer to take possession of the property. Since a seller would not want to warrant against acts of the contract purchaser during the contract period, the deed used to convey title would usually be a special warranty deed. It would give the purchaser warranties, but relieve the seller of responsibility for any defects created by the purchaser during the contract period.

Statutory Bargain and Sale Deed

A grantor willing to convey title without any warranties of title may use a bargain and sale deed. The **statutory bargain and sale deed** form simply states the grantor conveys the real property to the grantee. This deed does not provide any warranties or covenants of title to the grantee or the grantee's successors. Therefore, it will not protect the grantee against title defects.

However, use of this deed implies that:
- the grantor conveys his entire interest in the property as set forth in the deed at the date of the deed;
- the grantor, and heirs, successors and assigns of the grantor, will not assert that the grantor had less than the interest set forth in the deed at the date of the deed; and
- the deed will pass any and all after-acquired title.

A tax deed (used to convey title as a result of a tax foreclosure), a sheriff's deed (used to convey title as a result of a sheriff's sale due to a judicial foreclosure) and a trustee's deed (used to convey title as a result of a trustee's sale due to a default of a trust deed) would be bargain and sale deeds since the grantors have no reason to assume responsibility for any encumbrances against the property.

Statutory Quitclaim Deed

A deed which provides even less assurances than the bargain and sale deed is the quitclaim deed. The quitclaim deed creates the least protection of any deed for the grantee and entails the least liability to the grantor. It has the least number of warranties and covenants of any deed. It passes any interest the signer may have in the property but does not tie him to any warranty. The interest could be fee simple, an easement, a claim of adverse possession, color of title, or any other interest the grantor may have.

In the **statutory quitclaim deed** form, the grantor releases and quitclaims to the grantee all right, title and interest in the real property. This has the effect of conveying whatever title or interest, legal or equitable, the grantor may have in the property at the date of the deed. Unlike the bargain and sale deed, this deed does not even imply that the grantor actually has the interest purported to be conveyed. In effect, this deed is stating that the grantor transfers any interest he might have, although he may have no interest at all and someone else may have a stronger claim. Therefore, the quitclaim deed might convey no ownership rights at all. The quitclaim deed merely releases any claims of the grantor to rights in the property.

For this reason a quitclaim deed is most commonly used to remove a cloud from the title. The term **cloud on the title** means an encumbrance, charge, or claim against the property, which could make it legally impossible for the owner to convey marketable title. (**Marketable title** is title which a reasonably prudent person, knowing the facts, would not hesitate to accept.) A cloud on the title might also be a minor defect, which prevents securing a clear title report, e.g., no record that a lien had been satisfied.

A properly executed quitclaim deed will always convey the existing interest of the grantor, i.e., the right the grantor may hold at the time the deed is delivered. The quitclaim deed will

 not transfer rights the grantor may acquire in the future. While the warranty, special warranty, and bargain and sale deeds all convey after-acquired interests and promise that the estate or interest held by the grantor is that which is purported to be conveyed, the quitclaim deed does not. The quitclaim deed will not transfer any after-acquired title or interest, and does not prevent the grantor or his successors, etc. from asserting that the estate or interest held by the grantor at the date of the deed was less than that purported to be conveyed.

----- RECORDING -----

State statutes permit the recording of documents relating to real estate to give constructive notice to the world of the existing interests and their respective legal priorities in a particular parcel of real estate based on order of recordation. The following may be recorded:

- Deeds
- Easements
- Liens (e.g., mortgages, trust deeds, and construction liens)
- Options
- Land sales contracts
- Restrictions
- Leases
- Other documents affecting interests in real property

Recording is allowed by law, not required by law. The recording system is designed to provide public notice concerning documents affecting the title to real estate and to prevent forgery in recorded documents.

Each county has a county recorder. Instruments affecting real property may be recorded with the recorder of the county in which that property is located, and in order to be effective, the recordation must be performed in the county in which the property is located. If the property were located in more than one county, a deed to that property would be recorded in each county in which the property lies.

There are four elements the recorder will require in order to accept a deed:
1. Acknowledgment by the grantor
2. Statement of the consideration
3. Name and address of the person to whom future tax statements are to be mailed
4. Legal description

None of these items are required for the deed to be valid. They are only required for the deed to be recorded. For a deed to be valid it must be written, signed by a competent grantor, and have a granting clause, identification of the grantor and grantee, and an adequate description of the property.

Every deed executed to convey title in Oregon must show an acknowledgment of the grantor before it will be accepted for recordation because an acknowledgement is proof of execution of the deed by the grantor and reduces the possibility of the deed being forged. An **acknowledgment** is a formal declaration by a person who has signed a document certifying that the signing is a genuine and voluntary act. This person would be the grantor of a deed, the lessor of a lease, the mortgagor of a mortgage, etc. The acknowledgement may be made in or out of the state but must be witnessed by an authorized public officer who does not have a direct interest in the transaction, usually a notary public.

A deed that is not acknowledged is valid, legal and effective between the parties to the transaction; however, it will not be accepted for recordation by the county clerk.

To be recorded, a deed must also contain the name and address of the party to whom the property tax statement will be sent. This is important because the property could be foreclosed upon due to nonpayment of property taxes even if the owner never received a tax statement. An owner of leased property would want the tax statement for that property sent to him rather than to the property. An owner who makes tax payments to his lender would want the tax statement sent to the lender.

In order to enable the tax assessor to obtain data regarding sales activity for assessment purposes, the law generally requires that the deed state the actual consideration paid by the grantee (consisting of the cash and any existing liens assumed by the grantee) in order to be recorded. However, there are certain types of transactions in which the consideration would not be useful in establishing fair market value of the property. These would include transactions involving gifts for nominal or no consideration and exchanges of property where the parties are more concerned with the difference in the values of their property than in the actual values. Therefore, the law requires that the consideration must be stated in dollars on the face of the deed in order for the deed to be recorded, except if the deed is given by gift or through an exchange. If the deed were given by gift or through exchange, then it must have noted on its face that other property or value was part or the whole consideration. In such instances, neither the dollar amount nor the description of the property or value need be given.

> **For Example**
>
> If a property is sold for $140,000, the deed must show the consideration as $140,000 for it to be recorded. If the same property were deeded to the grantor's child as a gift, it might state the consideration was $10 and other good and valuable consideration. (The term "good consideration" refers to consideration arising from love, affection, generosity, etc.) If the property were involved in an exchange, the deed need only state that the consideration includes other property without showing any dollar amount.

While a statement of consideration is not required for a deed to be valid, most deeds will show the consideration, because gift deeds, deeds used to make a gift of real property, might be challenged by creditors of a grantor when it appears that the grantor gave the deed to another for no actual value in order to defraud creditors.

For the deed to be accepted for recording, the description of the property in the deed must be a legal description, i.e., lot and block, government survey, metes and bounds, or reference to a public record in which the description may be found, or in any other manner in which the description is certain. Street address or tax lot number would not be acceptable.

The priority of a deed is established by the date the deed is recorded. When a deed is recorded, it is stamped with the time and date and indexed alphabetically under the names of the grantor and grantee. The recorder keeps a copy and returns the original to the grantee. Once recorded, the information in the deed is accessible to public inspection. The date and time stamped establish legal priority for interests in the property in the order in which they are recorded. While an unrecorded deed is valid and binding between the parties to the deed (the grantor and the grantee), it would be void against the rights of a bona fide purchaser for value who first records his deed.

A **bona fide purchaser for value** is a purchaser who pays valuable consideration in good faith and has no notice of the existence of another person's claim to the title.

| For Example | Adam sells property to Ben. Ben does not take possession of the property or record the deed. Ben's deed is valid. However, two years later Adam dies and his personal representative, unaware of the deed to Ben sells the same property to Clyde. Clyde has no way of knowing Ben owns the property. Clyde records the deed he gets from the personal representative. As a result, although Ben's deed was valid between Ben and Adam, it is void against Clyde's claim to the title. Because Clyde's deed is recorded first (and it was Ben's fault the sale to Clyde occurred), Clyde's claim has priority over Ben's. Clyde is the owner. Ben can attempt to get his money back from the personal representative.

The same results would occur if Adam were to have sold the property twice, once to a person who did not record or take possession and again (fraudulently) to a second person who does record the deed. The second person would own the property, and the first would have to chase after Adam. |
| --- | --- |

In order to be a purchaser for value, a person must also be a purchaser without notice. A person is without notice if he has no actual knowledge of another's rights to the property, e.g., he has not seen a recorded or unrecorded deed, and he has no reasonable means of obtaining that knowledge.

Brain Teaser

Reinforce your understanding of the material by correctly completing the following sentences:

1. Ownership and use of water in states where water is scarce is often determined by the doctrine of _____ _____.

2. _____ water is water on the surface of the earth, as well as spring water which flows in a normal channel over a property, or off the property on which it surfaces.

3. When a tenant in common dies, his interest passes to his _____, if he leaves a will.

4. If any deviations from or modifications to a statutory deed form are necessary, the client should be advised to seek the assistance of an _____ to make the changes.

5. An _____ is a formal declaration by a person who has signed a document certifying that the signing is a genuine and voluntary act.

Brain Teaser Answers

1. Ownership and use of water in states where water is scarce, is often determined by the doctrine of **prior appropriation**.

2. **Surface** water is water on the surface of the earth, as well as spring water which flows in a normal channel over a property or off the property on which it surfaces.

3. When a tenant in common dies, his interest passes to his **devisees**, if he leaves a will.

4. If any deviations from or modifications to a statutory deed form are necessary, the client should be advised to seek the assistance of an **attorney** to make the changes.

5. An **acknowledgment** is a formal declaration by a person who has signed a document certifying that the signing is a genuine and voluntary act.

Review — Oregon Property Law

This lesson explores the effects of Oregon laws on real property ownership and interests.

Water Rights

Water in Oregon is considered to be owned by the general public with some exceptions. Oregon is an appropriation doctrine state, in which the state grants, or appropriates, rights to use water to riparian and nonriparian owners. Beneficial use of water is the basis, measure and limit for the use of water. An Oregon water right may be lost by nonuse over a continuous period of five years. Water right priorities are on a "first come, first served" basis. However, if there is a conflict between two water right holders with the same priority and permits with identical dates of claims, a domestic user is favored over an industrial or commercial user. After a certificate of water right is issued, the water right is appurtenant to the place of use for which the right was established.

Surface water is water on the surface of the earth, as well as spring water which flows in a normal channel over a property or off the property on which it surfaces. Ground water is water beneath the surface of the earth which is obtained through artificial openings or artificially altered natural openings. A water right permit is not necessary and will not be issued for use of ground water for livestock watering, use of ground water to water a lawn or noncommercial garden a half acre or less in size, single or group domestic uses in an amount not exceeding 15,000 gallons per day, or any single industrial or commercial use in an amount not exceeding 5,000 gallons per day.

Tenancies

Since Oregon does not recognize community property, in Oregon a spouse may own property in severalty. If two individuals accumulate real property in severalty while they are single, after they are married the property remains as their separate property and will pass to their heirs or devisees upon their death.

A tenant in common is free to sell, transfer, convey or encumber his interest without the consent of any other co-owners.

A tenancy by the entirety is a tenancy that can only be created between a husband and wife. A married couple could choose to have one own the property in severalty or they could have both own it as tenants in common by having the deed specify that they wished to be tenants in common. When a husband and wife have a tenancy by the entirety each spouse has an equal interest in the property and holds title with a right of survivorship that cannot be destroyed by either party alone. Neither spouse may transfer his or her interest by will, since an interest in the entirety is not inheritable.

Adverse Possession

Oregon statute provides a person may acquire fee simple title to real property by adverse possession if he can prove by clear and convincing evidence that he and his predecessors in interest had (1) maintained actual, open, notorious, exclusive, hostile and continuous possession of the property for 10 years, and (2) at the time he or his predecessors in interest first entered into possession of the property, the person entering into possession had the honest belief that he was the actual owner of the property and that belief by him and his predecessors in interest had continued throughout the 10-year period, had an objective basis, and was reasonable under the particular circumstances.

Succession

Under Oregon's laws of intestate succession, when the decedent leaves a surviving spouse, the spouse gets the entire net estate if there are no children of the decedent or if all the children are children of the decedent and spouse.

Statutory Deeds

In 1973, the Oregon legislature enacted laws establishing statutory deed forms for the voluntary conveyance of real property. The purpose of the laws were to create shorter deed forms which could be uniformly interpreted. However, the laws do not require that a statutory form be used. A real estate licensee may not advise a client on the selection of a statutory deed form to use. If any deviations from or modifications to a statutory deed form are necessary, the client should be advised to seek the assistance of an attorney to make the changes. However, a real estate licensee may help the client fill in blanks on the statutory deed form.

A statutory warranty deed provides that the grantor conveys and warrants to the grantee, the real property free of encumbrances except as specifically set forth in the deed, and contains covenants of seizen, against encumbrances, and warranty. A statutory special warranty deed conveys and specifically warrants to the grantee the real property free of encumbrances created or suffered by the grantor, except as specifically set forth in the deed. A statutory bargain and sale deed form states the grantor conveys the real property to the grantee, without any warranties or covenants of title to the grantee or the grantee's successors. A statutory quitclaim deed releases and quitclaims to the grantee all right, title and interest in the real property but does not imply that the grantor has the interest purported to be conveyed.

Recording

State statutes permit the recording of documents relating to real estate to give constructive notice to the world of the existing interests and their respective priorities in a particular parcel of real estate based on order of recordation. The recording system is designed to provide public notice concerning documents affecting the title to real estate and to prevent forgery in recorded documents. Instruments affecting real property may be recorded with the recorder of the county in which that property is located. Elements the recorder will require in order to accept a deed for recordation are: acknowledgment by the grantor, a statement of the consideration, the name and address of the person to whom future tax statements are to be mailed, and a legal description.

The priority of a deed is established by the date the deed is recorded. The date and time stamped establish legal priority for interests in the property in the order in which they are recorded.

Oregon Subdivision and Condominium Regulation

Overview

This lesson explores the requirements for subdividing land and developing condominiums, including conversion condominiums, in Oregon.

Objectives

Upon completion of this lesson, the student should be able to:

1. Explain the difference between subdividing and partitioning land.
2. Describe the process of obtaining approval for a subdivision.
3. Identify the documents relating to condominium ownership.
4. Describe the nature of general and limited common elements.
5. Identify the rights of tenants in conversion condominiums.

Subdivision and Partition Process

----- SUBDIVISION AND PARTITIONS LAW -----

A real estate licensee may become involved in subdivisions and partitions when:
- an owner wishes to partition a parcel of land and list it for sale.
- a potential buyer wants property with the potential for division and resale.
- a developer wants to hire a real estate broker to market lots in an approved subdivision.

In each instance, the licensee would need a basic understanding of the essential rules relating to subdividing, partitioning and marketing of such property.

Chapter 92 of the Oregon Revised Statutes (ORS) regulates the legal separation and marketing of subdivisions and partitions of land in Oregon. The law has two purposes:
1. Give the local jurisdictions, cities and counties, authority to regulate the legal separation of land into smaller lots or parcels. This authority is contained in the portion of the statute known as the **Subdivisions and Partitions Law**.
2. Give the Real Estate Commissioner authority to oversee the marketing and sale of undeveloped, legally separated land to consumers. This authority is contained in the portion of the statute known as the **Subdivision and Series Partition Control Law**.

Partitions and Subdivisions

This law applies when land which exists as a unit of land or contiguous units of land under single ownership at the beginning of a calendar year is divided during the calendar year. When land is divided into two or three units, the process is called **partitioning** and the units are called **parcels**.

> **For Example**
>
> Rocky Beaches owns a single parcel at the beginning of the calendar year and in May partitions it, creating two parcels. In August, Rocky partitions one of the two parcels creating a third parcel. If Rocky does not create another parcel until after the first of the following year, it will continue to be considered a partition because he will have created a total of three parcels in that calendar year. After the first of the next year, the partitioning process can be started again by dividing one of these parcels.

When a tract of land that existed as one unit or contiguous units of land under single ownership at the beginning of a calendar year is divided into four or more units within a calendar year, the process is called **subdividing**, and the units are called **lots**.

Once lawfully created, a lot or parcel will remain a separate lot or parcel unless the boundary lines are changed or vacated or the lot or parcel is further legally divided.

Regulation

The law exempts the following transactions from the definition of a partition:

- A division of land resulting from a lien foreclosure, foreclosure of a recorded contract for the sale of real property or the creation of cemetery lots
- An adjustment of a property line by the relocation of a common boundary where an additional unit of land is not created and where the existing unit of land reduced in size by the adjustment complies with any applicable zoning ordinance
- A division of land resulting from the recording of a subdivision or condominium plat
- A sale or grant by a person to a public agency or public body for state highway, county road, city street or other right-of-way purposes
- A sale or grant of excess property resulting from the acquisition of land by a public agency or public body for right-of-way purposes
- A sale or grant as part of a property line adjustment incorporating the excess right of way into adjacent property

Cities and counties must regulate partitions and subdivisions and approve any street or road created for the purpose of partitioning. They have the right to adopt standards and procedures governing approval of subdivision and partition plats, including requirements for:

- placement of utilities, width and location of streets or minimum lot sizes and other requirements needed to lessen street congestion.
- securing safety from fire, flood, slides, pollution or other dangers.
- providing adequate light and air.
- preventing overcrowding of land.
- facilitating adequate provision of transportation, water supply, sewerage, drainage, education, recreation or other needs, and the protection and assurance of access to wind for potential electrical generation or mechanical application.

Before regulations may be adopted, the planning commission must hold public hearings. After a hearing the planning commission has 60 days to make recommendations to the governing body, which has the authority to adopt the regulation after holding another hearing.

----- APPLICATION -----

The first step in applying for approval of a subdivision or partition is the application stage. A person or his authorized agent or representative will apply in writing to the city or county for approval of a proposed partition or proposed subdivision, showing the true name of the owner and developer of the property and that the requirements of state law and the local governing body would be met by the development. The application is accompanied by a map, called a **tentative plan**, showing the general design or layout of the proposed partition or subdivision.

Action on these applications is considered to be a judicial act; therefore, quasi-judicial hearings must be held in accordance with their procedural rules. A governing body of the city or county may delegate its power to approve applications for subdivisions and major partitions to its planning commission or to a city or county official, subject to appeal directly to the governing body.

In reviewing the tentative plan, the governing body will ascertain whether or not the proposal complies with state law. The proposed subdivision name cannot be similar to or pronounced the same as the name of another subdivision in the county unless the:
- land platted is contiguous to and platted by the same party that platted the previous subdivision.
- consent of the previous party is filed and recorded, and all block numbers of the previous plat of the same name are to be continued.

For Example	Sherwood Estates could not be so named if Sherwood Hills existed in the same county unless the two subdivisions were platted by the same person and next to each other or unless approval was obtained from the developer of Sherwood Hills.

The streets must conform to plats of adjoining property in all respects, including width and general direction unless the city or county determines that modification of the street or road pattern is in the public interest. Streets and roads held for private use must be clearly indicated on the tentative plan. Any reservations or restrictions relating to such private roads and streets must be set forth. In addition, the tentative plan must comply with the applicable zoning ordinances or regulations, including the comprehensive plan of the city or county.

Approval
The second stage of the approval process is approval of the final plat of the proposed partition or subdivision. A plat includes a final map and other writing containing all the descriptions, locations, specifications, dedications, provisions and information concerning a subdivision or partition.

Approval of an application and tentative plan is binding on a city or county for purposes of the preparation of a plat. Therefore, as long as the development conforms to the approved plan and all conditions required for approval of the application and tentative plan, the city or county is committed to approving the final plat for recording, even if a more restrictive land use law is imposed after approval.

Before granting plat approval, the governing body will determine that the plat complies with applicable zoning ordinances and regulations and is in substantial conformity with the approved tentative plan.

Also, all streets and roads for public use are dedicated without any reservations or restrictions other than the right to regain possession, if they are vacated by the governing body, and other than easements for public utilities. All common improvements, such as streets, roads, parks, sewage disposal and water supply systems, are donated if that was a condition of approval of the tentative plan.

This donation is called a dedication. **Dedication** is the act of setting aside for public use such property as streets, utility easements, school sites, parks, recreational facilities and the like. Dedication can be provided on the plat or by a separate dedication or donation document on a form provided by the city or county. Explanations of all common improvements required as conditions of approval of the tentative plan must be referenced and recorded. These explanations are necessary to show the exact intention of the dedicator or public agency.

> **For Example**
>
> A notation that the owners dedicate all areas shown for public purposes would not indicate whether the areas are for public utility easements only or could be used by private telephone and TV cable companies. Showing an area on a plat as a common area or as being reserved for park purposes would not indicate whether the land is to be used only by the residents of the subdivision or by the general public as well.

A dedication creates an easement over the property. The dedicator retains a fee interest in the property, and he or his successors have the right to full title to the property if the dedicated area is vacated. Plat approval does not constitute acceptance of a dedication. An ordinance or order is necessary to show acceptance.

In order to approve a subdivision plat, the city or county must also receive and accept with regard to both a water supply system and a sewage disposal system, one of the following:
- A certification by a city-owned system or by the owner of a privately owned system that is subject to regulation by the Public Utility Commissioner of Oregon, that water will be available to the lot line of each and every lot depicted in the proposed plat
- A bond, contract or other adequate assurance by the subdivider to the city or county that the system will be installed by or on behalf of the subdivider to the lot line of each and every lot depicted in the proposed plat
- A statement that no such system will be provided to any purchaser. While this option is provided by state statute, the city or county may adopt more stringent requirements for water or sewer installations and their availability to each lot. Also, the DEQ must approve method of sewage disposal even if the statement is given.

In order to have a final plat approved and recorded, there are a number of detailed requirements with which the subdivider must comply:
- The survey for any subdivision or partition plat must be made by a registered professional land surveyor based on Federal Geodetic Control Committee guidelines. Each lot or parcel must be numbered consecutively, with lengths and courses of all boundaries of each lot or parcel shown and each street named.
- Locations and descriptions of all monuments must be recorded on the plat, with distances and angles of all boundary lines conforming to the surveyor's certificate

shown. The plat must also show the location, dimensions and purpose of all proposed or existing easements and the area of each lot or parcel.

- A surveyor must certify he has correctly surveyed and marked the land with proper monuments of either concrete, galvanized iron pipe or an iron or steel rod.

- A subdivider must provide a notarized declaration stating the plat has been prepared and the property subdivided or partitioned in accordance with the law and stating any dedications, easements, or restrictions created. If the declarant is not the fee owner of the property, the fee owner and the vendor must also execute the declaration, consenting to the partition. Finally, if there is any dedication or donation of land to public purposes, the holder of any mortgage or trust deed must also sign the declaration.

- All ad valorem taxes and special assessments, fees or other charges which have or will become a lien in that tax year must have been paid. If the amount cannot be determined at that time, an amount estimated by the assessor for taxes, special assessments, fees and other charges must be paid, or a bond not to exceed twice the amount of the previous year's total charges must be deposited with the tax collector to assure payment of the taxes.

- The county or city surveyor has approved the plat, after checking the site and the plat, taking measurements and making any computations necessary to determine that the plat and survey are accurate.

- The county assessor, irrigation, drainage, water control and improvement districts, and the governing body have approved the plat.

When recorded, subdivision plats are indexed in the deed records by owner name and subdivision; partition plats are indexed by owner name and plat type or plat name.

If the comprehensive plan and land use regulations of the jurisdiction have not been acknowledged, the city engineer, city surveyor or county surveyor must immediately notify the Real Estate Commissioner in writing of receipt for approval of the subdivision plat.

Recorded plats may be amended by an affidavit of correction to show courses or distances omitted from the plat, to correct errors in the courses or distances or in the property descriptions shown on the plat, or to correct any other errors or omissions ascertainable from the data shown on the final plat. The amendment cannot be made to change courses or directions in order to redesign the lot configurations. The surveyor who filed the plat (or the county surveyor if the original surveyor has died) must prepare the affidavit, and the county or city surveyor must certify that they examined it. The surveyor must also have the affidavit recorded.

To change the configuration of lots, parcels or easements of a recorded plat, a person must follow the procedures for replatting. In general, these are the same as those for the original plat approval.

----- SALES -----

The law restricts certain sales activity involving partitions and subdivision. A subdivider may negotiate a lot sale after the tentative plan is approved. This means he may advertise, solicit or promote the sale of the land but may not execute a binding sales agreement. He may sell the lots, or otherwise dispose of or transfer interests or estates in the land, only after the subdivision has been approved and the plat has been acknowledged and recorded. He may not sell any lots in the subdivision until final approval of the plat has been granted.

With regard to parcels in partitions, he may negotiate the sale prior to approval of the tentative plan but may not sell the parcels until the plan has been approved.

In negotiating lot or parcel sales, he may use the approved tentative plan. However, in selling the land, it is not permissible to refer to, exhibit or use an unrecorded plat.

What is a Condominium?

The **Oregon Condominium Act**, found in ORS Chapter 100, regulates the creation, marketing and operation of condominiums. It applies to all property located in Oregon which a person elects to submit to the condominium form of ownership, as well as condominiums located outside Oregon, but sold in Oregon.

A **condominium** includes:
- the land, if any;
- any buildings, improvements and structures on the property; and
- any easements, rights and appurtenances belonging to the property.

A **unit** is a part of the property that is intended for independent ownership and has described boundaries. It must have legal access to a public street or highway and have an interest in the common elements; it may not include any portion of the land. It may be a building or part of a building; a space used to park or store automobiles, trucks, boats, campers or other vehicles or equipment; moorage space for a watercraft, floating home or other structure; or a floating structure, including a structure formerly used as a ship or other vessel.

----- DECLARATION -----

To submit property to unit ownership, a person must record a **declaration** in every county in which the property is located. The declaration is the most important of all condominium documents as it creates the condominium and the covenants, conditions and restrictions (CC&Rs) for the condominium. When recorded, it converts the property to a number of single deed estates.

The person who records a declaration is called a **declarant**. If the declarant is not the fee owner of the property, the fee owner and the vendor under any instrument of sale must also execute the declaration to show their consent.

A declaration contains:
- a description of the property, including property on which a unit or a limited common element is located.
- a statement of the interest in the property being submitted to the condominium form of ownership, whether fee simple, leasehold, easement and/or other interest.

It also contains the condominium name. The name must include the word "condominium" or "condominiums" or the words "a condominium" and cannot be the same as or deceptively similar to the name of any other condominium located in the same county.

The declaration states the use, residential or otherwise, for which any building or unit is intended and also states that the designated agent to receive service of process is named in the Condominium Information Report filed with the Real Estate Agency.

Unit Description

The declaration will provide a general description of each unit and all buildings, including the number of stories and basements of each building, the total number of units and the principal construction materials. It will also contain a unit designation (i.e., a number and/or letter designating the unit), a description of the boundaries and square footage of each unit, and any other data necessary for proper identification of the unit.

The unit includes within its boundaries:
- all spaces.
- nonbearing interior partitions.
- windows and window frames, exterior doors and door frames.
- all fixtures and improvements.
- utility service line outlets for power, light, gas, hot and cold water, heating, refrigeration, air conditioning and waste disposal.
- if walls, floors or ceilings are included but do not contribute to the structural or shear capacity of the condominium:
  - all lath, furring, wallboard.
  - plasterboard, plaster and paneling.
  - tiles.
  - wallpaper, paint.
  - finished flooring.
  - any materials constituting any part of the finished surfaces.

Except as set forth above, all other portions of the walls, floors or ceilings are a part of the common elements.

Each unit may be individually conveyed and encumbered and may be the subject of ownership, possession or sale. A unit deed, entitling the owner to the exclusive ownership and possession of the unit contains:
- the name of the property.
- the recording index numbers and the date of the recordation of the declaration.
- any applicable supplemental declaration or declaration amendment.
- the unit designation.
- any other details which the grantor and grantee consider desirable.

A unit owner may make any improvements or alterations to his unit that do not impair or lessen the structural integrity or mechanical systems of the condominium. He may not make repairs or alterations or perform any other work on the unit which would jeopardize the soundness or safety of the property, reduce its value, impair any easement or increase the common expenses of the unit owners' association without prior consent of all the other unit owners affected.

Common Elements Description

A declaration will describe the general common elements and the method used to allocate an undivided interest in the common elements to each unit. It will allocate to each unit a fractional, or percentage, undivided interest in the common elements (e.g., each of 10 units may be allocated a 10% or 1/10 interest in the common elements). The undivided interest is appurtenant to and cannot be separated from the unit, so it is conveyed or encumbered with the unit even if it is not expressly mentioned or described in the deed.

General Common Elements

The **general common elements** are all portions of the condominium that are not part of a unit or a limited common element. They include:

- the land;
- the foundations, columns, girders, beams, supports, bearing and shear walls, roofs, halls, corridors, lobbies, stairs, fire escapes, entrances and exits of a building;
- the basements, yards, gardens, parking areas and outside storage spaces;
- central services installations for power, light, gas, hot and cold water, heating, refrigeration, air conditioning, waste disposal and incinerating;
- all apparatus and installations existing for common use, such as elevators, tanks, pumps, motors, fans, compressors, and ducts;
- premises for lodging of janitors or caretakers; and
- all other elements necessary or convenient to the existence, maintenance and safety of a building and the condominium or normally in common use.

> **For Example**
>
> Sarah Miller purchased a condominium which included several common facilities, including a swimming pool, tennis courts, and a putting green. These common elements would be owned by Sarah and the owners of the units of the condominium in the form of undivided fractional or percentage interests, even if nothing were stated in their respective unit deeds.

Each condominium unit with its allocation of undivided interest in the common elements is considered a parcel of real property, no matter how title is held, subject to separate assessment and taxation in the same way as other parcels of real property. The common elements are not considered a separate parcel for tax purposes. In determining the real market value of a unit with its undivided interest in the common elements, the county assessor may allocate each unit's undivided interest in the common elements based on the declaration.

Limited Common Elements

The declaration also designates any **limited common elements**. These are common elements, such as balconies, patios, party walls, and assigned parking spaces which are reserved for the use of a certain unit or number of units to the exclusion of the other units.

The declaration states the nature of the limited common element, the unit to which the use of each limited common element is reserved, and the allocation of use of any limited common element which relates to more than one unit.

 A unit owner may use common elements for the purposes for which they are intended. He may not change the appearance of the common elements or the exterior appearance of a unit without the permission of the board of directors, unless otherwise provided in the declaration or bylaws, and cannot hinder or encroach upon the rights of the other unit owners.

Common Elements Responsibilities

The **unit owners' association** has the right to maintain, repair and replace common elements and make additions or improvements to common elements, as provided in the bylaws. The association also has the right to assess each unit for funds necessary for maintenance, repair or replacement of the common elements, for emergency repairs required for public safety or to prevent damage to the common elements or to another unit.

The declaration also establishes the method of determining liability for common expenses and the right to common profits. Common expenses include:

- expenses of administration, maintenance, repair or replacement of the common elements.
- agreed-upon expenses common to all unit owners.
- expenses declared common by the law or by the declaration or bylaws.

Unless otherwise provided in the declaration, unit owners receive common profits and are charged common expenses based on their unit's share of the undivided interest in the common elements. An owner cannot unilaterally refuse to contribute towards the common expenses by waiving the use of any of the common elements, by abandoning the unit, or by claiming an offset against an assessment for common element expenses on the basis that the unit owners' association failed to perform its obligations.

The unit owners' association assesses each unit for its share of common expenses. The declarant is responsible for assessments due for operating expenses on all unsold units from date the first condominium unit is conveyed. For a staged (a condominium which provides for annexation of additional property) or flexible (a condominium containing property that may be reclassified or withdrawn) condominium, he is responsible for those assessments from the date the applicable supplemental declaration and supplemental plat is recorded. The declarant is also responsible for paying assessments for reserves on all unsold units.

Any unpaid association assessment and interest on the assessment will create a lien on the unit and its undivided interest in the common elements. In addition, fees, late charges, fines and interest are also enforceable as assessments. In most instances, an assessment lien has priority to a homestead exemption and any other liens or encumbrances on the unit except tax and assessment liens and a prior recorded mortgage or trust deed.

To claim an assessment lien, the unit owners' association would record a claim. The recorded claim will automatically accumulate any subsequent unpaid assessments and interest without any further filings until the full lien is paid.

Proceedings to foreclose assessment liens are similar to those to foreclose construction liens. An assessment lien may stay in force for up to six years from the date the claim is filed or from when any subsequent unpaid assessment became due.

The bylaws may provide that, in any foreclosure suit against a unit, the owner must pay a reasonable rental for the unit and the plaintiff may appoint a receiver to collect the rent. Unless prohibited by the declaration, the board of directors, acting on behalf of the unit owners, may bid at the foreclosure sale and acquire and hold, lease, mortgage and convey the unit.

A unit owner is personally liable for all assessments imposed on him or assessed against the unit by the association. However, when a purchaser gets title to the unit as a result of foreclosure of the first mortgage or trust deed, that purchaser and his successors and assigns are not liable for assessments imposed prior to his acquisition. Those unpaid assessments will be a common expense shared by all the unit owners including the purchaser.

In a voluntary conveyance, the grantee and the grantor are both held liable for all unpaid assessments against the grantor up to the time of the conveyance. However, the grantee would have the right to recover from the grantor any payments he had to make. If a prospective purchaser requests a statement of unpaid assessments against the grantor or the unit, he would not be liable for, and the unit would not be subject to, any subsequent lien for unpaid assessments against the grantor in excess of the amount shown on the statement.

Declaration Amendments

Generally, an amendment of the declaration is not effective unless it is approved by at least 75% of owners, the Real Estate Commissioner and county assessor and is certified by the chairperson and secretary of the unit owners' association, acknowledged and recorded.

In addition, unless the declaration requires a greater percentage, an amendment to change a general common element to a limited common element or change the boundary of a limited common element requires approval of at least 75% of owners and 100% of the owners of all units to which the limited common element relates. An amendment to change any part of a limited common element to a general common element requires approval of the owners of 100% of the units to which the limited common element relates and the board of directors.

An amendment that changes the boundary of the property or a unit requires approval of 100% of the unit owners, while an amendment adding property owned by the association to the condominium as a common element requires approval by at least 75% of owners.

 The allocation of undivided interest in the common elements, method of determining liability for common expenses, and the right to common profits or voting rights of any unit can be amended only with the approval of the owners of the affected units. The declaration establishes the voting rights allocated to each unit, as well as the method of amending the declaration and the percentage required to approve an amendment. Unless otherwise provided in the declaration, each unit gets one vote in condominium matters requiring a vote of the owners.

----- RECORDING -----

Any declaration, supplemental declaration or amendment must be approved in writing by the county assessor and tax collector and the Real Estate Commissioner before it can be recorded. The county assessor checks to see that the name, plat and floor plans comply with the requirements of the law. The tax collector checks to see that all taxes, assessments, fees, and other charges due have been paid. The Commissioner checks to see that the declaration or amendment, bylaws, plat and floor plans and, if appropriate, the procedures used for a conversion condominium comply with the requirements of the law. It must be recorded within two years from the date of approval by the Commissioner or the approval expires.

When a declaration or a supplemental declaration is recorded, an exact copy is also filed with the county assessor. A plat of the land, including floor plans, must be recorded with the declaration or supplemental declaration and a copy filed with the county assessor and county surveyor.

----- RESERVE ACCOUNT -----

The declarant must establish a **reserve account** for replacement of common elements including exterior painting of painted common elements and for any other items as required by the declaration or bylaws. The need for replacement is based on, among other things, normal wear and tear of the elements. The reserve account need not take into account items that can reasonably be funded from operating assessments or limited common elements which are the responsibility of one or more unit owners.

The reserve account, established in the name of the association of the unit owners, must be funded by assessments against the individual units. These assessments are the property of the unit owners' association and are not refundable to sellers of units. The association board of directors must conduct an annual reserve study to determine whether the current reserve account is adequate for upcoming expenses and then make adjustments accordingly.

The reserve account must be kept separate from other funds, but funds from the reserve account may be borrowed by the board of directors to meet high seasonal demands on the regular operating funds or to meet unexpected increases in expenses which will later be paid from assessments.

The condominium declaration or bylaws may provide for a period of declarant control of the unit owners' association. In a single-stage condominium this period cannot last longer than three years from the date the first unit is conveyed or the date 75% of the units have been conveyed to persons other than the declarant. Upon expiration of the declarant control period, the declarant's right passes automatically to the unit owners.

Operation of a Condominium

----- REPORTS -----

After a condominium is in operation, two reports must be delivered to the Real Estate Agency for filing. These are:

- a **Condominium Information Report**, filed within 90 days after the declaration is recorded, showing the name of the association; the name of the condominium and the county in which the condominium is located; the mailing address of the association; the date the condominium declaration was recorded and the recording index numbers; the name and residence or business address of the agent to receive service of process in any legal proceeding relating to the condominium or association; and the number and type of units.

- an **Annual Report**, showing the same information plus the names and addresses of the chairman and secretary of the owners' association and, if the designated agent has changed, a statement that the new agent has consented to the appointment.

Any amendment to these reports must be delivered within 30 days after there is a change in the information contained in a report.

----- UNIT OWNERS' ASSOCIATION -----

The unit owners' association is the means through which the unit owners administer, manage and operate the condominium. It may be organized as a corporation for profit, a nonprofit corporation or an unincorporated association. Only unit owners may be association members. A unit owner is one owning a fee simple interest in a unit, the holder of a vendee's interest in a unit under a recorded installment contract of sale and, in the case of a leasehold condominium, the holder of the leasehold estate in a unit.

The association has the following powers:
- Adopt and amend bylaws, rules and regulations
- Budgets for revenues, expenditures and reserves
- Levy and collect assessments from unit owners to pay insurance premiums for the policy covering common areas, as well as repair, maintenance and redecorating expenses for the common areas
- Hire and fire managing agents and other employees, agents and independent contractors
- Defend against any claims, proceedings or actions brought against it, and initiate or intervene in litigation or administrative proceedings in its own name
- Make contracts and incur liabilities

- Regulate the use, maintenance, repair, replacement and modification of common elements, and cause additional improvement to be made as a part of the common elements
- Acquire, hold, possess and dispose of real or personal property or an interest in it
- Impose and receive payments, fees or charges for the use, rental or operation of the common elements, and impose charges for late payments of assessments, attorney fees for collection of assessments and levy fines for violations of the declaration, bylaws and rules and regulations of the association
- Terminate rights of unit owners to receive utility services and use recreational and service facilities for violation of rules
- Grant leases, easements, rights of way, licenses and other similar interests

The affairs of the association are governed by the board of directors. The board of directors may modify, close, remove, eliminate or discontinue the use of a general common element facility or improvement or a portion of the common element landscaping.

The unit owners' association must keep within Oregon all required documents, information and records. It must keep financial records sufficient for proper accounting purposes. All assessments must be deposited in a separate bank account in Oregon, in the association's name, and its expenses must be paid from this account. Within 90 days after the end of the fiscal year, the board of directors must give each unit owner a copy of the annual financial statement (a balance sheet and income-and-expense statement) for the preceding fiscal year.

The association must provide, within 10 business days of a written request from an owner, a written statement that shows the amount of unpaid assessments due from the owner, the interest rate charged on unpaid assessments, and any charge for late payment.

Required records must be available for examination by a unit owner and any mortgagee and, upon the written request of an owner or mortgagee, must be available for duplication during reasonable hours. The association must maintain a copy of the declaration, bylaws, association rules and regulations and their amendments or supplements, the most recent annual financial statement, and its current operating budget.

If entered into before the turnover meeting, any agreement or contract made by or for the association, the board of directors or the unit owners as a group cannot exceed three years and may be terminated without penalty by the association or the board of directors with 30 days' written notice given within 60 days after the turnover meeting.

----- BYLAWS -----

Each unit owner and the declarant must comply with the bylaws, administrative rules and regulations, and covenants, conditions and restrictions (CC&Rs) in the declaration or in the deed to the unit. Failure to comply is grounds for an action by the association or by an aggrieved unit owner.

The declarant must adopt on behalf of the association initial bylaws governing the administration of the condominium and record them with the declaration. Unless otherwise provided in the declaration or bylaws, amendments to the bylaws may be proposed by a majority of the board of directors or by at least 30% of the owners. They require approval by at least a majority of the unit owners.

In condominiums which are exclusively residential, the bylaws may not provide that more than a majority is needed to amend them. However, the following would require approval by at least 75% of the owners:

- Age restrictions
- Pet restrictions
- Limitations on the number of persons who may occupy units
- Limitations on the rental or leasing of units

For five years after recording the initial bylaws, any amendment to them must be approved by the Real Estate Commissioner for compliance with the law before it may be recorded.

The bylaws provide for:
- the organization of the association of unit owners. This includes determining when meetings will be held, e.g., the initial meeting, the turnover meeting, the annual meeting and any other unit owner meeting; the method of calling the meetings; the percentage of owners that constitutes a quorum; and the election of officers of the association.
- preparation and adoption of a budget. Unless otherwise provided in the bylaws, the board of directors at least annually must adopt a budget for the association.
- maintenance, repair and replacement of the common elements and association property, including employment of personnel necessary for the maintenance and repair, payment for their expense and other expenses of the condominium, and the method of approving payment vouchers.
- the manner of collecting assessments from the unit owners; insurance coverage; preparation and distribution of the annual financial statement; the reserve account and the preparation, review and update of the reserve study; the filing of an Annual Report and any amendment with the Real Estate Agency; the method of adopting and amending administrative rules and regulations governing the operation of the condominium and use of the common elements; restrictions on and requirements respecting the use and maintenance of the units and the common elements; any restrictions on use or occupancy of units; the method of amending the bylaws; and any other details regarding the property the declarant considers desirable.
- election of a board of directors, the number of persons constituting the board, their terms of office, their powers and duties, their compensation, if any, the method of their removal from office, the method of filling vacancies on the board, and the method of calling meetings of the board. The board acts on behalf of the association and must exercise the care required of fiduciaries.

The bylaws may provide the board with the authority to decide whether to repair or reconstruct a damaged unit or that a unit is in need of repair or reconstruction for some other reason. If the board has that authority, it must obtain and pay for property and liability insurance, covering both the common elements and individual units, paying for that insurance with monies from the common expense fund.

The property insurance must cover at least fire, extended coverage, vandalism and malicious mischief. The liability insurance must be comprehensive liability insurance covering the association, the unit owners individually and the manager including, the board of directors, the public and the unit owners and their invitees or tenants. If the bylaws require the individual unit owners to obtain insurance for their units, they will require the board of directors to get property and liability insurance for the common elements.

----- LIENS -----

Once the declaration is recorded, liens and encumbrances may be created only against each unit and its undivided interest in the common elements instead of against the entire property. A mechanic's lien or materialman's lien arising out of labor contracted for or materials purchased by one owner cannot be placed against the unit of another owner unless that owner also consented to the work and/or materials or the board of directors initiated emergency repairs. If a lien is placed against two or more units, each individual unit owner can clear the lien against his unit by paying his pro rata share of the lien.

----- LEASEHOLD INTERESTS -----

Where the condominium involves a leasehold interest, the master lease must have independent default clauses, so that a unit owner cannot be evicted because another unit owner or the board of directors has defaulted as long as that unit owner has paid his pro rata share of the funds necessary to correct the default. The master lease must also contain the procedure for a unit owner to purchase the fee simple interest in the unit if the lease includes an option to purchase. The master lease must be recorded before the declaration for the property.

----- TERMINATION -----

A condominium may be terminated if all of the unit owners execute and record an instrument of termination signed by the county assessor, obtain the consent or agreement of all unit lienholders, and file a copy of the recorded instrument with the Commissioner.

A portion of the property may be removed from the provisions of the law by recording an amendment to the declaration and an amended plat.

Property may also be removed from the provisions of the condominium law if:

- 90% of the unit owners agree that it is obsolete and to sell it; or
- 60% of the unit owners agree that damaged or destroyed property is not to be repaired, reconstructed or rebuilt by the unit owners' association.

Property removed from the provisions of the law is considered owned in common by all the unit owners. Each unit owner is entitled to the total of the fair market value of his unit and his share of the common element interest. This is determined by dividing the fair market value of the unit and common element interest by the total fair market values of all units and common element interests. The fair market value of each unit and common element interest can be determined by:

- an agreement of all of the unit owners; or
- by an independent appraiser selected by the association board of directors.

For Example	Mrs. DeBeck owns a unit in a condominium that, per the agreement of 90% of the owners, is obsolete, to be removed from the provisions of the Oregon Condominium Act, and to be sold. Her unit has been appraised at $62,700. The total appraised value of all the units is $2,598,000 and of the common elements is $222,300. Two percent (2%) of the common elements relate to her unit. As a result, she would get $67,146 ($62,700 for her unit plus $4,446 [2% of the $222,300 value of the common elements]). This would amount to 2.38% of the total net proceeds ($67,146/$2,820,300).

----- CONVERSION CONDOMINIUMS -----

Conversion condominiums are condominiums in which there is a building, improvement or structure (such as an apartment) that was occupied prior to any negotiation. The restrictions of the condominium law apply to conversion condominiums that are at least residential in nature and are not wholly commercial or industrial in nature.

The declarant of a conversion condominium must give every existing tenant notice of intent to convert the tenant's building to a condominium at least 120 days before recording the declaration, bylaws and floor plans for the conversion condominium. He must also provide a copy of the notice to any new tenant before the start of the tenancy.

A notice of conversion states that the declarant intends to create a conversion condominium and provides general information relating to the nature of condominium ownership. It does not constitute a notice to terminate the tenancy and must include a statement to that effect. If the declarant will offer the condominium for sale, the notice will set forth the tenant's rights, provide good faith estimates of the approximate price range for which the unit will be offered for sale to the tenant and estimates of the monthly operational, maintenance and any other common expenses or assessments applying to the unit.

The notice of conversion is for the sole purpose of providing general information about the anticipated acquisition costs and monthly expenses. It is not an offer to either sell the unit to the tenant or to sell the unit at a particular price.

A declaration may be recorded before the end of the required 120-day period with the written consent of all tenants who received the notice of conversion less than 120 days before the date of consent.

If a dwelling unit is to stay as a unit in the conversion condominium without substantial alteration in its physical layout, the tenant who occupies the unit has a **right of first refusal**. This means the declarant must first offer to sell the unit to that tenant. The offer to sell cannot be presented to the tenant earlier than 30 days after the notice of conversion was delivered to the tenant.

An offer to sell a conversion unit to the tenant will terminate 60 days after the tenant receives it or gives written rejection of it, whichever occurs earlier. The offer must be accompanied by a copy of all applicable disclosure statements issued by the Real Estate Commissioner and does not constitute a notice to terminate the tenancy.

After the tenant gives notice that he does not wish to purchase the unit or the 60 days has elapsed and the offer to the tenant is terminated, the declarant may not sell the unit to anyone else during the following 60 days at a price or on terms more favorable to the purchaser than the price or terms offered to the tenant.

Brain Teaser

Reinforce your understanding of the material by correctly completing the following sentences:

1. When land is divided into two or three units, the process is called _____ and the units are called _____.

2. To submit property to unit ownership, a person must record a _____ in every county in which the property is located.

3. A Condominium Information Report must be filed within ____ days after the declaration is recorded.

4. The declarant of a conversion condominium must give every existing tenant notice of intent to convert the tenant's building to a condominium at least ____ days before recording the declaration.

Brain Teaser Answers

1. When land is divided into two or three units, the process is called **partitioning** and the units are called **parcels**.

2. To submit property to unit ownership, a person must record a **declaration** in every county in which the property is located.

3. A Condominium Information Report must be filed within **90** days after the declaration is recorded.

4. The declarant of a conversion condominium must give every existing tenant notice of intent to convert the tenant's building to a condominium at least **120** days before recording the declaration.

Review — Oregon Subdivision and Condominium Regulation

This lesson explores the requirements for subdividing land and developing condominiums, including conversion condominiums, in Oregon.

Subdivisions and Partitions

Chapter 92 of the Oregon Revised Statutes gives local jurisdictions, cities and counties, authority to regulate the legal separation of land into smaller lots or parcels. When land is divided into two or three units, the process is called partitioning and the units are called parcels. When a tract of land that existed as one unit or contiguous units of land under a single ownership at the beginning of a calendar year is divided into four or more units within a calendar year, the process is called subdividing and the units are called lots. Cities and counties must regulate partitions and subdivisions and approve any street or road created for the purpose of partitioning. Before regulations may be adopted, the planning commission must hold public hearings. After a hearing the planning commission has 60 days to make recommendations to the governing body, which has the authority to adopt the regulation after holding another hearing.

The first step in applying for approval of a subdivision or partition plan is the application stage. The application is accompanied by a map, called a tentative plan, showing the general design or layout of the proposed partition or subdivision. The second stage of the approval process is approval of the final plat of the proposed partition or subdivision. Before granting plat approval, the governing body will determine that the plat complies with applicable zoning ordinances and regulations and is in substantial conformity with the approved tentative plan.

A subdivider may negotiate a lot sale after the tentative plan is approved. He may sell the lots or otherwise dispose of or transfer interests or estates in the land, only after the subdivision has been approved and the plat has been acknowledged and recorded.

Condominiums

The Oregon Condominium Act, found in ORS Chapter 100, regulates the creation, marketing and operation of condominiums. It applies to all property located in Oregon which a person elects to submit to the condominium form of ownership, as well as condominiums located outside Oregon, but sold in Oregon.

To submit property to unit ownership, a person must record a declaration in every county in which the property is located. The declaration is the most important of all condominium documents as it creates the condominium and the CC&Rs for the condominium.

General common elements are all portions of the condominium that are not part of a unit or a limited common element, and include elements such as premises for lodging of janitors or caretakers and all other elements necessary or convenient to the existence, maintenance and safety of a building and the condominium or normally in common use. Limited common elements are common elements, such as balconies, patios, party walls, and assigned parking spaces, reserved for the use of a certain unit or number of units to the exclusion of the other units. The declaration states the nature of the limited common element, the unit to which the use of each limited common element is reserved, and the allocation of use of any limited common element appertaining to more than one unit.

The unit owners' association has the right to maintain, repair and replace common elements and additions or improvements to common elements, as provided in the bylaws, and to assess each unit for funds necessary for maintenance, repair or replacement of the common elements, or for emergency repairs required for public safety or to prevent damage to the common elements or to another unit. The unit owners' association assesses each unit for its share of common expenses.

Generally, an amendment of the declaration is not effective unless it is approved by at least 75% of owners, the Real Estate Commissioner and county assessor and is certified by the chairperson and secretary of the unit owners' association, acknowledged and recorded.

Any declaration, supplemental declaration or amendment must be approved in writing by the county assessor and tax collector and the Real Estate Commissioner before it can be recorded.

Each unit owner and the declarant must comply with the bylaws, administrative rules and regulations, and covenants, conditions and restrictions (CC&Rs) in the declaration or in the deed to the unit. Bylaws govern the administration of the condominium.

A condominium property may be terminated from provisions of the condominium law if all of the unit owners execute and record a termination instrument signed by the assessor, obtain the consent of all unit lienholders, and file a copy of the termination with the Commissioner. Property may also be removed from the provisions of the condominium law if 90% of the unit owners agree that it is obsolete and to be sold, or 60% of the unit owners agree that damaged or destroyed property is not to be repaired, reconstructed or rebuilt by the unit owners' association.

Conversion condominiums are condominiums in which there is a building, improvement or structure (such as an apartment) that was occupied prior to any negotiation. The declarant of a conversion condominium must give every existing tenant notice of intent to convert the tenant's building to a condominium at least 120 days before recording the declaration, bylaws and floor plans for the conversion condominium. A notice of conversion does not constitute a notice to terminate the tenancy and must include a statement to that effect. If a dwelling unit is to stay as a unit in the conversion condominium without substantial alteration in its physical layout, the tenant who occupies the unit has the right of first refusal. An offer to sell a conversion unit to the tenant will terminate 60 days after the tenant receives it or gives written rejection of it, whichever occurs earlier.

Property Ownership

Overview

In this lesson we explore the concept of property ownership. Real property and personal property are defined. Property owners' rights and the four governmental limitations on those rights are itemized. The relationship of personal property to real property is clarified. Five tests to determine if personal property has become a fixture (part of the real estate by virtue of its attachment) are listed. Drainage, air, mineral, easement, and water rights are defined. Discussions on planned unit development (PUD), townhouse, condominium, and cooperative ownership conclude the lesson.

Objectives

Upon completion of this lesson, the student should be able to:

1. Define and describe land, real estate, and real property.
2. State the difference between the feudal system of land ownership and the allodial system of home ownership.
3. Define the concept of real estate as a bundle of rights.
4. Identify the powers of government that may limit ownership of real property.
5. Define fixtures and apply the legal tests of a fixture.
6. Define and describe personal property.
7. Define and describe such land rights as easements, air rights, mineral rights and water rights.
8. Describe the differences between PUD, townhouse, condominium and cooperative ownership.

Types of Property Defined

Since a real estate agent is in the business of buying, selling, leasing, managing and exchanging real property, it is necessary for the agent to understand what real property is. When real property is being bought and sold, it is also necessary for the agent to be able to explain to buyers and sellers what is included as real property, and what is not. Otherwise, a seller may take items that should belong to the buyer and the buyer may expect to receive items that properly belong to the seller, and both parties will blame the agent for any misunderstanding.

Property is anything that can be owned, i.e., anything that can be exclusively possessed, used, controlled and disposed of. Property is either real or personal. Therefore, property that is not real property is personal property, and property that is not personal property is real property.

----- REAL PROPERTY -----

Real property, also called real estate or realty, is property that is basically immovable. It includes the land and everything permanently attached to the land. Therefore, real property includes:

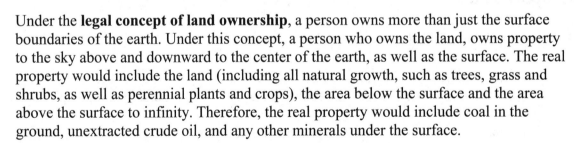

- land in the physical sense.
- airspace above the earth's surface.
- improvements to the land.
- rights belonging to the land (appurtenances), including all rights to own the land as well as the improvements on it and the minerals below the surface.

Under the **legal concept of land ownership**, a person owns more than just the surface boundaries of the earth. Under this concept, a person who owns the land, owns property to the sky above and downward to the center of the earth, as well as the surface. The real property would include the land (including all natural growth, such as trees, grass and shrubs, as well as perennial plants and crops), the area below the surface and the area above the surface to infinity. Therefore, the real property would include coal in the ground, unextracted crude oil, and any other minerals under the surface.

Real property would also include all the improvements on the land. In real estate, the term **improvements** generally means everything artificial or constructed on the land. If an owner purchases some stones, sand and cement, and builds a concrete walk on his parcel of real estate, this walk is an improvement and therefore is real property.

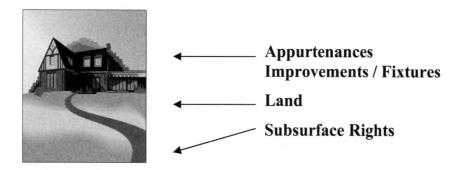

Appurtenances
Improvements / Fixtures

Land

Subsurface Rights

Improvements include buildings, fences, walls, drains, orchards, utilities, and roadways, as well as additions to these, i.e., fixtures. Land with improvements is called improved property, while raw land is called unimproved property.

Real estate also includes certain intangible rights. Items and rights that belong to the real property are called appurtenances. An **appurtenance** is any item or right that belongs to and goes with the land. Rights that are appurtenances are used with the land for its benefit and pass with the land when the ownership of the land is transferred. Such appurtenances include the right of lateral support and subjacent support, certain easements, air rights, mineral rights, the right to natural drainage, and, in many states, water rights.

Real property may be sold and may be used as security for a loan. When real property is sold, the document used to transfer the ownership rights (or title) to the real property is a **deed**. The deed will describe the surface boundaries of the property sold, and need not describe the improvements, appurtenances, or fixtures included with the land. Because these are all part of the land, they are automatically included in the transfer.

A real property owner may offer his real property as security for a loan. In exchange for the loan, the owner would give the lender a **note** promising to repay the loan. In addition, the owner would give the lender a written contract making the real property security for the loan. This would allow the lender to foreclose on the property if the borrower did not repay the loan as promised in the note. The written contract used may be a mortgage or trust deed (also called a deed of trust).

> **NOTE:** A trust deed, used as security for a loan, is different from a deed, which transfers ownership rights.

When a borrower gives a lender a mortgage or deed of trust, the borrower is hypothecating the property. To **hypothecate** is to pledge a thing as security for a loan without the necessity of giving it up.

If a person were to give property to the lender in return for a loan, such as when a person gives property to a pawnbroker, the person is pledging the property. However, when a person gives his property as security for a debt, but does not give up possession, he has hypothecated the property. Therefore, when a person buys real estate and gives the lender a mortgage or deed of trust, that buyer remains the owner of the real estate and has the exclusive right of possession. The lender holds an interest in the property, called a **lien**. Real property may be owned by the government or by private parties:

- Property owned by the government is called public property. So, property owned by the state would be public property.
- Property owned by private parties is called private property.

Much of the law relating to real property has evolved from English common law. During the Middle Ages, the King owned all the land. He would parcel it out to lords in return for their services or loyalty. These lords (or landlords) would then grant rights to vassals and serfs to farm the land in exchange for a share of the produce, services, or other payment. This concept of land ownership by the King, with rights granted to others in return for services, is considered the **feudal system** of land ownership. The interest held on the condition of performing services was referred to as a fief, fee or feud.

The holding of the property in return for services to be rendered was called a tenure, so the person holding the property came to be called a **tenant**. Eventually, holders of the fees acquired the right to sell their rights in the property to others who would agree to provide the same services. At the time, the fee holder was considered a freeman and his interest in the property was called a freehold.

By the time the English came to the United States, the feudal concept had been replaced by the allodial system of ownership. The **allodial system** is the system of ownership that allows land to be owned and controlled by individuals. Under the allodial system, land is owned absolutely and is not subject to any rent, service, or other tenurial right of a feudal ownership. In other words, under the allodial system an individual may own the land outright, subject only to certain rights held by the government.

Under the allodial system of ownership, the landowner has a **freehold estate**. This may be in the form of a:
- fee (or fee simple) estate, which includes a right to pass the property to others by will.
- life estate, which does not include the right of inheritance.

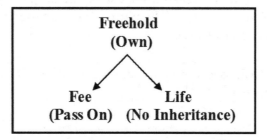

Either type of freehold estate is a real property interest and provides the owner with rights of ownership of the land. These rights of ownership include the right to use, possess, enjoy, and dispose of the land in any legal way and to exclude everyone else without rights from interfering.

These rights of ownership are referred to as a **bundle of rights**. This is because the rights may be held or disposed of together or separately, just like a bundle of sticks.

Included in the bundle of rights concept are the:

- air rights above the owner's property.
- mineral or subsurface rights below.
- right to lease the property to another.
- right to devise the property (i.e., to pass the real property to another in a will).
- right to encumber the property (such as by allowing a lender to have a lien against it).
- right to build on it.
- right to let or refuse to let others use it.

Therefore, the landowner has the right to sell or lease certain rights, while still remaining the owner of the land. A landowner could sell or lease subsurface rights or air rights so that he remains the owner of the land while another person(s) would own or possess the air rights and/or subsurface rights. The owner may lease the property to another, giving the tenant the right of possession while retaining the right to get the property back upon termination of the lease.

The bundle of rights, however, is not unlimited. It may be limited by **encumbrances** that give others rights in the property.

Encumbrances would include:
- private restrictions that limit uses of the property.
- easements that provide others with irrevocable rights to use the property.
- liens that give others rights to foreclose against the property if the owner does not pay a debt owed.

----- PERSONAL PROPERTY -----

Items of personal property may also be referred to as personalty or chattels, and rights in personal property may be referred to as chattel interests. **Chattel** is a movable article of property, or any tangible property other than land, buildings, and things annexed to land. The key feature of **personal property** is that it is movable in nature, because it is not physically or legally attached permanently to the land.

Tangible and Intangible Property
Personal property may be tangible, i.e., it can be seen or felt, or it may be intangible, such as contractual rights.

Tangible personal property would include house plants growing in tubs on the property, gardening tools, curtains and draperies suspended from curtain rods, a plug-in microwave oven sitting on a kitchen counter, a refrigerator, household furniture, a portable electric space heater, an electric washer or dryer, a television set connected to a cable outlet, a stack of lumber on a lot, a window air conditioner, or a three-ton piece of manufacturing equipment.

Intangible personal property includes rights in, or claims against, real estate held by anyone other than the owner of the real property.

> **For Example**
>
> When real estate is leased or rented to a tenant, the tenant (the "lessee") has a leasehold estate in the real property. Since this leasehold estate does not make the tenant the owner, it is personal property. Therefore, a lessee's interest under any lease is personal property.

In addition, a tenant may have ownership rights to annual crops (emblements) he planted or may have ownership rights to trade fixtures he installed for use in his business. A trade fixture is an article installed by a tenant under the terms of a lease and removable by the tenant when the lease expires. Emblements and trade fixtures would be personal property of the tenant.

Persons who have liens against real property have personal property interests in the real property. The **note** given to a lender, promising to pay a debt, is personal property of the lender. The mortgage or deed of trust creating a lien against the property is also personal property of the lender.

Sale and Security

Like real property, personal property may be sold and used as security for a loan. Personal property may be sold separately or in the same transaction with real property. In either case, the personal property should be adequately described in the purchase agreement to avoid legal problems, since it would be relatively easy for a seller to remove the item the buyer expected to receive and substitute another in its place.

Ownership of personal property is not transferred in the deed transferring ownership of the real property. When ownership of personal property is transferred or conveyed to another, the document used to show evidence of the transfer is called a **bill of sale**. A bill of sale is an instrument that conveys title (the rights of ownership) to personal property. It will:

- describe the property.
- state that ownership is transferred to the buyer.
- be signed by the seller.

Therefore, when a broker sells personal property, such as a refrigerator or furniture, along with the real property, the broker may have the seller use a bill of sale to convey the title to the personal property.

Personal property may be pledged as security for a loan. A pledge occurs when the borrower gives up possession of property in exchange for a loan. Upon repayment of the loan, the property is returned.

Ida Hunch built a house on speculation and sold it for $182,000. She received $32,000 in cash and a $150,000 promissory note secured by a mortgage. In order to build a house on another lot, Ida wants to borrow $70,000. She decides to use the $150,000 note as security for that loan. The note used in this manner would be a pledge.

Personal property may also be hypothecated as security for a loan, i.e., pledged without actually giving it up.

Luke Warm bought a furnace, and wished to finance the purchase. Since the furnace was to be installed in Luke's real property, it could not be given to the lender, so it would be hypothecated.

The Uniform Commercial Code establishes uniform procedures and documents to be used in personal property transactions. This law provides for use of a document called a **security agreement** to create a lien against articles of personal property. The security agreement has replaced the chattel mortgage as the instrument creating a lien on personal property. The security agreement makes the personal property security for the loan.

	Real Property	Personal Property
Sale	• Deed	• Bill of Sale
Lien	• Note • Mortgage/Trust Deed	• Security Agreement (formerly Chattel Mortgage)

Governmental Limitations on Real Property

----- GOVERNMENTAL LIMITATIONS -----

In addition, there are four **governmental limitations** to the private rights of ownership of real property. These limitations are in the form of public powers or rights. One can remember these rights by remembering PETE.

P	olice Power
E	minent Domain
T	axation
E	scheat

Police Power

Police power is the right of the government to enact legislation for the health, safety and general welfare of the public. Building codes, health laws, zoning ordinances, safety and traffic laws are all examples of police power. These laws are constitutionally valid as long as they are uniformly applied, nondiscriminatory and for the public welfare.
In real estate, the most common exercises of police power involve subdivision regulations, zoning, and building codes:

- Cities and counties set criteria for subdivisions. Before a developer can divide land into residential lots, he must get the approval of the city or county.
- Zoning ordinances regulate and control the use of land.
- Building codes establish standards and requirements for constructing new buildings and repairing existing ones.

> **NOTE:** Deeds and other private restrictions on property are not part of police power but are encumbrances imposed by private parties.

Governmental entities have a responsibility to arrange for growth in a methodical manner, while encouraging participation from people living in the area. They try to solve current problems and avoid foreseeable problems. The potential for the growth of commerce, the availability of jobs, and whether there is an adequate infrastructure are taken into consideration when developing the future plans of a community.

Not only does the government deal with growth, it also deals with controlling growth. Natural elements that enhance the lives of the people in an area must be respected. The land should not be overbuilt for the resources available.

Because police power does not involve the taking of property, a property owner is generally not compensated for the loss of use or value of his property as a result of the restrictions. However, in a number of states, laws provide for payment to landowners when the value of their real property is reduced by zoning or other land use regulation.

Eminent Domain

Eminent domain is the right of a governmental agency, or even a private entity, to acquire ownership of privately held real estate for public use regardless of the owner's wishes, upon payment of compensation to the owner. This allows the government to take land for streets, highways, airports, schools or public buildings. In addition, private companies serving a public purpose, such as utility companies, railroads, and communication and water companies, can also be granted the right of eminent domain. For example, a utility company could take a portion of land or an easement to use a portion of land to install and maintain gas or electric lines to a house.

The actual act of taking property is handled through **condemnation** proceedings. When the property is taken, the owner must be fairly and justly compensated. If the price offered is not acceptable to the owner, he has the right to appeal to the courts.

Taxation

A third government right is **taxation**. The government has the right to raise money to support itself through taxes, including general assessments against almost all property in the taxing district and special assessments against only specified properties benefited by certain public improvements.

Escheat

The fourth governmental right is escheat. **Escheat** (pronounced ĕs-chēt') is the right of the government to acquire title to the property when the owner dies intestate (without a will) and has no heirs eligible to inherit the property.

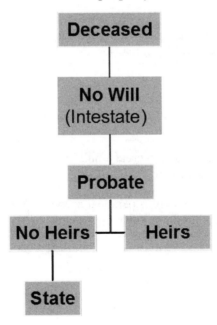

What is a Fixture?

Real property may be converted to personal property and personal property may be converted to real property.

Severance

Real property is converted to personal property by actual severance or by constructive severance. **Actual severance** occurs when an item is physically severed from the land.

> **For Example**
>
> Will Power tore down a fence with the intention that it be permanently removed and then piled the material on the land. That material has become personal property by the act of actual severance.

Constructive severance occurs when an item is detached by intent only, rather than physically severed.

> **For Example**
>
> Trees may be sold while still growing. Upon sale, they are constructively severed from the land and become personal property. A person who then purchases the land would not get the trees with the land.
>
> When air rights are sold separately from the land, they are constructively severed and are the personal property of the purchaser.

Attachment

Personal property can become real property, by attachment to the land.

> **For Example**
>
> Lumber from a tree when used to erect a building or fence becomes real property again when it is attached to the ground.
>
> A gas stove on display in a store is personal property. When that stove is installed in a permanent manner in a building, it is real property.

Fixtures

When personal property is attached to a building so that in a legal sense it becomes real property, it is called a fixture. A **fixture** is an article of personal property that has become part of the real estate by virtue of its attachment to the real estate.

Cabinets, plumbing fixtures, shelves, stoves and hot water heaters installed in a building are common examples of fixtures. They were personal property when purchased and became real property when they became attached to the building. If they had been attached to a travel trailer, they would have remained personal property, since the travel trailer is not attached to land.

Fixtures are a potential source of problems for real estate licensees, in part because it is often difficult to determine if an item is a fixture or personal property, and in part because the owner or seller may not understand the law of fixtures. Personal property would not usually be included with the sale of a residence, as the owner would take it. Fixtures would be included, so the owner should leave them.

Problems with fixtures may arise when real property is bought and sold, leased, or used as security for a loan. A broker who is not careful could wind up in the middle of a dispute between a seller and buyer as to who owns the range, screens, wall mirrors, shrubs, drapes or carpets, because the buyer and seller cannot agree as to whether an item is a fixture or personal property. If the matter is taken to arbitration or to court, the arbitrator or judge will attempt to determine whether or not the item is a fixture by utilizing certain tests.

----- TESTS FOR FIXTURES -----

The following are tests to determine whether or not an article of personal property has become a fixture:

These tests can be remembered by remembering MARIA. The tests do not include the size or the cost of the item. Such factors are not relevant in determining whether an item is a fixture.

M	Method of Attachment
A	Adaptation
R	Relationship Between Parties
I	Intent of Annexor
A	Agreement of Parties

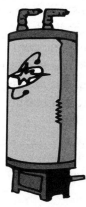

Method of Attachment

The test for method of attachment (or method of annexation) relates to the permanence of the annexation. If the attachment is permanent (e.g., by cement, nails, bolts or screws), and the removal of the item would cause substantial damage to the property, the item would be classified as a fixture. Plumbing would be considered a fixture under this test. Damage caused by removal itself is not a test, as items that can be removed without damage can be fixtures and items that can be removed only with resulting damage might not be fixtures, depending on the other tests.

Adaptation

A second test is adaptation of the item to the real estate and the nature of the use of the item. Under this test, fixtures would be items:

- essential to the purpose for which the building was intended, such as central air conditioning or the heating unit.
- custom-built for the building, even if they could be severed from the building, such as aluminum windows that are custom made and installed in a particular building, built-in ranges, wall-to-wall carpeting, screens, mini-blinds, and the keys to the doors to the structure.

On the other hand, freestanding ranges, area rugs and curtains would be considered personal property.

Relationship of the Parties

A third test is the relationship of the parties involved. The relationship could be that of buyer and seller, landlord and tenant or borrower and lender.

If the parties are the seller and buyer, items attached to the real property by the seller before entering into the contract to sell the property will be considered fixtures and will pass to the buyer with the land, unless there is an agreement to the contrary. In determining what is a fixture, courts generally will determine doubtful items in favor of the buyer. A buyer who inspects property with the intent of purchasing it, is entitled to assume that whatever is attached to the structure and is essential for its use is a fixture, even if the item could be somewhat easily removed without physical damage or lasting injury to the building or the article.

 If the parties are the borrower and lender, fixtures bought, paid for and installed by the property owner before or after execution of a mortgage usually become subject to the mortgage lien. Since fixtures are part of the real estate and the mortgage lien applies to all the real estate, any fixtures in the property at any time during the period of the lien are automatically subject to the lien. Therefore, gas stoves installed in an apartment building would be subject to the lien against the real property whether installed before or after the execution of the mortgage.

If fixtures are bought and installed but are not paid for, the rules are different. If the item was financed and the borrower gave the lender a security agreement, the item would usually remain personal property until the debt was paid off. Therefore, it could be removed by the holder of the security agreement if the borrower defaulted on the loan. The exception is when the item was installed and the holder of the security agreement has not filed a financing statement on the public records before another lender recorded a mortgage on the property in which the item is located. In that case, the holder of the security agreement could not remove the item, since he did not enable the mortgage lender to learn that the item had not been paid for.

If the parties are landlord and tenant, the general rule is that a fixture belongs to the owner of the land when there is no agreement to the contrary. Therefore, a tenant who puts fixtures into the premises cannot remove them when he leaves, without the consent of the owner. There are however, important exceptions to this rule. The tenant may normally remove domestic fixtures, agricultural fixtures and trade fixtures:

- Domestic fixtures are items installed by the tenant to make the dwelling more comfortable and attractive during his lease period. They may be for decoration or domestic use.
- Agricultural fixtures are items installed by the tenant to enable him to farm or graze the land that he has leased.
- Trade fixtures are items such as machinery, equipment, counters, and shelves, installed by a tenant for use in the business conducted on the leased premises. These items are utilized in his business as tools of the trade. In law, a trade fixture is personal property and not an appurtenance to real property.

Items that may properly be termed trade fixtures are intended to remain the property of the tenant. They are not a permanent part of the building and are not owned by the owner of the real estate.

Domestic, agricultural and trade fixtures may be removed by the tenant any time prior to the expiration of the lease.

For Example	Bennie Fishel has decided to move his business to a new location when the term of his lease expires. Bennie wants to move his display cases, which he purchased as equipment for the store, before the lease expires and install them in his new store. Bennie may remove the cases whether or not they are attached to the premises. He need not obtain the landlord's consent or reimburse the landlord for their value, as they belong to Bennie.

In addition, these fixtures may be removed when the lease expires or even within a reasonable time after the lease expires. If not removed within a reasonable amount of time afterward, they will become the property of the landlord.

For Example	Claire Voyant leased store space to M.T. Callory for a restaurant. M.T. installed his ovens, booths, counters and other equipment to operate the restaurant. These items would become Claire's property if M.T. does not remove them within a reasonable amount of time after expiration of the lease. If he damages the real property when removing domestic, agricultural or trade fixtures, the exiting tenant must restore the premises to their original condition.

Intention of the Annexor

The fourth test for fixtures is the intention of the annexor (the person who attached the item). This test is usually considered the most important. In fact, it is the criterion upon which all of the other tests are based. The intention can be found in statements, conduct, or custom (i.e., the intent of most people in similar situations).

A light bulb when screwed into a ceiling fixture is considered real property, because the intent of most owners is to keep the bulb in the fixture as long as it lasts. The same light bulb installed in a table lamp is personal property, since the table lamp is personal property.

Wall-to-wall carpeting is also considered a fixture, since it has been altered to fit one particular area, and most people would not remove it from that area. However, if the carpeting has been installed over hardwood floors in such a manner that it could be removed without damage to the floors, the party who attached the carpet could show that his intent was not to make the carpet a fixture. A court could rule that the carpeting was personal property rather than a fixture. The test of intention also makes kitchen appliance packages furnished by builders as part of a new home, fixtures. A built-in or freestanding range, refrigerator, dishwasher and disposal have been ruled to be fixtures where they were considered to be so by the builder. When the home is resold, these appliances would be considered part of the real property unless excluded from the sale in the sales contract.

Also, in apartments, those appliances normally furnished to the tenant as a part of the unit would be considered fixtures. If the building were sold, the new owner would receive title to those appliances as part of the real property, since they are vital to the operation of the structure, even though they are not specifically designed to be part of the unit or permanently attached to the unit.

Agreement

The fifth test is agreement between the parties involved. When a landlord and tenant enter into a lease, they may include a provision stating who will own the trade fixtures and any other fixtures installed by the tenant. In preprinted purchase and sale agreements common fixtures are listed so that the seller and buyer are aware of what would normally be transferred with the land. This list can be amended to allow the seller to remove fixtures or to require the seller to leave additional items that are not clearly fixtures. The agreement of the parties will determine their intent in the transaction.

A real estate agent can avoid problems by ensuring that the parties in the transaction express their intentions clearly and in writing with regard to items that might or might not be determined to be a fixture, since the agreement will override any legal considerations.

If a lease were to state that trade fixtures become property of the landlord, they will. If a purchase and sale agreement states the seller will remove the house from the lot, he can.

----- TREES, PLANTS AND CROPS -----

A real estate agent should also be aware of the fact that trees, plants, and crops may be real property or personal property, depending on the circumstances.

Natural growth (fructus naturales) and perennial plantings are normally considered real property. Therefore, trees, grasses and fruit orchards, uncultivated groves of trees, standing timber, a hedge of lilac that blooms annually, and apple trees in the back yard would be real property.

Annual crops (fructus industriales) such as grain, vegetables or fruit from orchards, are normally considered personal property. Therefore, a grape crop sold on contract to a winery, a wheat crop on leased land, and a crop of apples harvested and ready for market would be personal property. Another term for such annual crops is emblements. **Emblements** are crops that are grown on land and require annual planting and cultivation. These crops would be personal property.

The word "emblements" in some types of real estate leases means the right of a tenant farmer to go on the land to harvest his crop. The tenant farmer may exercise the right either before or after the lease is terminated. Therefore, when a farm is operated by a tenant under a lease, the crops requiring annual plantings and cultivation would be the personal property of the tenant. If a lease of uncertain duration were terminated by the landlord after a crop had been planted, the tenant (the lessee) would have the right to harvest the crop. In order to prevent tenants from returning to the property after expiration of a lease, the lease may have provisions to specifically limit or even remove the right of emblements.

Crops may be used as security for crop loans for purchase of seed and fertilizer, before or after planting. If the borrower defaults, the lender may attach, harvest and sell the crop, without affecting the title to the land. In addition, these crops may be sold separately from the land.

For Example	Dusty Rhodes owned 40 acres of land on which he grew onions. He sold the onion crop to Sandy Loam who agreed to harvest the onions. Before the onions were harvested, Dusty sold the land to Meadow Lark, and Meadow recorded the deed. The crop of onions would belong to Sandy. Meadow would own the real property, the land, without the crop.

Property Ownership Rights?

----- APPURTENANCES -----

Rights appurtenant to the land include the rights to lateral support, subjacent support, natural drainage, air rights, easements, and in most states water rights and mineral rights.

Lateral Support
The law guarantees a property owner the right to lateral support and subjacent support. **Lateral support** is support from the side. In effect, an owner has legal protection against acts of neighbors that would cause damage to his property.

Property A   **Property B**

<table>
<tr><td>For Example</td><td>Your neighbor cannot excavate on his property in such a manner that would remove natural support for your land, causing trees to topple or improvements to move. If natural support were removed, your neighbor would have to replace it with artificial support (e.g. a retaining wall) to prevent damage to your property.

Also, your neighbor could not construct a structure on his land that would be so heavy that it would cause excavations on your property to cave in.</td></tr>
</table>

Subjacent Support
The right to **subjacent support** is the protection of not having one's property disturbed by losing support from below the surface. Therefore, if a property owner sells mineral rights to another, the person having those rights may mine underground, but must provide support to prevent damage to improvements on the surface.

Natural Drainage
The right to **natural drainage** provides that a property owner has the right to a natural drainage of surface waters derived from rain or snow. A person's neighbors cannot:
- dam the flow of water so that it backs up and accumulates on his property.
- change the natural channel of water so as to cause the water to drain off onto his property causing damage to that property.
- create a reservoir to collect the water and then release it causing damage to his land.

- drain water into a natural watercourse so as to unreasonably increase the volume or accelerate the flow of water so that his property suffers damage.

A person may replace natural drainage with tile drainage to improve his property or make it usable, but he cannot change the water flow so as to damage someone else's property. Usually, the water is channeled into an underground pipe that deposits it in a public storm sewer system. This would cause no harm to neighboring properties. Neighbors do have the right to allow surface water to flow naturally from their property onto another's property, and are not obligated to stop the natural flow. They also have the right to direct water onto adjacent land, if that water would have flowed naturally over that land anyway. This may result in the water flowing more rapidly, but not in a different direction. In accelerating the flow they must act with prudent regard for the neighboring landowner and not cause unreasonable inconvenience.

Air Rights

Air rights are also appurtenant to the land. Because the legal concept of land holds that ownership extends to the center of the earth and the sky above the land, a landowner has the right to use the air space above his land. However, air rights can be restricted by zoning ordinances that limit the height of construction, as well as by federal laws that reserve the use of air space for aircraft. Air rights can be sold separately from the surface rights or leased separately from the land. Also, air rights can be reserved by the seller when he sells the land. When deeding the property to a grantee, the grantor can reserve the air rights while conveying title to the land.

Just as land can be divided vertically, air rights can be divided horizontally. As a result, in some areas, railroad companies have sold air rights above railroad tracks, to allow construction of buildings above the tracks. In other areas, railways have been constructed in air lots above existing buildings. Horizontal divisions are used to create condominiums. An individual who buys a condominium purchases a cube of air enclosed by the walls of a building. The rest of the owners of condominium units share the ownership of the shell of the building and the land on which the building sits. Each owner can sell his cube, lease it and even encumber it.

Mineral Rights

Just as a person has the air rights allowing use of air space, in most states he has the subsurface rights to **minerals** under his land. Solid minerals (e.g., coal and metal ore) are real property. They remain real property until they are removed from the earth or sold or leased to others. Then they become personal property. When real property is transferred, the rights to minerals under the ground go with the land, unless otherwise specified. The owner of the land has the right to sell the land to one person and the mineral rights to another, or may sell the mineral rights and keep the land, or may sell the land and keep the mineral rights.

Easement

Ownership of real property may include an easement, such as:

- a right of way to cross a neighbor's land in order to get to a main road.
- a party wall connecting adjoining dwellings.
- passages for light, air and heat from or across another's land.

An easement is an irrevocable right to use another person's land for a particular purpose. When the easement is permanent and benefits the land of the holder of the easement, it is appurtenant to that land, and is called an easement appurtenant. When the ownership of the land is transferred, the easement is included in the transfer to the new owner. When land with a right of way is sold, the new owner of the land would acquire the right of way. The seller would not take the easement with him; it stays with the land.

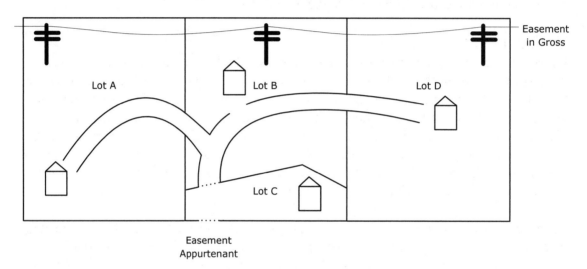

Easement in Gross

Easement Appurtenant

Water Rights

In the United States, each state has its own system for granting and recognizing the right to use water. Some states subscribe to the common law doctrine of riparian rights. However, the ownership and use of water in states where water is scarce is often determined by the doctrine of prior appropriation. Most western states use the prior appropriation system.

In many states, by virtue of state statute, water is considered to be owned by the general public, and not the person who owns the land through which the water passes. The public has the right to use the water for navigational and recreational uses, e.g., boating, swimming, fishing, etc., which do not reduce the normal quantity of flow of the water. However, a private person may obtain the right to use the water in such a way as to reduce the water flow.

In a riparian rights state, the riparian owner (the person owning land over which water flows or bordering on a waterway, such as a river or stream) has the right to use, i.e. take, that water. A **riparian right** is the right the owner of real property has to use the water from an adjacent waterway. The riparian owner gets the riparian right automatically because of the location of his land. Therefore, riparian rights are not listed in the warranty deed giving the owner title to the property, nor are they recorded. So, they are not found in the public records. Riparian rights only give the riparian owner the right to a reasonable use of water; they do not allow a right to use an unlimited amount of water. The riparian right holder does not have absolute ownership of the water and does not have an absolute and exclusive right to use the water. Therefore, he does not have the right to waste the water, divert it, or deprive other riparian owners of their right to use it.

In states operating under the doctrine of **prior appropriation**, a riparian owner does not automatically have the right to use water. Instead, the state grants, or appropriates, rights to use water to riparian and nonriparian owners. Therefore, under the prior appropriation concept, the state may give permission to a nonriparian owner of a farm to use water from a nearby lake.

Prior appropriation is a system of water rights primarily based on the order in which people initiated their use. This provides simple mechanisms for determining who has the right to use water in times of short supply. Under the doctrine of prior appropriation, a landowner must apply to a state department for a water rights certificate, in order to be able to divert water for private use. If the application is approved, a certificate is issued setting forth the period during which the right may be exercised, the point of diversion, the place of use, the maximum quantity of water that may be diverted, and the land to which the water right is appurtenant.

RIPARIAN	PRIOR APPROPRIATION
Automatic	Application Process
Reasonable Use	Specified Amount
Not Recorded	Recorded

Subdivisions and Condos

----- COMMON INTEREST SUBDIVISIONS -----

Today, many property owners prefer to own real property with a reduced lot size in return for common recreation areas and facilities and reduced individual maintenance requirements. Developers have responded with **common interest subdivisions** in which the owners own interests in or portions of the property in common. These include planned unit developments, townhouses, cooperatives, and condominiums. They provide for more efficient use of the land and for reduced construction costs by placing a number of units side by side with shared walls or all inside the same building.

Planned Unit Developments
In a **planned unit development (PUD)** each lot is sold separately. In addition, open space property and property used in common by the property owners (e.g., a club house or pool) is owned by a homeowners' association (HOA). All homeowners are members of the HOA. Many PUDs are zoned to allow a combination of various land uses (residential, commercial, retail, recreational) to serve the needs of the homeowners. They may also combine various housing types, including detached, semidetached, attached and/or multistory units. PUDs often have cluster zoning, which allows a number of dwellings to be clustered together in order to create a larger amount of land to be used for common areas.

Townhouses
Townhouses, or rowhouses, are dwellings constructed side by side with abutting walls, or party walls (shared walls). Each owner owns his unit and the land comprising the lot on which it was built, just as if the units were detached. With a party wall, each owner owns the portion of the wall on his property and has a party wall easement for support in the other portion.

Cooperatives
In a **cooperative** arrangement, a building containing a number of living units is owned by either a trust or a corporation.
- If title were held by a trust, a person wanting to occupy one of the living units would purchase a certificate of beneficial interest in the trust.
- If title were held by a corporation (as is the case with most cooperatives), a person would purchase shares of stock in the corporation that owns the building. More desirable units require the purchase of more shares of stock than the less desirable ones.

Whether a purchaser buys a certificate of beneficial interest or shares of stock, he has a personal property interest in the entity owning the building and not a real property or fee interest in any of the units. The units are owned by the trust or corporation. Therefore, the purchaser will not get a deed to any apartment.

However, with the share of ownership, the purchaser will get an exclusive right to occupy one of the units. This right to occupy is granted in the form of a long-term lease, called a proprietary lease. A **proprietary lease** is a lease held by a proprietor, or owner, of the company owning the building. Because the owner will have the right to occupy the unit for as long as he remains an owner in the trust or corporation, it is not uncommon to see such a person referred to as the owner of a cooperative apartment, even though technically, he is a tenant.

Because the trust or corporation owns the building and all the units in the building, it will obtain one loan to build or acquire the building, and it will receive one property tax bill for the entire building. It will then make the payments of mortgage interest and principal on the loan, pay the property taxes and property insurance premiums, and pay all operating and maintenance expenses on the property.

Each owner is assessed a pro rata share of these expenses. This results in one of the disadvantages of this form of ownership; that is, ultimately each owner is connected with the financial stability of his neighbors. If one owner does not pay his share of the expenses, all of the other owners must contribute to make up the amount needed. If the owners are unable or unwilling to do so, the unpaid lienholders may foreclose on the entire property.

To reduce this risk, most cooperatives maintain a reserve account and have bylaws that provide that an owner may be foreclosed against by the corporation or trust for failure to pay the assessment. As an additional safeguard, but also a disadvantage to an owner, the bylaws may provide that an owner may sell his unit and assign his proprietary lease, or even lease the unit, only with the approval of a majority of the cooperative's board of directors or owners.

Advantages of cooperative ownership include the following:
- Land costs are lower
- The owner may sell his interest and assign the lease, and upon sale, any profit is subject to tax treatment as a capital gain
- The owner's share of property taxes and mortgage interest is tax deductible
- The owner is not personally liable for the debts of the trust or corporation

Condominiums

Condominiums may be residential, industrial, commercial or resort properties. They may be any building type: detached, semidetached, multistory, etc. What makes a property a condominium is the fact that the units (the dwelling unit, office space, industrial space, etc.) are sold separately, and the land is owned by all unit owners in common.

Compare this to the PUD, townhouse or cooperative:
- In a PUD, the units with the land under them are owned separately, and the remaining land in the development is owned by the HOA, rather than the unit owners directly.

- In a townhouse, the units and the land under them are owned separately, and there is no land owned in common.
- In a cooperative, the units are not owned separately. Owners own shares of ownership in the entire building and lease their units.

The purchaser of a condominium unit will receive a unit deed granting fee title to the air space within and all finished surfaces of the walls, floors, and ceiling of the unit, and an undivided fractional or percentage interest in common with the other unit owners in the common areas and facilities of the property. He would obtain title insurance and property hazard insurance for the unit, just as the owner of a detached home would.

The common areas and facilities are referred to as **common elements**. The common elements would be all portions of the condominium other than the units. They may be general or limited.

General common elements are common elements used by all unit owners:
- The land on which the building is located
- Yards, gardens, parking areas, and outside storage space
- Premises for the lodging of janitors or caretakers of the property
- All elements of the building needed or convenient for its existence, maintenance and safety, or normally in common use (e.g., the exterior of the building, basements, foundations, columns, girders, roofs, main walls, halls, stairs, central utility services, elevators, swimming pool, recreation hall, etc.)

Limited common elements are common elements reserved for the exclusive use of one or more units. They would include party walls, patios, balconies, and parking spaces reserved for certain unit owners.

Common elements are owned by the owners of the units in the condominium in the form of percentage or fractional interests. The declaration filed in order to create the condominium establishes the method of allocating these interests and of determining liability for common expenses and the right to common profits. It also allocates to each unit owner voting rights in a unit owners' association. Generally, the unit owners association manages the property, enforces the condominium bylaws and rules, and provides for maintenance and repair of the common elements. Each owner is assessed fees periodically to cover the association's expenses. The association would normally use the fees it collects to pay premiums for a property insurance policy covering the common elements.

In a condominium, unit owners are responsible only for those liens (e.g., for construction, mortgage indebtedness and property taxes) involving their own units and the fee to cover a proportionate share of the expenses of the property held in common. Each unit owner will receive a separate tax bill that covers the value of his unit and his proportionate share of the commonly held property. Liens against the individual units or unit owners are not liens against the entire property. Therefore, failure to pay a lien against a unit could result in foreclosure of the unit but would not affect the other owners. The owner may hypothecate the unit as security for a mortgage without creating a lien on the title of the other unit owners.

Unless the condominium is built on leased land, the owner of a condominium unit has a freehold interest in the unit. This interest is generally fee simple, but it could be an estate for life. If the building were on leased land, the purchaser of the unit would have an estate for years, for the period of the lease.

The title to the individual condominium unit may be conveyed and financed just as if it were an individual building on a separate parcel of land. Unlike in a cooperative, the purchaser may later convey freehold title to a grantee without the need for any approval from the condominium owners' association.

In many resort areas, interests in condominium units or other properties may be marketed on a timeshare basis. Timesharing is a modern form of property ownership that involves the guaranteed right of occupancy and use of a specific property for a specific portion of each year for either a fixed number of years or forever. This right may specify the exact time of the year for the use or may allow use on a first-come, first-serve basis. There are various forms of timeshares. Some involve ownership while others involve only use, through a vacation license, vacation lease or club membership.

Condominiums may be sold as real estate investment contracts. These are a form of real estate security in which the investors are inactive participants who are led to expect profits (income, tax benefits and appreciation) solely from the efforts of the promoter or a third party. Real estate securities include rental pools, time-sharing agreements, limited partnership interests and certain forms of tenancy in common ownership. Condominium sales are securities if they are coupled with participation in a rental pool agreement where:
- a promoter or third party agrees to rent the condominium unit on behalf of the owner.
- the income and expenses of all units are combined.
- each owner receives a share of the profits.

These securities may have to be registered with state securities regulators or with the Securities and Exchange Commission, and persons may have to be registered or licensed to sell them. Even if exempt from registration, they may be subject to laws regarding sales practices.

Brain Teaser

Reinforce your understanding of the material by correctly completing the following sentences:

1. _____ is anything that can be owned.

2. The concept of land ownership by a king, with rights granted to others in return for services, is considered the _____ _____ of land ownership.

3. The document used to show evidence of a transfer of ownership of personal property to another is called a _____ _____ _____ .

4. _____ support is support from the side, while the right to _____ support is the protection of not having one's property disturbed by losing support from below the surface.

5. In a cooperative, a _____ lease is a lease held by one of the owners of the company owning the building.

Brain Teaser Answers

1. **Property** is anything that can be owned.

2. The concept of land ownership by a king, with rights granted to others in return for services, is considered the **feudal system** of land ownership.

3. The document used to show evidence of a transfer of ownership of personal property to another is called a **bill of sale**.

4. **Lateral** support is support from the side, while the right to **subjacent** support is the protection of not having one's property disturbed by losing support from below the surface.

5. In a cooperative, a **proprietary** lease is a lease held by one of the owners of the company owning the building.

Review — Property Ownership

In this lesson we review the concept of property ownership.

Basics of Real, Personal, and Public Property

Real property is property that is legally or physically immovable. It includes the land and everything permanently attached to the land. Under the legal concept of land ownership, a person who owns the land, owns its surface, plus airspace above and minerals below the surface, all improvements (anything artificial or constructed on the land), and rights (appurtenances) to the land.

Personal property is property that is not real property. It may also be called chattel, and rights in personal property may be called chattel interests. All rights in real estate held by persons other than the owner of the real estate are personal property, including the right of a lender given a mortgage or trust deed as security for a loan.

Real and personal property may be sold in the same transaction or separately. A deed would convey title to real estate, while a bill of sale can be used to convey title to personal property. Both types of property may be hypothecated (used as security for a debt, without giving up possession). A mortgage or trust deed can be used to create a lien against real property, while under the Uniform Commercial Code, a security agreement can be used to create a lien against personal property.

Property owned by the government is called public property. Property owned by private parties is called private property. Under the allodial system of ownership land can be owned and controlled by individuals. A landowner has a freehold estate, giving him a bundle of rights. These rights include the right to use, possess, enjoy, and dispose of the land in any legal way, allowing him to sell, lease, use, enjoy, exclude, encumber or devise (will) his interest.

Government Limitations

The government has four basic limitations on the rights of private ownership of real property:

- **P**olice power is the right to enact legislation for the health, safety and general welfare of the public.
- **E**minent domain is the right to acquire ownership of privately held real estate, for public use, upon payment of compensation to the owner.
- **T**axation is the right to raise money to support itself through taxes, including general and special assessments.
- **E**scheat is the right to acquire title to property when the owner dies intestate (without a will) and has no heirs eligible to inherit the property.

Differences Between Personal Property and Real Property

Trees and crops may be real property or personal property, depending on circumstances. A tenant may have ownership rights to annual crops (emblements) he planted or to trade fixtures he installed for use in his business. Emblements and trade fixtures would be personal property of the tenant and can be removed by him when, or a reasonable time after, the lease expires.

Real property can be converted to personal property by severance (either actual physical separation or constructive separation, such as when air rights or subsurface mineral rights are sold separately from the land).

Personal property can be converted to real property by annexation, such as a fixture. A fixture is an article of personal property that has become part of the real estate by virtue of its attachment to the real estate. Tests to determine if an item is a fixture are the following:
- **M**ethod of attachment
- **A**daptation of the item to the real estate
- **R**elationship between the parties involved
- **I**ntent of the annexor
- **A**greement between the parties involved

A property owner's rights include: lateral support, or the right to support from the side; subjacent support, or the right to support from below the surface; the right to natural drainage; air rights; and rights to minerals below the surface.

Land ownership may also include an easement appurtenant, or right to use another person's land for a particular purpose such as a right-of-way, and water rights.
- **Riparian**: In states that grant water rights under the system of riparian rights, landowners have an automatic right to reasonable use of water on, under or adjoining their property
- **Appropriation**: In an appropriation doctrine state, landowners must apply for a right to a limited and specified use of water

Ways to Own Land

In a planned unit development, each lot is sold separately, but open space used in common by the property owners is owned by a homeowners' association.

Under townhouse ownership, each owner owns his unit and the lot on which it was built, and common walls are owned in common with the adjoining owners.

In a cooperative arrangement, a trust or a corporation owns a building and its living units, and pays the property taxes, mortgage payments and operating expenses. A purchaser gets shares of ownership in the entity owning the building and an exclusive right to occupy one of the units in the form of a long-term proprietary lease. His lease payments cover his share of the building expenses.

A condominium is a residential, industrial, or commercial project in which each unit owner receives:

- a unit deed conveying a freehold estate (usually fee) to the air space within and all finished surfaces of the unit.
- an undivided fractional or percentage interest in common with the other unit owners in the common areas and facilities of the property.

The owner may obtain title insurance and homeowner's hazard insurance on his unit. He pays his own taxes, mortgage payment, insurance and redecorating and maintenance for his unit. His tax statement covers the value of his unit and a proportionate share of commonly held property. Liens against him or his unit are not liens against the entire property, so if he defaults on a mortgage loan secured by his unit, it has no effect on any other unit owners.

Timeshares

Interests in condominiums or other properties may be marketed on a timeshare basis, guaranteeing a right of occupancy and use of a specific property for a specific portion of each year for a specified number of years or forever. Some involve ownership while others involve only use, through a vacation license, vacation lease or club membership.

Property Descriptions

Overview

In this lesson we explain the importance of an accurate, complete property description for inclusion in a real estate contract. Main methods of legally describing real property are detailed, including lot and block, metes and bounds, and government survey.

Objectives

Upon completion of this lesson, the student should be able to:

1. Describe the different methods for legally describing real property and how they are applied throughout the United States.
   - Lot and block
   - Metes and bounds
   - Government survey
2. Demonstrate proficiency in using various land units and measurements.

Property Descriptions

When writing a listing agreement or sales contract, a real estate agent must include a description of the real and personal property involved.

As a result of the Statute of Frauds, all elements in a real estate contract, including a description of the property, must be in writing. If the written agreement does not enable a surveyor to locate the property and establish its boundaries, the contract may be void.

----- ADEQUATE DESCRIPTIONS -----

An adequate property description will identify property with absolute certainty so as to avoid litigation or defeat of the parties' purpose. Identification would include location, boundaries and area, so that the parcel can be distinguished from all other land. When the property description enables a disinterested party to segregate the object being described from all other objects of its type, it is called a **legal description**. An adequate legal description will identify the property so that a court would compel a seller to give, or a buyer to accept, the property.

Personal Property

If personal property (such as a refrigerator or swing set) is to be included in the transaction, that item must be specifically identified and written in the offer. Specific identification may include the quantity, brand name, model, style, the serial number, the location of the item as of the date of the offer, the color of the item, etc. An extremely cautious person might attach a picture of the item to the contract. Any combination of these methods may be helpful in avoiding any dispute as to what is called for in the contract.

For Example	There would be no doubt as to what was intended if the buyer wrote, "One General Electric Avocado 'Frost-free' Refrigerator (Serial # 456-1785 FF) located in the kitchen of the subject property as of the date of this offer" or "One set of 9' Ivory Customweave drapes located in the living room of the subject property as of the date of this offer."

Real Property

A listing agreement or an offer to purchase real property will normally include the land and anything permanently attached to it (buildings, trees, fences, fixtures, etc.). The description of the real property in an offer to purchase or a deed, however, will be only of the surface of the land and not of all of the improvements and rights appurtenant to the land.

Property Survey Types

----- LEGAL DESCRIPTIONS -----

The best means of describing real property is to use a description based on a survey, so that the location is completely enclosed by surveyed boundaries. There are three types of property survey methods commonly found on deeds, preliminary title reports, and title insurance policies:

1. Lot and block (or recorded plat)
2. Metes and bounds
3. Rectangular (or government) survey

Lot and Block

The **lot and block** method is the shortest, easiest, and simplest method to describe real property. It is most commonly used in highly populated areas. It describes parcels in platted subdivisions by referring to the recorded plat (map) for the subdivision. Hence, it may be referred to as the **recorded plat method**.

When a tract of land is subdivided, a surveyor divides the property into streets, blocks and lots. A subdivision plat, showing the divisions, is recorded in the county or city in which the property resides and is available for public inspection. It contains a name or number for the subdivision. It shows the location name and width and centerline of each street. It shows the blocks and lots. The blocks are groups of contiguous or adjoining lots bounded by streets, physical barriers or other parcels of land. The blocks are divided into lots. These are the smallest parcels of land intended to be conveyed as a unit to a purchaser. Each lot and block is numbered. Once the entire subdivision is platted, the legal description of the property is written as the lot number, block number, the name of the subdivision, and the county and state in which the subdivision is located.

For Example	"Lot 7, Block 3, Section 2, Sunnyside Acres, Any County, Your State." The description may also refer to the book and page number of the county records in order to facilitate locating the records. So, the description may state, "as platted and recorded on page 42 of book 23, Any County, Your State, Plat Records."

A plat may contain a number of other features:
- The number of square feet contained in the lot
- The dimensions in feet, to the nearest hundredth of a foot inside the lot along the boundary line, of each lot's *frontage*, or *front lot line* (the line along the front of the lot, separating it from the street), the *rear lot line* (the boundary on the rear of the lot), and the *side lot line* (the boundary on the sides of the lot) (When describing the dimensions of a lot, the frontage is shown first, e.g., a rectangular lot described as 75' x 100' has 75' frontage and a depth of 100'.)

- Building restriction lines (**building lines** or **setback lines**) shown by long dashed lines with the distance of the setback (Setback lines, whether set by local zoning ordinance, subdivision restrictions or statute, are the minimum distance a structure must be set back from a street, lot line or other boundary.)
- Easements for streets, turnarounds, utility lines for water and electricity, sewer lines, flight paths, etc., shown as dashed lines with their width and purpose
- The direction of each boundary line, measured by its bearing from north or south points on a compass, in degrees, minutes, and seconds (A north arrow on a plat points to north in relation to the plat. If there is no arrow, presume that the top of the plat is north.)

To understand directions, picture a circle at the beginning of each line, with the point at which the line starts being the center of the circle. A circle has 360 degrees (360°). Each degree has 60 minutes (60'). Each minute has 60 seconds (60"). N 15° 35' 30" E is "North 15 degrees, 35 minutes, 30 seconds East."

> **NOTE:** Do not confuse these marks (' and ") with feet and inches, although they are written the same.

On a plat, the direction of a boundary line depends on where the surveyor started.

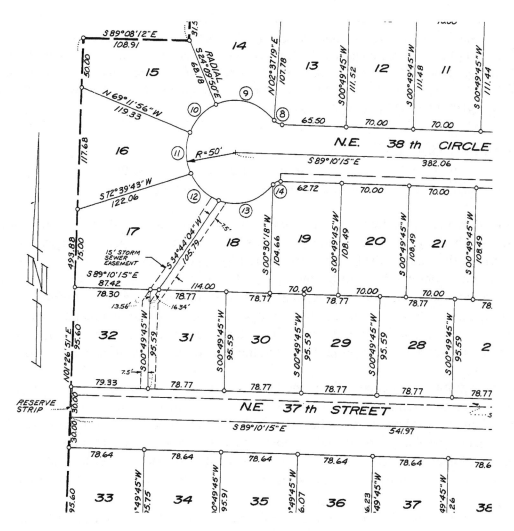

Air space above land may be divided into air lots. **Air lots** consist of airspace within specified boundaries above a parcel of land. A description of such air space is used for buildings constructed above railroad tracks and for platting condominium units where the owner of each unit will own the air space within the floor, ceiling and walls of his unit. Descriptions of air lots include elevations. Elevations can be measured using **benchmarks**. These are metal disks set in rock or permanent structures throughout the country by the National Geodetic Survey to precisely measure elevation.

Markers and Monuments

Parcels that have not been platted may be identified by describing their boundaries. Originally, this was done through what is called the **markers and monuments system**. A **monument** is a fixed object used to establish a real estate boundary. It may be natural (a river or rock formation) or man-made (a fence, building, or iron stake placed by a surveyor). It may be tangible (a point established by another surveyor) or intangible (the centerline of a street).

"Being all that parcel of land bounded on the north by the white picket fence of Samuel Johnson, bounded on the east of Horseshoe Lane, bounded on the south by the barbed wire fence of Elizabeth Hansen, up to the tall pine tree where Peter Smith was hung, and then along the stone fence back to Farmer's Lane, and bounded on the west by Farmer's Lane, containing five acres, more or less."

Metes and Bounds

A more accurate method of describing the boundaries of a property is provided by a **metes** (measurements) and **bounds** (boundaries) description.

This method describes the land by providing the measurement and direction (also called course and bearing) of each boundary line. It should contain the specific length and direction of the sides of the property (measured from north and south points to east or west points), a definite point of beginning and definite corners, and should start and finish at the same identifiable point. It begins at a permanent reference point (a **point of beginning**), which is a monument. If the property is not bounded by this point of beginning, the description will describe the distance and direction from the point of beginning to a corner of the property, called the **true point of beginning (TPOB)**.

The description will then describe a line that follows the boundary of the property to the corner or terminal (end) point, at which the direction of the boundary line changes. The word "thence" in a description indicates a shift to a new direction. The distance (in feet, miles, inches, or older forms of measurement such as chains, rods, and links) and direction of each boundary line is shown continuously from one corner to another until the last boundary returns to the true point of beginning, to produce a fully enclosed area.

"That portion of the southwest quarter of section 19, township 12 north, range 4 east, W.M., in _____ County, _____ State, described as follows: Beginning at the southwest corner of said section 19, thence north 0□06'24" west along the west line thereof, 275 feet; thence north 87□24'45" east 500 feet to the true point of beginning of this description; thence continuing north 87□24'45" east 193.40 feet; thence north 20□29'15" east, 162.12 feet to the southwesterly line of county road; thence north 35□43'25" west along said southwesterly road line, 190.63 feet; thence south 64□08'35" west, 221.00 feet; thence south 15□23'45" east, 227.12 feet to the true point of beginning.

A property boundary may include a waterway. Owners of property adjoining a river or stream are riparian owners. Owners of property adjoining lakes and oceans are called **littoral owners**. If the waterway is non-navigable, an adjoining property owner has title to the land to the center of the river or streambed. If the waterway is navigable, the state owns the land under the water between the mean high water marks. Adjoining owners own the land up to the mean high water marks and have a right to reasonable use of the water, secondary to the public's right to use the water for navigational purposes. The metes and bounds method is not brief or simple and may result in errors when copied onto new documents. Also, it may be interpreted differently by different persons; there may be a discrepancy between a line and an angle, or a distance and the location of a monument, resulting in disputes between the parties.

Government or Rectangular Survey

A third type of property description is the **government survey method** (or rectangular survey method, or section and township system).

In the late 1700s, the federal government started a survey of all lands *except* the 13 original states, the New England and Atlantic Coast states, West Virginia, Kentucky, Tennessee, Texas, and Hawaii. Under this system there are 36 fixed points in the country from which separate surveys begin. Through each point runs an imaginary line in a true north-south direction, called a **meridian** or **principal meridian**, and an imaginary line in a true east-west direction, called a **baseline**.

Parallel to the meridian, running north-south and six miles apart, are **range lines**. The area between each range line is called a range. Range lines and ranges are numbered consecutively from the meridian. On the west they are Range 1W, Range 2W, Range 3W, etc. On the east are Range R1E, Range R2E, etc.

Lines running east-west, six miles apart and parallel to the baseline are called **township lines**. They are numbered consecutively north and south from the baseline. The area between the township lines running east-west is called a tier or township. Below is an example of the baselines and meridians for the western half of the states:

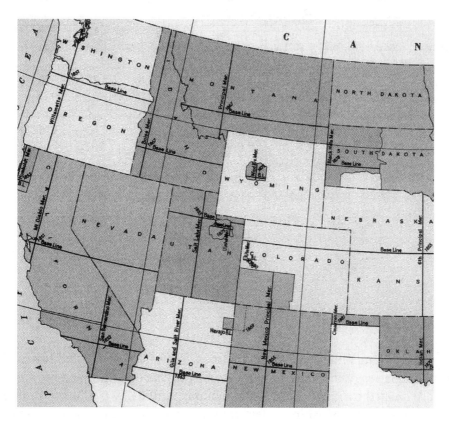

Township Grid
Principal Meridian and Baseline

				T5N R1W	T5N R1E				
	T4N R4W	T4N R3W	T4N R2W	T4N R1W	T4N R1E	T4N R2E	T4N R3E	T4N R4E	
	T3N R4W	T3N R3W	T3N R2W	**Principal Meridian**		T3N R2E	T3N R3E	T3N R4E	
	T2N R4W	T2N R3W	T2N R2W	T2N R1W	T2N R1E	T2N R2E	T2N R3E	T2N R4E	
1N 4W	T1N R4W	T1N R3W	T1N R2W	T1N R1W	T1N R1E	T1N R2E	T1N R3E	T1N R4E	T R4
T1S R4W	T1S R4W	T1S R3W	T1S R2W	T1S R1W	T1S R1E	T1S R2E	T1S R3E	T1S R4E	T1S R4E
T2S R4W	T2S R4W	T2S R3W	T2S R2W	T2S R1W	T2S R1E	T2S R2E	T2S R3E	T2S R4E	
	T3S R4W	T3S R3W	T3S R2W	T3S R1W	T3S R1E	T3S R2E	T3S R3E	T3S R4E	
	T4S R4W	T4S R3W	T4S R2W	T4S R1W	T4S R1E	T4S R2E	T4S R3E		
				T5S R1W					

6 Mi.² — Baseline — N, W, E, S

The intersection of range lines and township lines creates squares called **townships**. The north-south boundaries of townships are created by townships lines and the east-west boundaries are created by range lines. A township is 6 miles by 6 miles (6 miles square) or 36 square miles. Each township is identified by its township, range and meridian. T2S, R3W, WM would be the second tier south and the third range west of the meridian. (WM, the Willamette Meridian, is the principal meridian in this example.)

Government Survey System

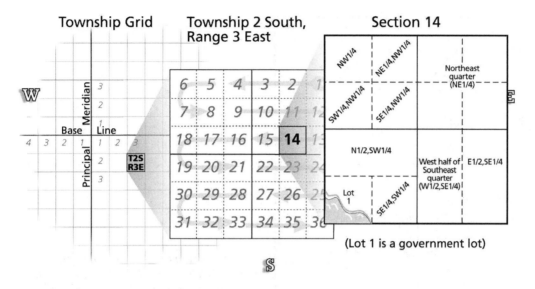

(Lot 1 is a government lot)

Each township is divided into 36 sections. A standard **section**:
- measures one mile by one mile (5,280 ft. x 5,280 ft.; or 1,760 yd. x 1,760 yd.).
- contains 640 acres. One acre is 43,560 square feet. If square, an acre has 208.71 feet on each side.

Sections are numbered in a special way. They always start with 1 in the northeast corner of the township. The numbering then goes in sequence westerly to Section 6 in the northwest corner, drops to the next row and goes back east. At the end of each row, the next number is directly below the last numbered section. The numbering proceeds, snakelike, to number 36 in the southeast corner of the township.

Each section can be divided into quarters. When a section is quartered, each quarter section is described by its position in the section. Therefore, there is a NW ¼, a NE ¼, a SW ¼, and a SE ¼.

Section Numbering Sequence

6	5	4	3	2	1
7	8	9	10	11	12
18	17	16	15	14	13
19	20	21	22	23	24
30	29	28	27	26	25
31	32	33	34	35	36

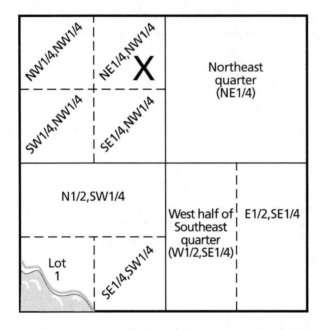

Section 14, Township 2
South, Range 3 East
Lot 1 is a government lot

The diagram to the left shows a section. The section is 640 acres. When it is quartered, and the quarter is quartered, the result is 40-acre parcels.

Each quarter may be divided into quarters or halves, which in turn could be divided as well. The section marked with an "X" above would be described as "the NE ¼ of the NW ¼ of Section 14, T2S, R3E, WM." Descriptions may show the words "of the" or show a comma as an abbreviation of the words "of the."

To find "X" start from the back of the description, the largest area, and move forward:

➔ Step 1 – Find the meridian, township, range and section 14
➔ Step 2 – Find the NW ¼ of section 14
➔ Step 3 – Find the NE ¼ of the NW ¼

Read the description like a street address, from left to right; but locate the parcel from right to left (as you would look for a street address).

From the description, one can determine the number of acres in a parcel. To do this, start at the end of the description and work forward, one step at a time.

For Example

To determine the acreage of N ½, NE ¼, SE ¼, section 12, start with the section (640 acres) and divide by 4, divide by 4 again, divide by 2, then press "=".

640 ÷ 4 ÷ 4 ÷ 2 = 20

N½, NE ¼, SE¼, Section 12

➔ Step 1 – Section 12 = 640 acres
➔ Step 2 – SE¼ = ÷ 4
➔ Step 3 – NE¼ = ÷ 4
➔ Step 4 – N½ = ÷ 2
20

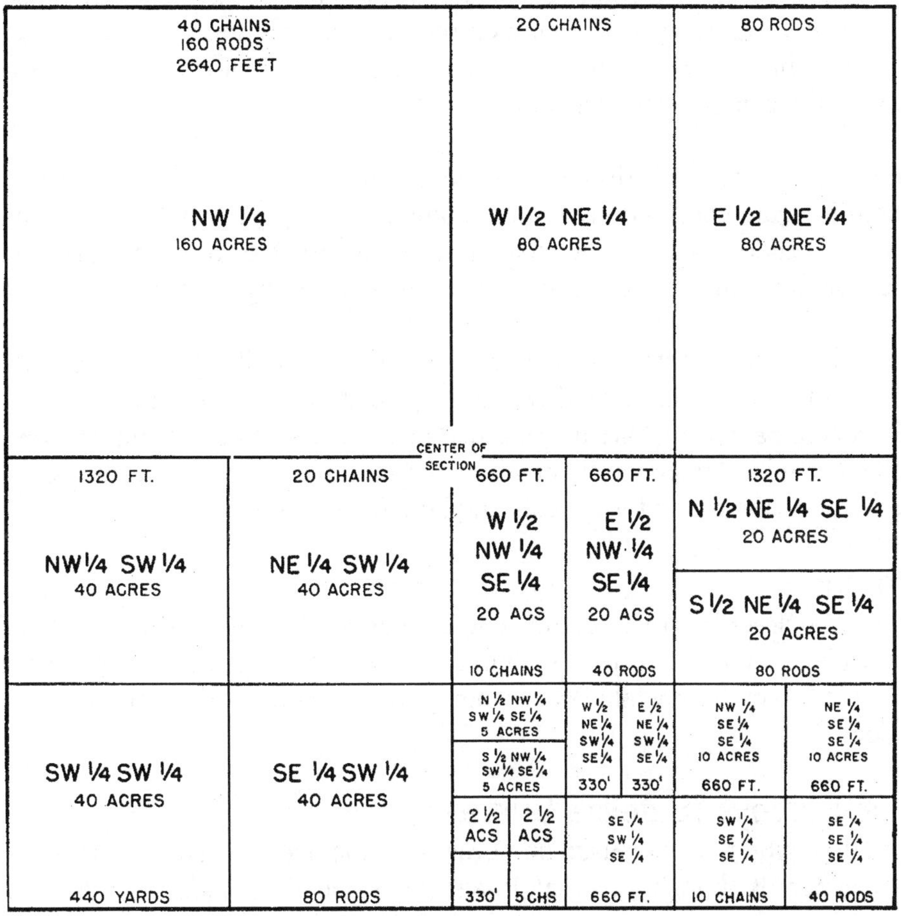

40 CHAINS
160 RODS
2640 FEET
20 CHAINS
80 RODS
NW 1/4
160 ACRES
W 1/2 NE 1/4
80 ACRES
E 1/2 NE 1/4
80 ACRES
CENTER OF SECTION
1320 FT.
20 CHAINS
660 FT.
660 FT.
1320 FT.
NW1/4 SW 1/4
40 ACRES
NE 1/4 SW 1/4
40 ACRES
W 1/2 NW 1/4 SE 1/4
20 ACS
E 1/2 NW 1/4 SE 1/4
20 ACS
N 1/2 NE 1/4 SE 1/4
20 ACRES
S 1/2 NE 1/4 SE 1/4
20 ACRES
10 CHAINS
40 RODS
80 RODS
SW 1/4 SW 1/4
40 ACRES
SE 1/4 SW 1/4
40 ACRES
N ½ NW ¼ SW ¼ SE ¼
5 ACRES
S ½ NW ¼ SW ¼ SE ¼
5 ACRES
W ½ NE ¼ SW ¼ SE ¼
E ½ NE ¼ SW ¼ SE ¼
330'
330'
NW ¼ SE ¼ SE ¼
10 ACRES
NE ¼ SE ¼ SE ¼
10 ACRES
660 FT.
660 FT.
2 1/2 ACS
2 1/2 ACS
SE ¼ SW ¼ SE ¼
SW ¼ SE ¼ SE ¼
SE ¼ SE ¼ SE ¼
440 YARDS
80 RODS
330'
5 CHS
660 FT.
10 CHAINS
40 RODS

Below, see how the number of acres is calculated in each of the following:

1. S ½ of SE ¼ of NE ¼ of Section 20 = 640 ÷ 4 ÷ 4 ÷ 2 = 20 acres
2. SE ¼ of the SE ¼ of the SE ¼ of Section 1 = 640 ÷ 4 ÷ 4 ÷ 4 = 10 acres
3. S ½ of the SE ¼ of the NW ¼ of the NE ¼ of Section 29 = 640 ÷ 4 ÷ 4 ÷ 4 ÷ 2 = 5 acres

When a parcel is in two quadrants of a section, the description will include the words "and the" or a semicolon as the abbreviation for those words.

Kay Tell owned a parcel which covered S ½, SE ¼, NW ¼, section 12 and SW ¼, SW ¼, NE ¼, section 12. It could be written as S ½, SE ¼, NW ¼ and SW ¼, SW ¼, NE ¼, section 12. To calculate the area, calculate each part of the description separated by the "and" separately and add the parts together.

S ½, SE ¼, NW ¼ and SW ¼, SW ¼, NE ¼, section 12.

640 acres ÷ 4 ÷4 ÷ 4 = 10 acres
640 ÷ 4 ÷4 ÷2 = 20 acres
10 + 20 = 30 acres

Because of the curvature of the earth, meridian lines would converge as they approach the North Pole. To keep townships as a square as possible, adjustments are made every 24 miles, or every four townships, using correction lines and guide meridians. The area created by these lines and meridians, called a "check, " is 24 miles by 24 miles (i.e., 24 miles square) and contains 16 townships.

Some rectangular survey descriptions have lot numbers. These parcels, called **government lots**, are considerably larger or smaller than the normal 40 acres in a quarter-quarter section of land. They usually exist due to an error in the survey or because normal designation and staking was prevented by a bordering waterway.

The government survey system is used primarily when describing rather large parcels of land, such as a farmland, timberland and grazing land. It is not used to describe irregular shaped parcels or parcels that are not oriented in a north-south direction. However, when the parcel is irregular, the government survey system may be used to establish the reference point of beginning for a metes and bounds description.

By Reference
Property may be described by a reference to a recorded document, such as a deed or mortgage, which contains a correct legal description, e.g., "lot and improvements known as 1410 Maple Street, Sunnydale, Your County, State, more particularly described in the attached deed."

Geodesic Surveys (Satellite Surveys)
Another method which may be used on occasion is the geodesic survey method. Geodesic surveys are generally thought of as satellite surveys. Geodesic points are determined by the GPS, or global positioning system, using satellites. The aim of geodesy is to determine the form and dimensions of the earth from a geometric viewpoint.

Real Property Measurements

----- General Descriptions -----

General descriptions may be used temporarily when a legal description is not readily available. They may describe the property sufficiently well between the parties, but they are not sufficient to properly identify the boundaries with reference to adjacent lands.

These may include a tax lot number assigned to property for the convenience of the assessor. Since this number may change when property is divided, a description using it should refer to the year in which the tax lot number appeared on the assessment rolls or the year of the tax map from which it was taken.

A street address may be used to describe the property when a contract is written and in most instances will help identify which property is involved.

One can usually obtain a legal description from a title company or from the present owner's deed, mortgage, contract for deed or title insurance policy.

----- Measurements Relating to Real Property -----

You should know basic linear, square and cubic measurements relating to real property.

Linear Measurements

Linear measurements relate to distance. They involve one dimension. Common linear measurements are inches, feet, yards, and miles. In working with these measurements, you may have to convert them. To do so, you need to remember a conversion factor.

Linear Conversion Factors
> 1 foot = 12 inches
> 1 yard = 3 feet
> 1 mile = 5,280 feet

To Convert Smaller Units of Measurement to a Larger One

Divide by the Conversion Factor:

5,280 feet to yards	divide by 3	5,280' ÷ 3 = 1,760 yards
7'6" to feet	divide 6" by 12	6" ÷ 12 = .5; 7'6" = 7.5 feet
36,960 feet to miles	divide by 5,280	36,960' ÷ 5,280 = 7 miles

To Convert Larger Units of Measurement to a Smaller One

Multiply by the Conversion Factor:

48 yards to feet	multiply by 3	48 yards x 3 = 144'
4 miles to feet	multiply by 5,280	4 miles x 5,280 = 21,120'

With this information, you can calculate the perimeter of a parcel of land. The perimeter is the distance around a parcel. To calculate perimeter, just add the length of the sides.

> **For Example**
>
> A 100' x 200' parcel is a rectangle with 2 sides of 100' and 2 sides of 200'.
> 100 + 100 + 200 + 200 = 600 feet.
> 600 ÷ 3 = 200 yards.
>
> If fencing around the parcel costs $5 per yard, the fencing cost is $5 x 200 yards = $1,000.

You can also calculate cost per front foot. A front foot is one foot along the frontage of a lot. (The depth of a lot is the distance from the front to the back of the lot.)

> **For Example**
>
> A lot measures 80' x 120' and costs $200 per front foot. The first dimension given is always the frontage. Therefore, the lot costs $200 x 80 front feet, or $16,000.

Square Measurements

Square measurements relate to the area of a surface. They result from multiplying two dimensions. Inches x inches = square inches; feet x feet = square feet, etc. For square measurement conversions, the conversion numbers must be squared.

Square Conversion Factors

1 square foot = 144 (12 x 12) square inches
1 square yard = 9 (3 x 3) square feet
1 acre = 43,560 square feet
1 square mile = 640 acres

To Convert Square Measurements

Square inches to square feet	divide by 144
Square feet to square yards	divide by 9
Square feet to acres	divide by 43,560
Acres to square miles	divide by 640

Squares and Rectangles

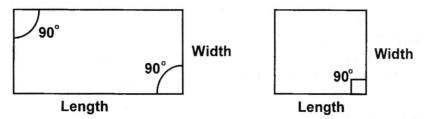

To calculate the area of a square or rectangle (figures with four sides at 90° angles to each other), multiply length by width.

Area = Length x Width

For Example

To calculate the area of a square parcel of land with 1,320 feet on a side:
➔ Multiply 1,320 x 1,320 = 1,742,400 sq. ft.
➔ To convert to acres, divide by 43,560 = 40 acres

To calculate the number of acres contained in an area measuring 220 yards by 220 yards:
➔ Multiply 220 x 220 = 48,400 sq. yd.
➔ To convert to sq. ft., multiply 48,400 x 9 = 435,600 sq. ft.
➔ To convert to acres, divide by 435,600 by 43,560 = 10 acres

To calculate the rent per year for office space with dimensions of 30 feet by 40 feet leased for $14.50 per square foot per year:
➔ Determine the sq. ft. and multiply by $14.50
➔ 30 x 40 = 1200 sq. ft; 1200 x $14.50 = $17,400 per year
➔ The rent per month would be $17,400 ÷ 12 = $1,450

To calculate the sales price of a tract of land 1,320 feet by 440 yards (if $500 per acre):
➔ Find the number of sq. ft. and convert to acres
➔ First convert 440 yards to feet: 440 x 3 = 1,320 ft.
➔ Then multiply 1,320 by 1,320 to determine sq. ft.: 1,320 x 1,320 = 1,742,400 sq. ft.
➔ Divide by 43,560 to get the acreage: 1,742,400 ÷ 43,560 = 40 acres
➔ Then multiply by $500: 40 x 500 = $20,000

Triangles

A second area formula to remember is for the area of a triangle (a figure with three straight sides and three angles). Each triangle has a base and height, i.e., any two sides that come together at a 90° angle. In some cases the height is an imaginary line, as none of the actual sides are at 90° to each other.

The area of a triangle equals the base x the height divided by 2.

Area = base x height
2

Cubic Measurements

Cubic measurements relate to volume and measure the space within a three-dimensional figure, such as the space within a warehouse. Cubic conversions entail multiplying a conversion number by itself three times.

Cubic Conversion Factors

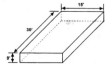

1 cubic foot = 12 x 12 x 12 (1728) cubic inches
1 cubic yard = 3 x 3 x 3 (27) cubic feet

To find volume, multiply the area by the height of the object.

----- BASIC MULTIPLICATION FORMULA -----

Calculation of area and volume involves basic multiplication formulas, where one number equals the product of other numbers. Here is how to work with any multiplication formula, regardless of the information given.

The basic multiplication equation is that one number = the product of two others, e.g.:

Area = Length x Width

When given width and length, multiply:
_____ = width x length

When given area, divide it by length to get width or by width to get length:
Area = width x _____ : divide area by width to get length
Area = _____ x length: divide area by length to get width

A rectangular lot containing 8,554 square feet has a width of 47 feet. The depth of the lot:

➜ Area = width x ?

➜ 8,554 ÷ 47 = 182 ft.

A rectangular lot contains 540 square yards and has a frontage of 45 feet. The depth of the lot:

➜ 540 x 9 = 4,860 sq. ft.

➜ Area = width x ?

➜ 4,860 ÷ 45 = 108 ft.

An acre divided into four equal rectangular lots, each 200 feet deep. The width of the lot:

➜ 43,560 ÷ 4 = 10,890 sq. ft. per lot

➜ Area = ? x length

➜ 10,890 = ? x 200

➜ 10,890 ÷ 200 = 54.45 ft.

Brain Teaser

Reinforce your understanding of the material by correctly completing the following sentences:

1. As a result of the Statute of _____, all elements in a real estate contract must be in writing.

2. _____ lines are the minimum distance a structure must be set back from a street, lot line or other boundary.

3. To convert 41,000 square feet to acres, divide by _____.

Brain Teaser Answers

1. As a result of the Statute of **frauds,** all elements in a real estate contract must be in writing.

2. **Setback** lines are the minimum distance a structure must be set back from a street, lot line or other boundary.

3. To convert 41,000 square feet to acres, divide by **43,560**.

Review — Property Descriptions

In this lesson we discuss the main methods of legally describing real property.

Property Descriptions

When writing a listing agreement or sales contract, a real estate agent must include a written description of the real and personal property involved. When the property description enables a disinterested party to segregate the object being described from all other objects of its type, it is called a legal description. An adequate legal description clearly identifies the property so that a court could compel a seller to give, or a buyer to accept, the property.

The best means of describing real property is to use a description based on a survey so that the location is completely enclosed by the surveyed boundaries. The three types of property survey methods commonly used are 1) lot and block (or recorded plat), 2) metes and bounds, and 3) rectangular (or government) survey. Such descriptions may be easily obtained from deeds, preliminary title reports and title insurance policies.

Surveying Methods

The lot and block method, also called the recorded plat method, is the shortest, easiest, and simplest method to describe real property. In urban and suburban areas, a surveyor divides the property into streets and blocks, divides blocks into lots, and gives each lot and block a number. A lot is the smallest parcel of land intended to be sold as a unit to a purchaser. A subdivision plat, or map, is then recorded in the county or city in which the tract is located and is available for public inspection. The lot and block description identifies the parcel by lot number, block number, the subdivision name, and the county and state.

A metes and bounds description is a method of describing a property by showing its "metes" (measurements) and "bounds" (boundaries). It uses angles, terminal points and established lines to describe the property. The first step in the process is to locate a permanent reference point, called a point of beginning. This is a monument, which may be tangible or intangible (not visibly identifiable). If the property is not bounded by this point of beginning, the description describes the distance and direction to a corner of the property, called the true point of beginning.

A third type of property description is the government (also called rectangular) survey method. This system applies to all of the contiguous western states and most of the mid-western states. It is used primarily when describing large parcels of land.

Under the government survey method there are 36 fixed points in the country from which separate surveys begin. Through each point runs an imaginary line in a true north-south direction, called a meridian or principal meridian, and an imaginary line in a true east-west direction, called a baseline. Range lines run north-south, parallel to the meridian, six miles apart. The area between each range line is called a range. Township lines run east-west, parallel to the baseline, and are also six miles apart. Range lines and township lines intersect to create townships that are six miles by six miles. Each township is divided into 36 sections. They are numbered snakewise, with the section in the upper right hand corner of the township numbered 1 and the section in the upper left hand corner numbered 6. Section seven is below 6, and section 12 is below 1 and to the east of 11. A standard section is a square measuring one mile by one mile (5,280 feet by 5,280 feet) and contains 640 acres. One acre is 43,560 square feet.

Each section can be divided into quarters. To read a description for a parcel, read from left to right. To find the location of a parcel, read the description from right to left, as you would look for a street address. To determine the size of a parcel, calculate from right to left, starting with 640 acres in a section. Therefore, S½, NE¼, SW¼, Section 25 is $640 \div 4 \div 4 \div 2 = 20$ acres.

Another way to legally describe property is to make reference to the description of the property contained in a recorded document.

General descriptions may also be used temporarily to describe the property when a legal description is not readily available. These include the street address and the tax lot number assigned to property for the convenience of the assessor.

Using Measurements

An agent should know how to use some basic measurements relating to real property, including linear, square, and cubic measurements.

- Linear measurements relate to distance and involve one dimension.
- Square measurements relate to the area of a surface and result from multiplying two dimensions (length and width). Calculate the area of a square or rectangle by multiplying length by width. Inversely, when the area is known, divide it by the length or width to find the other.
- The area of a triangle equals the base multiplied by the height divided by two.
- Cubic measurements relate to volume and measure the space within a three dimensional figure. Find the volume by multiplying the three dimensions (length, width, and height).

Real Estate Careers

Overview

In this lesson real estate is viewed from a larger perspective. Activities of varying types of real estate companies are outlined. A licensee's opportunity to pursue an array of real estate careers besides residential real estate is explained. In addition, the lesson highlights how federal and state regulations impact the real estate industry. The roles of professional associations and industry allies are reviewed. The lesson ends with a list of traits of successful real estate professionals.

Objectives

Upon completion of this lesson, the student should be able to:

1. Explain the services of various types of real estate companies.
2. Identify various local, state and national agencies involved in regulating the real estate industry.
3. Identify professional trade associations within the real estate industry and explain why they differ from regulatory agencies.
4. Identify related business activities associated with real estate.
5. Identify factors involved in real estate as a career.

Specialties in Real Estate

Within the real estate industry, various types of real estate companies provide a wide range of services. Some companies provide property management services, while others provide brokerage services. Some are consultants. Some are builder-brokers. Most operate as brokers.

Brokerage is an activity involving the sale or lease of a commodity through an intermediary who usually acts as an agent (or representative) of one of the parties. This intermediary receives compensation for the service. The dollar value of the compensation is negotiable and usually varies with the size and complexity of the transaction.

Because there is no uniformity throughout the country as to the name for the license given to a person in the real estate business, for purposes of this course, we will use the term:
- "agent" to refer to anyone licensed to transact real estate business.
- "broker" to signify the person licensed to supervise other persons conducting real estate activities.
- "licensee" to signify a person licensed to work under a broker's supervision.

----- TYPES OF REAL ESTATE COMPANIES AND SERVICES -----

Size of Operation

Real estate firms range in size from one-person companies to companies with hundreds, if not thousands, of licensees. Each size of operation has its advantages and disadvantages.

 A small office may have a number of advantages for the broker and licensee.

Advantages for the broker generally include:
- minimal supervisory time and training, since there are fewer producers.
- personal satisfaction from working directly with buyers and sellers to put together a transaction.

Advantages for the licensees generally include:
- working closely with the broker and being trained on a one-on-one basis.
- receiving a greater portion of the commission for a transaction due to the low overhead of the brokerage.

A small real estate brokerage has the disadvantage of being dependent on the broker being both a good salesperson and a good manager. With fewer licensees to produce income for the company, the broker must engage in sales activity. This may result in:
- little time to supervise licensees.
- competition with the licensees.
- limited opportunity to take time off.
- inability of the company to recover from a slump in the broker's production.

The firm may only be as good as the broker, as there is no one else to provide the skills the broker may be lacking. If he lacks the skill to avoid conflict, is unable to demonstrate concern for the welfare of the licensees, and cannot provide the assistance they require, licensees will transfer to other real estate offices, open their own offices, or leave the business.

 A medium-sized brokerage firm is customarily run by a sales manager/broker who will manage, but not compete with, the sales staff. In such a company there are enough licensees earning sufficient commissions so the broker need not have to produce commissions of his own.

 In a larger-sized company, the broker will generally perform only executive and administrative functions. A larger company will be headed by an executive specializing full time in real estate office administration, whether it is the broker or a manager hired for that function.

The executive will:
- set attainable goals for the company.
- see that financial, sales and personnel records are carefully maintained.
- oversee the company earnings and expenditures.
- make sure that licensees are receiving sales training and necessary technical support.
- develop and update a policy and procedures manual setting out company policy, procedures and rules.

In a larger firm, there will be others employed to train and manage licensees.

A large company has the advantage of diversification:
- It derives income from the production of many licensees.
- It often has a number of offices, so it can benefit from growth in different parts of the area and change in demand for different types of properties.
- Office staff can take time off.
- The presence of many office personnel and managers and licensees generates creative thinking.
- The greater opportunity available for company expansion and for promotion of individuals within the firm is an inducement for licensees to remain with the firm.

For the broker, disadvantages to a large firm may include:
- responsibility for the entire organization meaning greater liability.
- no longer being able to list or sell.
- a need for more capital to operate the firm as costs escalate.
- greater management skills are needed to effectively organize and operate a larger organization.

For the licensee, disadvantages of a large firm may include:
- limited flexibility.
- a reduced amount of personal attention from management.

Whether large or small, a successful real estate company will strive to develop and maintain a good reputation, provide exceptional service, and infuse the licensees with a spirit of cooperation. If well run:

- its broker or manager should have a professional attitude, be sensitive to changing market and business conditions, and have enough experience to have a good understanding of the fundamentals of the business.
- its managers and employees will strive to be efficient and effective.
- it will have sufficient capital to operate and compete effectively and provide the service necessary to ensure customer satisfaction.

Licensees in such companies generally receive considerate treatment because of uniform policies and procedures and contractual arrangements, as well as by training and educational programs offered to enable them to develop to their fullest capacity. Licensees often take advantage of online training to hone their skills as well.

Training programs may be formal or informal. While a large company may be able to
 offer a weeklong structured classroom-training program to twenty new licensees at a time, this would be impossible in a small firm. The small firm may offer to send a licensee to an off-site training program or may offer one-on-one training with the broker providing direct assistance. Such one-on-one training often begins with the licensee observing the broker, the licensee then performing with the assistance of the broker, and finally the licensee performing with the broker just observing. This may be more effective than classroom training if the broker is willing to devote the time and energy necessary.

Regardless of the type of training, the manager often will have an open door policy by which he makes himself available to provide guidance and assistance in solving problems during regular office hours.

Most of the licensees are expected to be:

- full-time professionals who are trained, confident, informed and up to date in knowledge, procedures and technology.
- people oriented, fair, cooperative, reliable, loyal and attentive to details.

A company with such managers and licensees will enjoy a significant amount of repeat and referral business.

One of the best means of determining the characteristics of a company is to attend a sales meeting to see:

- how management relates to the licensees.
- how the licensees relate to each other.
- their attitudes toward the public and the industry.

Single-Family Homes

Most real estate agents engage almost exclusively in purchase and sale transactions involving single-family residences. The single-family housing market provides the greatest number of sales opportunities and requires the least amount of professional knowledge and experience. Even the most inexperienced agent will be able to list a residence of a friend or relative. With the help of a broker or willing sales associate in the office, he can show properties to prospective buyers and write up a purchase and sale agreement. However, the fact that an agent can negotiate simple transactions and probably earn some commissions does not mean that the job of selling residences is easy or will be rewarding. A real estate agent paid to handle transactions for others is expected to be a specialist, capable of saving a seller or buyer time and money because of his knowledge of the details of property transfers, market conditions and methods of marketing real estate. If he does not quickly become such a specialist, he will not remain in the business.

Residential real estate brokerage sales operations include the following activities:
- Secure an inventory of property to sell through referrals, leads and direct canvassing and then having sellers sign listing agreements
- Prospect for buyers through advertising, marketing and referrals
- Negotiate to bring together a meeting of minds between the buyer and seller
- Assist the parties in satisfying the terms and conditions of their agreement, including obtaining financing, having appraisals and inspections made, having necessary repairs performed, and closing (transferring ownership of the property, usually through a neutral third party called "escrow") in a timely manner

In order to remain an effective force in the real estate marketplace, the broker and his licensees must act professionally and ethically in dealing with other agents. Real estate brokerage activities and services are generally provided in both a competitive and a cooperative manner. Brokers will compete with each other for listings and buyers. Yet they also cooperate with each other in order to create a sale.

> **For Example**
>
> Broker A competes with Broker B to obtain a listing. If Broker A gets the listing, he will allow other brokers, including Broker B, to bring in offers from buyers to purchase the property he has listed. Broker B, as a selling broker, will eagerly show property listed by Broker A in order to obtain a portion of Broker A's commission if the seller accepts an offer he submits.

A selling agent, who is not also the listing agent, may act as an agent of the listing broker (as a subagent) or as an agent of the buyer (as a buyer's agent), or in some states, as a facilitator (an agent of no one). In most instances the commission earned by the listing broker would be shared with the selling broker regardless of whom that broker represented. Because cooperative efforts between brokers result in improved service to both buyers and sellers of real estate, cooperative sales constitute a significant share of the transactions in any area.

While selling is the chief purpose of real estate brokerage, a considerable amount of administrative work and paperwork is required, including completing forms, preparing market analyses, ordering special reports, assisting buyers in obtaining financing, maintaining records and engaging in general correspondence. In a small office, these duties will be performed by the broker or a licensee, perhaps with clerical assistance or with the aid of a personal assistant employed by one or more licensees. In a larger office, these functions may be performed by clerical staff, transactional coordinators employed by the broker, or personal assistants employed by the licensees. They may also be delegated to specialized departments.

To assure that the sale and transfer of ownership of the property will take place without unnecessary complications, the residential real estate agent must have detailed knowledge of:
- financing and financing institutions.
- real estate law.
- agency law.
- contract law.
- residential real estate valuation.

Additionally, he should know his community well so he can answer questions as varied as the location of shopping centers, schools, city services, and recreational opportunities, the approximate charge for utilities, and the location of nice restaurants.

For this reason many agents will select geographic areas, called "farm" areas, in which they will specialize and become the experts. They will obtain information regarding the properties in the area such as the names and addresses of the owners, the last tax assessment and tax amount, the last price paid, and the age and size of the structure. This information is received from title insurance companies, online public records, or the multiple listing service (MLS). By contacting owners in the area and becoming acquainted with them, the agent can expect that, when a need for a real estate agent arises, the owners will call upon him, the person they know who specializes in their area. Many agents specialize in various types of residential property instead of, or in addition to, specializing in certain geographic areas. Most agents sell existing homes, but some will specialize in:
- new homes. These agents must have knowledge of construction and quality of construction, and an ability to work with builders and buyers as they attempt to work out the final details of an uncompleted house or resolve problems with construction arising after construction is completed.
- second homes. These agents must have knowledge of tax laws, financing sources, and laws affecting rental and management of such property.
- land for residential construction. These agents must be knowledgeable about the subdivision process, subdivision and land use laws, financing strategies for land purchases, and environmental impact laws.
- condominium or cooperative units. These agents must have knowledge of community ownership laws, financing, and other issues unique to these types of housing.

In all cases, the professional residential real estate agent must have knowledge of the current real estate market in the community. Real estate markets change continuously,  due to changes of seasons, changes in interest rates and local tax rates, commercial and residential construction activity, road construction, or positive or negative school events. Changes in the market may result in higher or lower sales prices and longer or shorter periods required for property to sell or sales to close. These changes may be for all properties at any time or for only certain types of properties.

For instance, in an active market, there may be a steady rise in prices for less expensive properties, but no increase in prices for properties above a certain price and maybe even a decrease in prices for such homes. It may take 60 days for a lower priced home to sell, but 120 days for a more expensive home to sell. A sudden burst of activity in the market may cause delays in closings. The knowledgeable agent is aware of all of these market conditions and makes clients aware of what to expect.

The residential real estate agent also knows how to market the real estate. He knows how to find prospects for listed property, is able to relate to prospective buyers as individuals, and is able to determine and promote those features that make the property most desirable.

Other Functions of an Agent

An agent can be trained in fields besides residential real estate sales. Many agents enjoy managing other persons. They can supervise other licensees (once they are able to satisfy any state requirements to supervise real estate activities).

Some agents specialize in helping investors buy and sell income-producing property or land through the use of IRS Code Section 1031 tax-free exchanges. Other agents act as leasing agents, and still others act as property managers.

Commercial Property

Many real estate companies specialize in sales of commercial property including:
- raw land to be held for appreciation, subdivision or future development.
- residential income properties, such as apartment buildings, acquired for cash income and/or future capital gain.
- stores, motels, and other real estate used in business.
- office buildings, shopping centers, mobile home parks, and other commercial properties held for lease income.

In firms specializing in commercial property, real estate agents may specialize in certain aspects, such as development of shopping centers, sales of small office buildings, or acquisition and development of fast-food operations.

Industrial property includes warehouses, manufacturing plants, organized industrial parks, redeveloped industrial parcels in core urban areas, and industrial acreage held for business use or for lease income.

Industrial sales brokerage requires technical knowledge of:

- special industrial construction features.
- industrial transportation and utility requirements.
- land use restrictions affecting industrial properties.

Those who engage in commercial property brokerage need a sound knowledge of real estate practices. They also need skill and confidence in estimating the value of commercial property and performing financial analysis of such property. A seller's agent wants to ensure that the sales price represents a fair price to the seller. A buyer's agent wants to ensure that the price and terms are reasonable and consistent with the buyer's goals.

Because the dollars involved are much larger, brokerage commissions for each commercial real estate transaction are generally larger than for a residential property transaction. However, because the process of negotiating and then closing the transaction is longer, the commercial property agent would be expected to engage in fewer transactions each year than a residential agent.

Some firms specialize in commercial property management services. Other firms provide sales services as well as property management services, offering complete service to those they have dealt with in the sales transaction.

Farm and Land Brokerage

A number of firms specialize in farm and land brokerage. Specialists in rural properties provide skilled services in appraising and negotiating the purchase and sale of operating  farms, ranches, orchards, recreational property, unimproved acreage, and timberlands. The most effective agent will probably have knowledge of the local situation, where no two properties are the same, and will have education or experience in agriculture or animal husbandry. While both buyers and sellers of farms and ranches may be knowledgeable about agribusiness operations, they may be less qualified in valuation of the land. A knowledgeable real estate agent who is able to provide sound estimates of value will provide a valuable service in the market, while the agent who creates inflated land valuations based on highly speculative projections of future events is considered a hazard to the industry and to the public.

Farm and land brokerage may include transactions in both rural and urban land. Skilled agents will analyze the use of the land for its highest and best use and determine its feasibility for development and use for a particular purpose.

Subspecialties of farm and land brokerage range from ranch management to land investment, financing, and taxes. This specialist will be comfortable discussing the client's needs for cattle property or for the growth of various crops. A specialist in land management has knowledge of climate, soils, crops, irrigation, animals, and marketing. An investment land agent or counselor has knowledge of economic and political matters and trends, subdivision and development techniques, financial feasibility analysis, research and statistics.

Another specialized area of land brokerage is that of recreational properties, including raw land, unimproved lots, and interests in resort developments.

Recreational Land Brokerage

While many specialists in farms and land deal in subdividing large tracts of rural land and marketing parcels primarily for their recreational benefits, some brokers and licensees have concentrated their efforts exclusively in the recreational land marketing field. Sales techniques have in the past followed two patterns:

1. Mail order sales or direct representation sales of the property
2. Tours of the property, often with a promise of a free gift to the prospective buyer, followed by intensive, sophisticated on-site closing conferences, designed to convert prospects into buyers in a single sitting

Both techniques require that the seller allocate a large proportion of the selling price to sales promotion and selling commission expenses. Those expenses, sometimes reaching 50% of the price, are feasible only because of the large markup in the land price to the customer and the relatively little development expense.

Timber and Mineral Rights Brokerage

Standing timber is often marketed through experienced timber brokers, who may also be licensed real estate brokers. However, the timber is ordinarily acquired under options or contracts that do not include any rights or interests in the land. These convey rights to sever the timber from the land, with title passing to the buyer when the timber has been converted to personal property.

 Rights to subsurface oil, gas and minerals are often conveyed in the form of leasehold interests in the land. The lease periods are intended to provide time for exploration, followed by new agreements with the owner of the land in the event any mining is commenced. An agent of the prospective lessee who negotiates a lease for him, may be engaging in activity the state defines as real estate brokerage, and if so, would be required to be licensed.

Mobile Home Brokerage

A number of brokers provide mobile home brokerage services. In most states, licensed real estate brokers and their licensees are permitted to negotiate the purchase, sale, or exchange of a used mobile home in conjunction with the purchase, sale, exchange, rental or lease of the land upon which the used mobile home is located.

Sale of Timeshares

A timeshare is an interest in a development held by a person entitled to use of a unit in the development for a limited period of time each year. Most states regulate the sales of timeshares. They may require that a timeshare salesperson hold a real estate license or timeshare registration.

Business Opportunities Broker

A business opportunities broker is a person who acts for another in listing, offering for sale, or negotiating the purchase, sale, exchange, lease or rental of a business opportunity. A **business opportunity** is a business, an existing opportunity and/or the good will of an existing business.

Depending on state law, a person may need a real estate license to sell any business opportunity or to sell a business opportunity if it includes a transfer of title to real estate and/or a transfer of a lease of real estate. While the seller of a business is exempt from licensure, he is regulated by other laws, such as the Uniform Securities Act, which may make his offer to sell a part interest in his business an offering of a security subject to the Act.

Business opportunities brokerage requires many skills that may be developed in brokerage of commercial property. But an agent handling a business opportunity transaction must have knowledge of various accounting and business financial practices and be capable of estimating the value of a business from analysis of its assets and liabilities, its income and expenses, the quality of its management and operations, and outside influences.

Business opportunity brokerage involves the use of specialized forms, reports, and contractual documents and provisions, such as protective covenants to assure the buyer that the seller will not compete with the business he has sold. Business brokerage requires knowledge of public use restrictions relating to:

- zoning, building codes, etc.
- regulations relating to the transfer of a license, franchise, or distributorship.
- provisions of the Uniform Commercial Code (UCC) relating to assignments of accounts receivable, existing leases, and the stock of the business.

Affiliates

----- RELATED FIELDS -----

From time to time, real estate agents need to call upon other specialists who operate in related fields. The following specialists may be among those performing functions required to complete a transaction:

- Surveyors and engineers
- Appraisers
- Financial institutions furnishing funds for making transactions possible
- Title companies assisting in effecting transfers of property
- Escrow agents facilitating the actual closing of transactions
- Architects, contractors and builders
- Home and pest inspectors examining the property for structural and insect damage
- Cleaning companies and landscapers
- Computer technicians and web designers
- Professional real estate organizations
- Credit reporting agencies determining the credit of contracting parties
- Lawyers assisting in the legal phases
- Accountants preparing financial statements
- Government personnel providing assistance or information in the areas of:
    - taxation and assessment
    - acquisition
    - sale
    - leasing and management of government property
    - city/county planning and land use regulation

Financing
Real estate financing activity is performed by mortgage brokers and by mortgage loan representatives or loan officers representing various lending or government institutions. A loan officer will take loan applications, prequalify, precertify and qualify loan applicants, and supervise the administrative work involved in processing the loan. Loan representatives working for mortgage bankers or mortgage brokers will spend a considerable amount of time in marketing their services to real estate agents in an attempt to have business referred to them. Mortgage brokers will arrange for borrowers to be placed in contact with a lender who may offer terms of financing suitable to the borrower's needs and may provide loan consulting services for a fee. They can assist a borrower in selecting the source and type of loan and in applying for that loan.

Escrow and Title Insurance
Escrow and title insurance activities provide opportunities for those who like to pay attention to details and derive satisfaction from overcoming obstacles and seeing a job to

its completion: in this case, the closing of a transaction. Escrow and title agents work with real estate agents, as well as buyers and sellers, to gather information needed to complete closing documents (e.g., the deed) and financing documents (e.g., the note and mortgage), and to clear clouds that appear in the title search. Often, they work under the pressure of deadlines imposed by buyers eager to move in and sellers eager to move out, while coordinating the closing of multiple transactions which are all contingent upon each other. They must also coordinate with lenders to arrange for payment of current loans against the property as well as payment of new loan proceeds to the seller.

Appraisal

Appraisal is another field populated by those who appreciate detailed work. Appraisal is often chosen by those who enjoy the fieldwork involved in real estate. They are analytical and have good judgment; they do not necessarily have good sales skills. An appraisal involves a detailed analysis of market data, construction cost factors, and the income-producing potential of property to arrive at an informed estimate of property value. Appraisers may be salaried employees of lenders, government agencies, the county tax assessor, etc. Others are independent and are hired to perform appraisals for lenders, lawyers, courts, sellers or buyers.

As a result of federal laws, each state must license or certify appraisers who perform appraisals for loans made for just about any lending institution. Most states have expanded this requirement to apply to almost every real estate appraisal for any purpose. Different levels of licensing and certification, each with different levels of education, experience and examination requirements are necessary to perform appraisals of residential and/or commercial properties. The license or certification required is based on the value of the property.

Urban Planners

A number of government agencies and corporations hire urban planners to develop plans for future growth and land use developments. Urban planners develop plans and recommend changes relating to streets, highways, utilities, schools, parks, civic buildings, and environmental protection. These people usually hold degrees in planning.

Asset Managers

Governments and corporate entities hire asset managers and others to deal with real property they own or intend to acquire. About a third of the land in the country, including forest property, recreational property, office buildings, highways, and municipal buildings, is owned by the government. Government workers are needed to negotiate purchases and sales, appraise or review appraisals of such property, arrange for financing, manage and maintain the property, and plan for future uses, development, and disposition of the property.

Property Management and Leasing

Property management is an activity that may or may not require licensure, depending upon who is employing the property manager and the relationship between the employer and manager. **Property management** involves supervising a property's operation in order to produce the greatest net return for the owner. It may be performed as an employee of a management company, as an independent property manager or as an employee of the owner. The property manager advises the owner regarding the operation of the property, rental rates and tenant policies. He will establish the rental schedule, check credit reports, lease the property on a short-term or long-term basis, collect rents, arrange for maintenance, repairs and remodeling, and pay bills for the owner. Some people operate as leasing agents. Their only service is leasing the property for which there is a fee. They do not manage the property after it is leased.

Land Development and Construction

Land development is another related area. Those involved in **land development** locate land, negotiate its purchase, develop plans for its use, get approval for subdivision, and then either market the lots to builders or actually have the construction performed and then market the finished product to the final user. Those who divide the land into smaller parcels and sell it to others before construction are called subdividers. Those who actually build on the land are called developers.

The subdivider's expenses are typically limited to the cost of acquiring the land, having it surveyed and staked, and preparing a plan for submission to the local governing body for approval.

The developer's function is much more extensive and involves much greater expense. The developer prepares the lots for construction by filling and grading, if necessary, and by having streets graded and paved, and curbs, gutters and utilities installed before selling the lots. Developers need to possess knowledge of the market, population and growth trends, and have an acute sense of timing so as to acquire the land before the cost becomes exorbitant and sell the land without undue delay and at a profit.

Often real estate licensees who have acquired some degree of expertise in construction through experience or courses may actually engage in construction. This requires managerial skills and a solid knowledge of construction in order to ensure that the finished product is well made, at a reasonable cost, and in demand.

Construction may be speculative or custom. **Speculative construction** entails buying lots and building structures on them with the goal and hope of selling the property at a profit. **Custom construction** entails building a home on a lot owned by the person contracting for the home or on a lot owned by the builder and sold as part of a package custom home.

Licensees may purchase property in need of repair and/or renovation in order to increase the value of the property and realize a profit, in excess of acquisition and repair costs, from the sale.

Development and construction are both high-risk endeavors which, when performed properly, can reap high rewards.

Home Inspections

Those with knowledge of construction may also work in the business of home inspections. Homebuyers are generally advised to make their offers to purchase subject to a satisfactory inspection of the property by a qualified inspector. For existing homes there may be just one "whole house" inspection for each sale. However, if there are suspected environmental problems, there may be inspections or tests by persons trained to test for such hazards as asbestos and lead. If there are suspected problems with a roof, a foundation, or other aspect of the property, a specialist may be hired to inspect that particular item.

Education

Another field related to real estate is education. Successful agents continually take real estate related courses and additional training.

As a result, there are opportunities for agents to work as:
- teachers of real estate in colleges and real estate schools, teaching prelicense or continuing education courses.
- sales trainers employed by brokers to train new agents in sales techniques.
- independent motivational speakers or personal marketing advisors, teaching techniques for personal improvement.

----- LAWS AND REGULATORY AGENCIES -----

Because a real estate agent is affected by many laws created from a number of sources, he must be alert to events occurring in many areas.

Laws applicable to real estate come from the following principal sources:
- The U.S. Constitution
- Laws passed by Congress
- Federal regulations
- The Constitution of the state
- Laws passed by the state legislature
- Rules and regulations of state and local agencies
- Ordinances
- Court decisions

In the United States, two separate basic systems of law are in force: federal law and the state law.

Except in a few circumstances, federal law operates uniformly throughout the United States. State law varies between states since each state has its own Constitution and its own statutory and case law reflecting the economic, political, and social background and conditions of that particular state.

Federal Laws

The U.S. Constitution is the supreme law of the land. Many rules of law pertaining to real

property are based on provisions of the Constitution and its amendments. For example, in <u>Shelley vs. Kraemer</u>, the Supreme Court ruled that judicial enforcement by state courts of covenants restricting the use or occupancy of real property to persons of the Caucasian race violated the equal protection clause of the 14th Amendment.

The Bill of Rights contains a provision restricting the power of the government to deprive a landowner of his title to real property without just compensation. Thus, under the power of eminent domain, when the government acquires a parcel of land for public use, it must pay the owner the market value of the property.

In addition, Congress has enacted numerous legislative measures that have an effect upon real property. For example, when Congress enacted the Uniform Bankruptcy Act, it excluded state governments from establishing any laws which would conflict with that legislation. In the Civil Rights Acts of 1964 and 1968, the Fair Housing Amendment Act of 1988, and the Americans with Disabilities Act, Congress prohibited discrimination in real estate dealings against various groups of people.

In the federal Truth in Lending Law and the Real Estate Settlement Procedures Act, Congress has required uniform loan and closing disclosures to be adopted throughout the country.

Numerous federal administrative bodies have the power to impose rules and regulations necessary to carry out the provisions of the laws. For example, the regulations of both the Department of Housing and Urban Development (HUD) and the Department of Veterans' Affairs establish criteria for residential property loans insured or guaranteed by those agencies. HUD administers fair housing and interstate land sales disclosure laws, making rules to implement them and conducting investigations to enforce them.

The Federal Reserve Board has tremendous influence over the amount of mortgage money that may be made available at any particular time, as well as the interest rates charged by commercial banks.

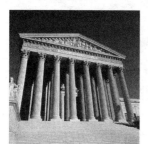

Even the federal court system has an impact on the real estate industry. The United States District Court, the Circuit Court of Appeals, and the U.S. Supreme Court all have made decisions affecting the rights to buy, sell, or use real property.

In several types of cases, the federal courts have exclusive jurisdiction, and these proceedings often affect title to real property. The federal courts have exclusive jurisdiction over all bankruptcy cases, all civil actions in which the United States is a party, such as a condemnation action brought by the United States government, and all cases involving disputes between persons of different states where the amount involved is over $10,000.

State and Local Laws

States and their various governmental agencies have a huge impact upon real property. Many measures in a state's constitution relate directly to real property, and state legislatures enact statutes controlling the ownership and use of real property.

Among the state agencies protecting consumers in real estate transactions are:
- those charged with ensuring that persons in the real estate business are licensed and regulated.
- those ensuring that persons are not unfairly discriminated against in residential real estate transactions.
- those regulating financial institutions, as well as mortgage brokers, mortgage companies, consumer lending companies, and escrow companies.
- those regulating and licensing contractors.
- those dealing with environmental issues.
- those enforcing any unfair business practices and/or consumer protection laws.

Local governments may regulate activities in their jurisdiction through orders of county commissioners or ordinances of city councils. Many of these, such as zoning, subdivision ordinances, health codes, building codes, and sign codes, have a direct effect on the use of real property.

Although the courts do not make the law, they do interpret the law. Therefore, it is often necessary to examine the decisions of the appellate courts to determine the meaning and effect of a law pertaining to real property. A considerable portion of the law relating to real property is civil law (as opposed to criminal law) and is contained in the decisions of the state appellate courts.

Because our legal system does not contain a civil code, most of the law relating to the rights of parties in a dispute has evolved through court decisions.

----- TRADE ASSOCIATIONS -----

Numerous professional trade associations help to promote ethics, education and professional practice in the real estate industry. Membership in these organizations is voluntary and is not required in order to engage in the business of real estate.

The major real estate trade organization is the **National Association of Realtors**®. Only a member of a National Association of Realtors® may call himself a Realtor®, or use the term Realtor® in his business name.

The local association of Realtors® belongs to a state association of Realtors®. The state association conducts many functions on behalf of its member local associations. It lobbies for the statewide industry, creates model forms and provides educational opportunities for its members. The state association belongs to the National Association of Realtors®. The national association lobbies at the national level for the industry and also creates model forms and policies and provides educational opportunities for members.

The National Association of Realtors® has a code of ethics through which it attempts to promote ethical behavior among its members. However, it does not have the power to take away licenses or determine that a person may or may not engage in the real estate business.

The National Association of Realtors® has also created a number of institutes, societies, and councils (e.g., the Institute of Real Estate Management and the Real Estate Brokerage Management Council) that keep members informed of developments in particular areas of special interest.

Real estate agents may also join other professional organizations that have no official connection with the National Association of REALTORS®, such as the Mortgage Bankers Association of America (MBA), the National Association of Home Builders (NAHB), and the National Multi-Housing Council.

What Makes a Good Agent?

Broker Expectations

Brokers have a number of expectations relating to what a new licensee is to contribute to their firm. At a minimum, they generally expect that a new licensee will:

- have a fundamental knowledge of real estate.
- be motivated to succeed.
- be able to set reasonable goals.
- be able to organize time effectively.
- be dependable, cooperative, loyal, and honest.
- be sensitive to laws affecting real estate transactions in order to avoid creating unnecessary risk for the broker.
- strive to become a good producer.

New Licensee Expectations

A new licensee is expected to learn many things concerning the actual practice of selling real estate quickly.

He must learn ethical and effective real estate sales techniques. Even those with sales experience in other lines will find that the selling of real estate differs from the selling of other products in a number of significant ways. The real estate transaction is more complex and individualized.

Every transaction is unique. There are no standardized units as there are for other products. The products (i.e., properties) differ in terms of their construction, condition, location, etc. Yet in each instance, the licensee must become knowledgeable about the specific product being marketed, including its value, its construction, its neighborhood and the general type of buyers who will be attracted.

The transactions themselves differ in terms of financing used, contingencies for financing or the sale of other property, compliance with zoning, environmental and building regulations, etc.

There is no limit to the number or type of products that can be sold by the licensee. Usually every property available for sale can be sold by the licensee. This includes properties being sold For Sale By Owner (FSBO), through the MLS, or through direct contact with an owner of property that the licensee's client would like to acquire. Unlike a person who sells from a certain limited product line, a real estate licensee is expected to be aware of all products available and, if working with a buyer, assist that buyer in narrowing down the choices until the best one becomes apparent. The licensee must have knowledge of the city, the parts of the city and neighborhoods in which he will operate, plus awareness of and/or access to current facts and projections for amenities and services, new developments and trends in the local real estate market.

Because real estate is such a large investment for the parties involved, the parties are concerned, nervous, in need of reassurance and, as a result, quick to apply pressure on the  licensee. The real estate agent must act in the best interests of the party being represented and be able to convey to that party that those interests are being protected. There is a big difference between selling a product priced by the owner of a store and selling a house on which the licensee has provided the market analysis to arrive at a recommended price or suggested that a price lower than the list price be accepted by your seller.

The sales process for real estate takes longer and is more tedious than for other types of sales. It requires a great deal of patience on the part of the broker, his licensees and their families, the property owner and the prospective purchaser.

The psychology of predicted behavior of the parties involved in a residential sale is more complex than in the sale of less personalized consumer goods. The seller may have a considerable number of emotional ties to the home he has improved, remodeled, renovated, and/or decorated. The buyer, on the other hand, sees the property merely as the seller's house, which will probably be altered in some respect to reflect his taste and eliminate the personal touches of the previous occupants. The greatest emotional involvement may come after he makes the offer and begins to suffer "buyer's remorse." **Buyer's remorse** is when a buyer questions the advisability of having committed to the largest investment of his life and doubts the wisdom of not waiting to see if better homes would come on the market in the following weeks. Every new ad seems to offer more value for the price requested, and he worries about whether he has paid too much. He questions the efforts of the agent to find the right property and to negotiate the best price and terms.

The transfer of real estate involves legal requirements that do not exist with other sales. These requirements vary with each transaction and, if not quickly recognized and satisfied, can have serious consequences.

Definite legal and ethical restrictions are imposed on the conduct of business to ensure that a licensee will act in the best interests of those he represents while treating other parties openly and honestly.

To succeed in the real estate business, a licensee should possess certain traits and skills that will enable him to adapt to the demands of the business. While no person can possess every quality advantageous to the job, a person entering the field should possess a sufficient number of these traits and skills and find enough strength in the ones they possess to overcome those that are lacking.

Function Independently

Real estate is not a salaried job where the agent is paid a salary for showing up on the job. Because the agent is paid a commission for producing results, he must be able to function independently and adapt to the pressure and stress that accompanies the uncertainty of receiving a paycheck. This means he must be a self-starter, organized, goal oriented, and capable of working both hard and smart.

Many people enter the field of real estate because they do not want to be confined to a nine-to-five job and the salary that goes with it. Real estate offers the potential to earn substantially more than in a salaried position, but as with all other ventures in life, the greater the reward potential, the greater the risk. If real estate were easy, compensation would be lower; everyone would earn close to equal amounts; there would be no good months and bad months and no good years and bad years. To reach for a six-figure income, a real estate agent must accept the prospect of a no-figure income.

Initially, a new licensee will need to call upon financial reserves of four to six months' income in savings or family members producing income upon which to live in order to relieve the pressure of unpaid bills or accumulating debt. Even if a new licensee were to make a sale the very first day in the business, it would generally take at least two months for that sale to close.

Because there will be months when earnings are exceptional and other months when there are no earnings, a licensee must be able to budget time and resources. He cannot spend money as if every month will be exceptional. He cannot slow down because  income has been good, become euphoric during good months or become depressed during the bad. He must achieve a balanced attitude and lifestyle that enables him to adjust to easily accommodate swings in income.

A real estate licensee also must balance out the amount of time devoted to the business and to personal life. Real estate business does not stop at 5:00 p.m., on weekends or holidays. Because clients and customers generally ask for the greatest amount of a licensee's time when they are not working, clients want to see houses on weekends or in the evenings. Offers are generally written and presented when all buyers or all sellers are available: after work or on weekends or holidays. The customer's and the client's free time is the licensee's work time. They expect the licensee to work at their convenience and not at his convenience.

A successful real estate licensee enjoys working at any time necessary to effect a transaction, whether it is an evening or weekend, but also recognizes the need to attend to a personal life. He must set out a block of time reserved for family and friends and convey to those with whom he is working that he is not available at those times. For example, many licensees will work one but not both days of a weekend and will take off one day during the week. This allows for quality personal time and time for working with clients or customers on a weekend. The licensee would expect to be treated as if he deserved compensation each time he was called upon for the use of his time. The licensee who makes all time available generally will be treated as if that time is worth nothing.

The proper attitude that develops as a licensee becomes more confident projects to the public. As he develops his skills, he becomes less likely to work with prospective buyers who are not committed to buy now or with sellers who are not motivated to sell at market price now. When he exhibits confidence and competence and shows he expects commitment and respect, buyers and sellers will become more considerate of the demands they place on his time.

The openness of the workday also requires that he be a self-starter, that is, self-motivated and disciplined. A licensee with these traits can start each day ready to seek new business, finish old business, and act with minimal supervision and without the need for constant encouragement. He is able to establish priorities and plan the work necessary to achieve his goals.

With all of this, the licensee also must be able to work hard and smart. Hard work without smart work is fruitless, and smart work must be accompanied by effort in order to be rewarding. Smart work entails organizing time effectively, so as to make one trip to a location instead of two or three, and spending time doing that which will have the highest potential for success at the times when the effort is most likely to be successful.

Hard work entails working long hours when necessary, taking the time to become better educated, and attending to all the details. Often a licensee who possesses very few of the traits one would expect of a successful real estate agent is able to achieve success through hard work. Real estate is often portrayed as being a numbers game. A licensee who makes so many contacts will obtain so many appointments; and for so many appointments, he will get so many listings or so many buyers with whom to work. A hard worker makes the calls and follows up. A hard worker, who is also a smart worker, can get more appointments with fewer contacts and effect more transactions from fewer appointments. As a smart worker, he will analyze the best times to make contact, analyze sales techniques to recognize the most productive, and utilize all available tools that might enable him to perform his tasks easier, faster, and more accurately.

Relate Well to People

A real estate agent is paid to solve problems, many of which are created by the people for whom he is working. If not for the problems that can arise in a transaction, there would be no need for real estate agents. The constant exposure to people with problems can cause a licensee continuous stress. Unless he likes and relates well to people, the stress of dealing with their problems will wear on him. He must enjoy solving problems, so the parties to the transaction can achieve their goals.

He will have to work with many different types of people, including those who are pleasant and those who are abrasive, those who are emotional and those who are analytical. This requires some degree of empathy and a great deal of tolerance.

Empathy is the ability to identify with another person so as to be able to look at a situation from that person's point of view. Empathy is necessary to understand what might be causing a person to act in a certain manner. It enables the licensee to react differently to people buying their first home than to people buying their fifth home. It enables him to relate to the stress of a seller who must have the home sold and the sale closed within one month as compared to the attitude of a seller trying to get as much as possible for a property without any constraint on when or if the sale must take place.

Tolerance is necessary to avoid trying to force people to behave in the way the licensee may think is best for them (e.g., to have them make an offer on a house they are not convinced they want or to have them make an offer they are not ready to make at that time). He may become frustrated, having spent days finding the type of property the buyers stated they wanted and he knows they want, only to have them avoid making the decision to make an offer. It can be frustrating knowing that the offer he has submitted is the best offer the seller will receive only to have the seller reject the offer. An ability to understand why people act as they do, to be able to tolerate their faults and attempt to resolve the difficulties created by their faults, is a valuable trait for success in real estate.

Listening Skills

To understand what motivates people to act in a certain way, a licensee must be a good listener. The most successful agents are not smooth talkers; they are smooth listeners. They can listen and actually hear what the buyer or seller is trying to say. Each buyer is different and has different wants and needs. A licensee must be able to listen to each client objectively and probe to determine whether he heard what is being said and whether what is being said is what was meant, in order to truly understand what that buyer is trying to say.

Five Most Important Traits in Sales

Many of these characteristics may be summed up in a few traits. Studies of successful agents indicate that these are the five traits that are most important in sales:

1. **Dependability and accuracy in attending to details**. He anticipates problems and spends the time and exerts the efforts necessary to prevent problems from arising.
2. **Diplomacy and tact in dealing with others**. Tactful negotiations with buyers or sellers make people feel comfortable with the transaction. Instead of bullying persons into making a decision or making them feel inadequate, he will lead, suggest and skillfully guide the parties to make choices that are best for them and in the end have parties who are pleased with those choices.
3. **Enthusiasm** to believe in what he is doing and to cause others to also believe in what he is doing. He has a positive attitude, is enthusiastic about his ability to get the job done, the company he works for, real estate in general, and the choices the parties are making. This enthusiasm spreads so that buyers and sellers share in the positive feelings about working with him and about the transaction.
4. **Self-reliance and self-confidence**. No mentor or class will inspire him to achievement for more than a brief moment. He must have inspiration from within which enables him to rebound and to think creatively to overcome obstacles. These traits provide him

with a willingness to change and try new ideas and new programs, to set goals and strive to achieve them, and to organize time and effort to maximize results.

5. **Assertiveness**. This is not aggression or domineering or abrasive behavior. It is resistance to intimidation. It is the ability to knock on doors, call on strangers, call on friends, be told "no" and not take it personally. It is the courage to keep trying to find new solutions to problems.

Brain Teaser

Reinforce your understanding of the material by correctly completing the following sentences:

1. _____ is an activity involving the sale or lease of a commodity through an intermediary who usually acts as an agent for one of the parties.

2. A selling broker, who is not also the _____ broker, may act as a buyer's agent.

3. In recreational land marketing, sales promotion and selling commission expenses sometimes reach _____ % of the price.

4. The _____ _____ _____ influences the amount of mortgage money available at any particular time.

5. _____ is the ability to identify with another person so as to be able to look at a situation from that person's point of view.

Brain Teaser Answers

1. **Brokerage** is an activity involving the sale or lease of a commodity through an intermediary who usually acts as an agent for one of the parties.

2. A selling broker, who is not also the **listing** broker, may act as a buyer's agent.

3. In recreational land marketing, sales promotion and selling commission expenses sometimes reach **50** % of the price.

4. The **Federal Reserve Board** influences the amount of mortgage money available at any particular time.

5. **Empathy** is the ability to identify with another person so as to be able to look at a situation from that person's point of view.

Review — Real Estate Careers

In this lesson we discuss what it means to be in the real estate industry.

Types of Real Estate Services

In the real estate industry, various types of real estate companies provide a wide range of services to include:

- property management services.
- brokerage services.
- consulting services.
- builder-brokerage.

However, most real estate companies operate as brokers. Brokerage is an activity involving the sale or lease of a commodity through an intermediary who usually acts as an agent for one of the parties. This intermediary receives compensation for the service, the dollar value of which usually varies with the size and complexity of the transaction.

Advantages of a small office for licensees generally include working closely with the broker and being trained on a one-on-one basis, and receiving a greater portion of the commission for a transaction, due to the low overhead of the brokerage. Advantages of a large company include structured training, supervision and procedures, and greater opportunity for promotion within the firm.

Real estate brokerage activities and services are generally provided in both a competitive and a cooperative manner. Brokers will compete with each other for listings and buyers. Yet, they also cooperate with each other in order to create a sale.

A residential salesperson must have detailed knowledge of:
- ✓ financing and financing institutions.
- ✓ real estate law.
- ✓ agency law.
- ✓ contract law.
- ✓ residential real estate valuation.

Additionally, he should know his community well.

Laws Governing Real Estate

In the United States, two separate basic systems of law are in force: (1) federal law, and (2) each particular state's law.

Laws applicable to real estate in any state come from the U.S. Constitution, laws passed by Congress, regulations from federal and state administrative bodies, court decisions, the state Constitution, and local ordinances.

The U.S. Constitution is the supreme law of the land. Many rules of law pertaining to real property are based on provisions of the Constitution and its Amendments. For example, the Bill of Rights contains a provision that restricts the power of the government to deprive a landowner of his title to real property without just compensation. Then there is the enactment of a Uniform Bankruptcy Act, in which the federal government has excluded state governments from establishing any laws in conflict with such bankruptcy legislation.

Federal laws prohibit discrimination against various groups of people in the purchase, sale, and closing of real estate. These are the:
- Civil Rights Acts of 1964 and 1968.
- Fair Housing Amendments Act of 1988.
- Americans with Disabilities Act.

Federal laws also require uniform loan and closing disclosures to be adopted throughout the country. These are the Federal Truth in Lending Law and the Real Estate Settlement Procedures Act.

Federal administrative bodies prescribe rules and regulations necessary to carry out the provisions of laws. For example, the regulations of the Department of Housing and Urban Development (HUD) and the Department of Veterans Affairs have a considerable impact upon a residential property loan insured or guaranteed by those agencies. HUD also administers the Fair Housing and Interstate Land Sales Disclosure Acts, makes rules to implement them, and provides investigations to enforce them.

The Federal Reserve Board has tremendous influence over the amount of mortgage money that can be made available at any particular time, as well as the interest rates that commercial banks charge.

Even the Federal court system has an impact upon the real estate industry. The United States District Court, the Circuit Court of Appeals, and the U.S. Supreme Court have all made decisions that may affect the rights of people to buy, sell, or use real property.

State Laws

Each state and its agencies have a tremendous impact upon real property. Many measures of the state Constitution relate directly to real property, and through the years, the state legislatures have created many legislative acts that control the ownership and use of real property. These laws are added to and become part of the laws of each state.

As a result of federal laws, each state must license or certify appraisers who perform appraisals on loans made for just about any lending institution. Most states have expanded this requirement to apply to almost every real estate appraisal for any purpose.

Associations

Professional trade associations also promote ethics, education, and professional practices in the industry. The major real estate trade organization is the National Association of Realtors®. The local association of Realtors® belongs to a state Realtor® organization. Only those licensees who are members of the National Association of Realtors® can call themselves Realtors®. The National Association of Realtors® has a code of ethics governing the behavior of its members, but does not have the power to take away licenses or determine that a person may or may not engage in the real estate business.

Real estate agents may also join other professional organizations, such as the Mortgage Bankers of America (MBA), the National Association of Home Builders (NAHB), and the National Multi-Housing Council.

What It Takes to be a Real Estate Agent

Traits most important in sales include dependability and accuracy in attending to details, diplomacy and tact in dealing with others, enthusiasm, self-reliance and self-confidence, and assertiveness. In dealing with others, the agent should have empathy, which is the ability to identify with another person so as to be able to look at a situation from that person's point of view.

Tenancies

Overview

In this lesson we explore a number of options available to hold an estate, called tenancies. Differences among individual ownership and concurrent forms of ownership, such as joint tenancy and tenancy in common, are clarified. The lesson ends with explanations of various types of real estate syndicate ownership.

Objectives

Upon completion of this lesson, the student should be able to:

1. Define ownership in severalty.
2. Differentiate among forms of co-ownership including joint tenancy, tenancy in common, tenancy by the entirety, and community property.
3. Define ways in which business organizations can hold ownership of real property, including syndicates, partnerships, corporations and joint ventures.
4. Explain how property can be held in trust.

Types of Tenancies

Now that we know what can be owned and how rights can be split up, we are ready to look at tenancies, the options of holding estates.

----- SEVERALTY -----

When a person purchases a parcel of land, he could buy it himself or he could buy it with someone else. When someone owns property to the exclusion of all other persons, that person is said to hold the property in severalty and may be said to have a **tenancy in severalty** (or **estate in severalty**). Severalty ownership of real estate means sole ownership by one person. That person can be a natural person (a human being) or a legal person or entity (e.g., corporation).

Property owned by the government would be held by a government corporation and therefore would be held in severalty. Property owned by a private corporation with many stockholders would also be held in severalty, since the corporation itself is one person.

Do not confuse the word "severalty" with the word "several." Severalty derives from the word "sever." In an estate in severalty, the owner's interest is severed from that of anyone else. Therefore, an estate in severalty is held by one person and exists when only one person owns a parcel of real estate.

A person who holds an estate in severalty may deed it to others or hold it until his death. Upon his death, the estate would be probated. It would pass to his:
- devisees if he died testate, leaving a will.
- heirs through descent and succession if he died intestate (without a will).

----- CONCURRENT OWNERSHIP -----

When two or more persons own the same property at the same time as co-owners they have **concurrent ownership**.

Depending on state law, persons having concurrent ownership may hold title as:
- tenants in common.
- joint tenants with the right of survivorship.
- community property.
- tenants by the entirety.
- tenants in partnership.

> **NOTE:** Not all states recognize community property, tenancy by the entirety, or joint tenancy.

In concurrent ownerships the co-owners have an:
- undivided interest in the property.
- equal right of possession.

Undivided interest means each co-owner (tenant) has a right to possession of the entire property, as each is a part owner of the entire property. Each owner has an interest in the land, but no specific interest in any one part of the land. None of the owners would be able to determine which portion of the land is theirs, since it is all theirs.

> **For Example**
>
> Guy and Barb Dwyer own a house together. They together own the whole house. They do not each own a separate part of it. If they did, they would each have separate interests, which would be estates in severalty.

The second item common to all concurrent ownership estates is an equal right of possession or **unity of possession**. This means that each co-owner has an equal right to occupy all or any part of the property. None of the co-owners can be excluded from occupancy. If one does occupy the property, he need not pay rent, unless there is an agreement otherwise. All co-owners must contribute to the cost of repairs, maintenance, taxes and other costs associated with the property. If the property is rented to someone else, all owners share in the rents and profits. If a co-owner had to pay more than his share of expenses, he could get a lien against the interests of the others, and foreclose on that lien if he was not reimbursed.

> **For Example**
>
> Fran and Ann Tick own a ranch as tenants in common. Each has an undivided half interest. Ann is in sole possession of the land and is operating the ranch. She would be liable to Fran for a share of any rents received from third parties for the use of a portion of the land, for any property expenses, for payments Fran makes on the mortgage executed by both, as well as for payments of any other liens against the land. She would not be liable for payment of rent to Fran for her own use of the land.

Tenancy in Common

One form of concurrent ownership is a tenancy in common. A **tenancy in common** exists whenever two or more natural or legal persons hold an undivided interest in an estate that is passable to their heirs or devisees. The persons holding the tenancy could be unrelated, related, husband and wife, and even corporations, because this tenancy has no right of survivorship. A **right of survivorship**, which exists in a joint tenancy or tenancy by the entirety, means that when one co-owner dies, the remaining (surviving) owners acquire that person's interest.

If four unrelated persons wish to purchase a parcel of land together and each wanted to be able to will his interest or pass his interest to his heirs, they would need to take title as tenants in common.

If a brother and sister held title to property and the sister had a will drafted, providing that upon her death her interest in the property was to pass to her son, the brother and sister would be holding title as tenants in common.

When a tenant in common dies, his interest passes to his devisees if he leaves a will, or to his heirs if he does not. Then his heirs or devisees would become tenants in common with the original surviving co-tenants.

Heather and Yon purchased property as tenants in common. When Heather died, her heirs or devisees received her interest and became tenants in common with Yon.

In a tenancy in common, the co-owners will share the right of possession, but their interests can be:

- acquired at different times.
- acquired in different ways (e.g., some by deed, some by will).
- equal or unequal amounts. While they will have undivided interests, they do not have to have equal interests.

A tenant in common is free to sell, transfer, convey or encumber his interest without the consent of any other co-owners. A tenant in common who wants to sell, but is unable to, may file a suit to partition the property. A **partition suit** would force a division of the property or a sale of the property with the proceeds being divided among the co-owners.

Joint Tenancy

When a **joint tenancy** exists, two or more natural persons are joint and equal owners of an undivided interest in property and have a right of survivorship. When one co-owner dies, his interest would be divided equally among the surviving co-tenants.

Four brothers owned property as joint tenants. When one died, the surviving three each had a one-third interest in the property. When another died, the two survivors each had a half interest. When one of the two died, the surviving brother owned the property in severalty.

The heirs of a joint tenant have no interest in the property, as the joint tenant cannot will his interest. This is both a disadvantage and an advantage:

- Disadvantage: A joint tenant cannot change his mind and leave his interest to his heirs.
- Advantage: The property will pass to the surviving co-tenants without the cost or delay of probate proceedings. The surviving co-tenants need only record a properly prepared death certificate to show they have acquired the interest.

In order to create a joint tenancy four unities must exist. All tenants must:

- have an equal right of possession.
- have an equal interest (e.g., if there are two co-owners, each must have a 50% interest; if there are four, each must have a 25% interest).
- acquire title at the same time.
- acquire title in the same deed or will.

4 Unities of a Joint Tenancy	
1.	Possession
2.	Interest
3.	Time
4.	Title

Despite the fact that a joint tenant cannot will his property, he can unilaterally sell, encumber, lease, or give away his interest during his lifetime. If he sold his interest, the purchaser would be a tenant in common with the other joint tenants.

> **For Example**
>
> X, Y and Z are joint tenants. X sells his interest to M. In this case, M would be a tenant in common, since he does not have a unity of time with Y and Z. However, Y and Z would remain joint tenants. If Y died, his interest would pass to Z as the surviving co-tenant. At that point M and Z would become tenants in common.

When a joint tenant incurs debts using the property as security for a loan, the creditor could force the sale of the tenant's interest during the life of the tenant if the debt were not paid. However, if the tenant died before he paid off the loan or sold his interest, the surviving joint tenants would receive his interest free and clear of the encumbrance.

Community Property

Community property ownership is a form of ownership recognized in only eight states: Washington, Idaho, California, Arizona, New Mexico, Texas, Nevada and Louisiana. Any real property acquired in these states would be subject to their community property law, regardless of where owners actually lived.

In these states, all property acquired during marriage by the industry and labor of either or both spouses belongs to both as community property. Neither spouse may sell, convey or encumber the community real property alone; any contracts for such purposes would require the signatures of both spouses to be valid.

Property not acquired during marriage by the industry and labor of either or both is separate property. **Separate property** is owned and may be conveyed individually by the husband or wife without the spouse's signature on the deed. It includes:

- property owned before marriage.
- rents and profits from separate property.
- property acquired with the proceeds of separate property.
- property acquired during marriage by devise, inheritance, or gift.

Tenancy by the Entirety

Most states do not have community property law. Some states have laws that provide for **tenancy by the entirety**. A tenancy by the entirety is a common law tenancy that can generally only be created by husband and wife.

The main advantage of a tenancy by the entirety is its right of survivorship. With this right, when one spouse dies, the other owns the whole property, without probate, free and clear of that spouse's debts (but not free of debts incurred jointly by both spouses). Because of this feature, when a husband and wife take title to property, unless otherwise specified, they automatically take title as tenants by the entirety.

While both spouses are alive, neither can destroy the right of survivorship by giving the property to someone else. However, a tenancy by the entirety may be terminated in a number of ways, including:
- sale or gift by one spouse to the other.
- divorce (upon which they become tenants in common).
- death of either spouse (upon which the survivor becomes a tenant in severalty).
- sale by both parties (joint conveyance).

Dower and Curtesy

In some states, there exist some forms of legal life estates created for the benefit of spouses under the common law concepts of dower and curtesy. The concepts of dower and curtesy were developed in order to provide a spouse who did not share ownership of the property with a means of support after the death of the spouse who owned the property.

Both dower and curtesy provide that the surviving spouse is entitled to a one-third life estate in the property owned during the marriage by the deceased spouse:
- **Dower** is the right of the wife to a life estate in the deceased husband's property.
- **Curtesy** is the right of the husband to a life estate in the deceased wife's property, provided the couple had at least one child.

These rights would exist and override the provisions of the deceased spouse's will, if the will conflicted with those rights.

Where the right exists, during their lifetimes the spouse with the right is said to have an **inchoate** (in <u>k</u>oit) right, i.e., an expected right, to the estate upon the spouse's death. As a result, both spouses generally must sign documents relating to the conveyance of real property, in order to ensure there is no future claim to the dower or curtesy rights.

Neither dower nor curtesy are recognized in community property states, nor in the majority of the remaining states which have adopted the Uniform Probate Code. Under the **Uniform Probate Code**, a surviving spouse is entitled to a certain share of the deceased spouse's estate, and that share is not merely a life estate interest.

Other Types of Ownership

----- SYNDICATION -----

Real property may also be owned through participation in a syndicate. A **syndicate** is a group of investors who join together to make and operate a real estate investment. Participation in a syndicate enables individuals to pool their abilities, experience, and resources, so they can engage in a larger investment than any one of them could separately. Through a syndicate, an individual can become an investor with only limited cash or perhaps under an arrangement where he contributes a small amount periodically.

Syndicates can be created through various forms of organization, including a general or limited partnership, corporation, trust, tenancy in common, joint tenancy, joint venture, or limited liability company (LLC).

Partnership

A **partnership** is an association of two or more persons to operate as co-owners of a business for profit. It may be a general partnership or a limited partnership.

In a **general partnership**, all partners are co-equals in ownership and management and have full authority to act on behalf of the partnership and other partners. Specific partnership property may be disposed of by all partners acting together, or by one partner acting as an agent of the partnership, if the sale is in the ordinary course of business. Each partner is entitled to a share of the profits and is jointly and severally liable for debts of the partnership. All partners may be sued jointly (together) or severally (individually) for the debts of the partnership. Therefore, the personal assets of each general partner can be claimed to pay partnership debts. If a partner dies, withdraws or declares bankruptcy, the partnership is dissolved. It may then be reorganized or closed down.

In a **limited partnership**, there is at least one general partner who manages the partnership and has personal liability for all partnership debts. In addition, there are limited partners. These limited partners have liability for partnership debts limited to no more than the amount they have agreed to contribute to the partnership. However, they cannot participate in the management of the partnership. In the event of the death or withdrawal of a general partner, the limited partnership may be dissolved or continued, based on the terms of the limited partnership agreement. Death of a limited partner has no effect on the limited partnership.

The advantage of general or limited partnerships to investors is that the partnerships are not taxable entities. All profits and losses are passed on to the partners for their own tax reporting.

The disadvantages are:
- partnership interests are not easy to sell.
- a general partner has full and unlimited liability for partnership debts (whether the partnership is general or limited).
- limited partners have no control over the management of the partnership.

Partners in either type of partnership may hold property belonging to the partnership as tenants in partnership. They may hold title in the name of the partnership or in their own names as partners. Each partner has an undivided interest in the partnership property and has the right to use the property for partnership purposes. A partner may transfer his interest in a partnership but cannot transfer partnership property without the consent of the other partners.

Corporation

A **corporation** is a legal entity. Regardless of the number of stockholders, a corporation is one entity and will hold title in severalty if it is the sole owner. In addition, a corporation may hold title to real estate with other corporations or individuals as a tenant in common or as a tenant in partnership. However, because of its perpetual existence, it cannot be a joint tenant.

There are a number of advantages to this form of ownership:
- The corporation exists in perpetuity, forever. Death of officers, directors, and stockholders does not affect the corporation's ownership of the property.
- The corporation has ways of raising money not available to individuals. In addition to obtaining loans from a lender, it can issue promissory notes and bonds, and issue and sell stock.
- The stockholders have limited liability. They can only lose what they have invested, no more.
- Stockholders' shares of stock are usually more liquid than interests in other types of business organizations.

But there are also disadvantages:
- Generally, corporations are expensive to establish.
- Unless a person is a major stockholder, he has little control over management. He can vote for a board of directors, but the board selects officers who actually manage the corporation's day-to-day operations.
- The shareholder does not receive tax deductions to which he would be entitled under other forms of ownership.
- There is double taxation. As a legal entity the corporation is taxed on its profits. Then any income it pays as dividends to stockholders is taxed (at a rate of up to 15%).

Corporate property may be sold by someone in the corporation who has authority to represent the corporation, granted by a resolution of the board of directors. This person may have a corporate seal, which implies his authority to act for the corporation, but the seal is not required on any documents.

One way to avoid double taxation is through an **S corporation**. This is a corporation that does not pay corporate income tax. Instead, each stockholder declares his share of the profits as personal income and can deduct his share of the losses. To qualify for this tax treatment, the corporation can have no more than 75 shareholders, and each shareholder must elect S corporation tax treatment. The advantages of this form of ownership are the limited liability of the shareholders and the elimination of the double taxation. The disadvantage is that the shareholders have to pay income tax on earnings, even if the corporation was not able to distribute the money to them.

Limited Liability Company

A **limited liability company (LLC)** is a business entity that combines the best features of a corporation and a partnership. The members of the LLC have the limited liability of limited partners or corporate shareholders but are taxed as if they were partners. In effect, an LLC acts as a limited partnership in which every member is a limited partner, but each has the ability to participate in management.

Although it is possible to have a one-person LLC, the LLC is generally created by an LLC agreement drawn up by two or more persons (called members). This agreement may provide for any or all of the members to be appointed to manage the company and may delegate any or all to bind the company to contracts. Unlike the general managers of partnerships, LLC managers have no personal liability for the company's obligations.

Joint Venture

A **joint venture** is an entity created to carry out one particular transaction, rather than a series of transactions or a continuing business. It may be in the form of a general or

limited partnership, a corporation, a REIT, a tenancy in common, or a joint venture agreement (which is very similar to a general partnership). Joint ventures are frequently used in construction projects where persons with expertise join with persons with the financing who want to participate in the management of the venture. Unlike a general partnership, a joint venture is terminated upon completion of the project and does not continue afterwards.

----- TRUSTS -----

Individuals or groups of individuals may hold title to real property in trust. Trusts may be created to hold title to property for unincorporated groups, such as churches, fraternal or investment organizations, or for individuals. They are often used to hold title to property left by a deceased trustor, until the heirs are old enough to assume responsibility for the property themselves.

A **trust** is created when a trustor conveys title to property to one or more trustees. If created during the trustor's lifetime through a trust agreement, the trust is called a living trust. If created upon the trustor's death through a will, it is called a testamentary trust.

The trustee may be a natural person or business firm. If there is one trustee, he would hold title in severalty. If there is more than one, they could hold title as joint tenants. The trustee manages the trust assets as authorized and limited by the terms of the trust document, as a fiduciary on behalf of a beneficiary.

The trust may be established for a definite term or for the lifetime of the beneficiary. If it is created for a definite term, the trustee may be required to deed the property to the beneficiary or to sell the property and provide the beneficiary with the sale proceeds at the time the trust terminates.

The beneficiary is entitled to all of the profits from the trust. He has a personal property interest in the trust, which can be:

- transferred to another by assignment.
- pledged as security for a loan.
- passed to his heirs or to his legatees (persons named in a will to receive personal property) upon his death, based on the laws of the state in which he resides, rather than the laws of the state in which the property is located.

In many states, a form of trust called a **land trust** may be created. With a land trust, legal title to the land is transferred to a trustee. The trustee would be the person signing the listing, sales agreement or deed on behalf of the trust. The only asset in the land trust is real estate. By utilizing a land trust, an owner's interest is converted from an interest in real property into an interest in personal property.

There are a number of advantages to holding property in this manner:

- Nonresidents can avoid ancillary probate of their estates.
- Partitioning may be prevented.
- There is confidentiality of ownership (the true identity of the owners on public records is avoided). Usually, the person creating the trust (the trustor) will also be the beneficiary, but the beneficiary is not named in the public records. Therefore, the land trust would often be used by a person who is attempting to acquire separate parcels and assemble them, without disclosing his identity.

- The owner of a beneficial interest may divide the property into smaller units and dispose of them over time.

Another type of trust is the **real estate investment trust (REIT)**. A REIT is formed to invest in real estate as a long-term investment, providing income from rentals as well as long-term capital gains when the property is sold. REITs provide investors with the benefits of corporate ownership without the double taxation, if certain conditions are met, including the following:

- At least 100 people must invest.
- Any five investors cannot own more than 50% of the shares in the trust.
- At least 75% of the trust's assets must be in real estate.
- At least 90% of the earnings must be distributed to shareholders each year.

Brain Teaser

Reinforce your understanding of the material by correctly completing the following sentences:

1. _____ ownership of real estate means sole ownership by one person.
2. When a _____ tenancy exists, two or more natural persons are joint and equal owners of an undivided interest in property and have a right of survivorship.
3. A _____ is a group of investors who join together to make and operate a real estate investment.

Brain Teaser Answers

1. **Severalty** ownership of real estate means sole ownership by one person.

2. When a **joint** tenancy exists, two or more natural persons are joint and equal owners of an undivided interest in property and have a right of survivorship.

3. A **syndicate** is a group of investors who join together to make and operate a real estate investment.

Review — Tenancies

In this lesson we discuss the tenancies through which persons hold their estates in real property.

Basics of Tenancies

Tenancies are the methods by which individuals, businesses, or governments hold, or own, real estate. Those who hold the real estate are called tenants.

Among the many ways individuals may own property are:
- ownership in severalty.
- joint tenancy.
- tenancy in common.
- community property.
- tenancy by the entirety.
- dower and curtesy.
- trusts.

Types of Tenancies

Ownership in severalty is the sole ownership of real property by one legal or natural person.

In any concurrent tenancy, which involves more than one owner, all co-tenants must sign legal documents relating to the property, such as sales agreements and deeds, for them to be legally binding on them.

Tenancy in common exists when two or more natural or legal persons hold an undivided interest in an estate that is passable to heirs and devisees. An undivided interest means all co-owners have an interest in the whole property, not just in parts of it. Each co-tenant has an equal right of possession to the property and cannot exclude another co-tenant or claim ownership of a specific portion of the property. Co-tenants need not pay rent for their use of the property, but will share in any income and expenses. Co-tenants may be related or unrelated persons; have equal interests or unequal interests; acquire title at different times and different ways; sell, encumber, and will their interests separately without consent of the other co-tenants. Any co-tenant can bring an action for partition to have the property divided up between the owners or sold at auction with each owner paid his share of the proceeds, if unable to sell his interest separately.

In a joint tenancy, two or more natural persons are joint and equal owners of an undivided interest in property and have a right of survivorship. A joint tenancy can only be created by a written instrument that expressly declares the interest created to be a joint tenancy.

Four unities must exist in order to create a joint tenancy:
- Possession (equal rights of possession)
- Interest (equal interests)
- Time (acquired at the same time)
- Title (acquired in the same deed)

Spouses

Each state has its own laws to deal with rights of spouses in real property. In community property states, all real property situated in that state and all personal property wherever situated, acquired by a husband and wife during a valid marriage, is community property belonging to both spouses, unless specifically acquired by one or the other as separate property.

In tenancy by the entirety states, a husband and wife may hold title as tenants by the entirety by placing both names on the deed. This tenancy gives each a right of survivorship, so upon the death of one spouse, the surviving spouse will own the property in severalty, without probate.

In states with dower and curtesy, dower rights give the wife a life estate in the deceased husband's property; curtesy rights give the husband a life estate in the deceased wife's property.

Syndications

When persons join together to make and operate a real estate investment, they form a syndicate. Syndicates can be created through such entities as a general or limited partnership, corporation, tenancy in common, joint tenancy, joint venture, or LLC.

Partners may hold title to property belonging to a partnership in the name of the partnership or in their own names as tenants in partnership. In a general partnership, each partner has an undivided interest in the partnership property and the right to use the property for partnership purposes. He is fully liable for all losses, and may transfer his interest in a partnership. However, he cannot transfer partnership property without the consent of the other partners. In a limited partnership, there is at least one general partner who manages the partnership and has unlimited liability. Limited partners, who perform no management function, provide investment capital, pay the general partner, share in profits, and have liability limited to only the amount of their investment.

A corporation, as a legal entity, may hold title to real estate by itself in severalty if it is the sole owner, or with other corporations or individuals as a tenant in common or as a tenant in partnership. A corporation cannot be a joint tenant because of its perpetual existence. Corporate property may be sold by someone in the corporation who has authority to represent the corporation, granted by a resolution of the board of directors.

A joint venture is an entity created to carry out a single particular transaction, rather than a series of transactions or a continuing business. It may be in the form of a general or limited partnership, a corporation, a REIT, a tenancy in common, or a joint venture agreement.

Title may also be held in trust. Trusts may be created to hold title to property for unincorporated groups, such as churches, fraternal or investment organizations, or for individuals. They are often used to hold title to property left by a deceased trustor, until heirs are old enough to assume responsibility for the property themselves.